Interpreting Local Culture and History

Interpreting Local Culture and History

Edited by
J. Sanford Rikoon and Judith Austin

Idaho State Historical Society
Boise
University of Idaho Press
Moscow

Published 1991 by the University of Idaho Press, Moscow, Idaho 83843 for the Idaho State Historical Society. Preparation of *Interpreting Local Culture and History* was funded in part by grants from the Steele-Reese Foundation and the Idaho Humanities Council (formerly the Association for the Humanities in Idaho).

Designed by Melissa Rockwood

Printed in the United States of America
95 94 93 92 91 5 4 3 2 1

Library of Congress Cataloging in Publication Data
Interpreting local culture and history / edited by J. Sanford Rikoon and Judith Austin.
p. cm.
ISBN 0-931406-06-4
1. Idaho—History, Local—Congresses. 2. Northwest, Pacific—History, Local—Congresses. 3. Idaho—Civilization—Congresses. 4. Northwest Pacific—Civilization—Congresses. 5. Local history—Congresses. I. Rikoon, J. Sanford. II. Austin, Judith, 1940- .
F746-I35 1991
979.5—dc19
86-34281
CIP

ISBN 0-931406-06-4

Contents

III. Rethinking Cultural Stereotypes

Foreword

Lawrence de Graaf

One of the more surprising developments in the realm of history has been the widespread interest in activities and studies collectively labeled "local history." A considerable portion of recent academic scholarship has used communities as the basis for analyses of past societies, culture, politics, and institutions. Inspired by such popular works as *Roots* and by the Bicentennial of the American Revolution, many people sought security in the recapture of their family and group heritage and provided a market for a steady stream of popular and illustrated history books and media productions, many of which focused on local areas. Interest in local history extended beyond the traditional media of written and pictorial works. A vigorous historic preservation movement was stimulated by legislation and tax benefits but drew much of its personnel from local community groups. A parallel interest developed in the preservation and exhibition of artifacts, reflected in the proliferation of locally based historical museums. Finally, several multifaceted projects designed to foster and improve a variety of undertakings in local history have been started. One of the most ambitious and successful of these has been the Working Together project, begun in September of 1981.

The conferences of the Working Together project, from which the papers in this volume have been drawn, epitomize the clientele of local history: they were attended primarily by nonacademic historians and by persons for whom history is an avocation. Participants' interest in local history tended to be an indigenous fascination with the state, region, or community, and their forte had traditionally been the collection and preservation of the historic resources of those areas. The aim of the conferences on Interpreting Local Culture and History was to expand the participants' awareness of interpretation in historical research and writing. It was hoped that this would lead them to examine topics and sources different from the classic western image and encourage them to work with academic historians, folklorists, and others taking an analytical approach to local history and culture. Each of the papers in this volume was intended to provide perspective on interpretation, demonstrate various methods of analyzing historical material, or suggest the value and broader significance of interpreting local history.

In the initial essay, T. Allan Comp notes some reasons why persons who are interested in the history of their community or region may not fully appreciate or utilize the resources available for its study. While his comments are directed specifically at museum personnel, they could easily pertain to anyone working in local history. The vital ingredients for successful work—an empathy with the locality and an active imagination that can see the story of the past in a variety of forms—are ones that several other essays also stress.

Another group of essays discusses specific resources in both rural and urban areas and how they might be used to shed light on local customs and experiences. Barre Toelken shows how simple structures can illustrate folk culture. Comp demonstrates the potential of industrial sites and buildings to explain local history. Jeff Simmonds notes the rôle of technological history. Other essays deal with how the historian uses various materials. William Lang and Laurie Mercier suggest techniques for obtaining reliable information in oral interviews. Jan Brunvand offers similar insights in the use of folktales, and the essay by G. Thomas Edwards provides tips on researching historical photographs.

Equally important to interpretation as historical resource and technique are the use of imagination in the perspectives from which one views a subject and the critical use of local history to question long-held views. Patricia K. Ourada reveals a little-known facet of Idaho's history in her essay on its Mexican population. Sue Armitage shows that the frontier experience that has shaped much of Idaho's heritage looks very different through the eyes of women. Sharon Boswell offers a fascinating example of the need to use a variety of resources and imaginative thought to recreate the past of a single site. The critical use of history is discussed by LeRoy Ashby in an essay on popular culture, in which he notes how a careful study of that subject can change the image of a decade, and by the refutations of popular stereotypes of Native American by Alan Marshall.

These essays offer to all who are interested in the history of their state or locality some excellent examples of the rich variety of topics and approaches in this field. They also suggest some more comprehensive questions that have long been debated by those who have worked in local history. The questions that need to be raised if these pieces of local history are to fit into a meaningful whole include: what do we mean by local history? What are the purposes and values to be gained by its study?

What types of historical research and writing are best suited to fulfill these purposes and realize these values?

"Local history" does not lend itself to a simple definition, for various areas have been subsumed under or linked with the term. These include incorporated towns and cities, "communities" that may range from a block or a neighborhood to a county, broader regions, and states. Some historians have reduced the scope of local history even further by noting that single buildings, sites, or physical artifacts may be interpreted so as to suggest the experiences of a locality, region, or era. In his second essay, Allan Comp notes: "Buildings—especially industrial buildings—can sometimes testify to remarkable chapters in our social history, chapters no better written than in the structures themselves." And Barre Toelken similarly notes in his essay that "our physical artifacts are touchstones to more complex beliefs and values."

How one defines local history will depend heavily on what one sees as the primary purpose or value of studying the past records of a city, community, or state rather than a nation or larger area. On this question, a large gap has long existed between most academic historians, on the one hand, and nonacademic professional historians and amateur practitioners of local history, on the other. The latter were the ones who began our tradition of recording the history of many local political units in the nineteenth century, establishing an extensive network of historical societies, archives, and local journals that are still the primary repositories for the study of cities, counties, and states. This tradition has been aptly labeled "biographical," for it regarded the primary purpose of the local historian as being "to re-enact, in his own mind, and portray for his readers, the Origin, Growth, Decline, and Fall of a Local Community."[1]

Local history so construed was usually a narration of the dramatic events, leading citizens, outstanding contributions, and prominent milestones or "firsts" in a community.[2] This approach presumed that each locality was in some ways unique and that its history deserved to be recorded for its own sake. Some academic scholars have concurred in this view that the history of a locality should not be used only to study national trends. These historians often also insist that the unique biography of a locality can only be fully written by going beyond the traditional documentary records and employing the ideas and resources of archaeologists, geographers, and those in other disciplines.[3]

Scholars in the history departments of universities have generally taken a very different view of the purpose and utility of local history. They have viewed their mission as the analysis of significant events and developments in human society. For many years, "significance" was seen only at the level of national and world events, and most university-based historians took no interest in local history.[4] More recently, many academic historians have shifted their interest from national and world politics to a concern for "undocumented, inarticulate groups" and the study of social structures, social change, and their components—especially cities, ethnic groups, and cultural trends. These "new" fields of history were accompanied by a shift in methodology to quantitative data and samples of national population groups. In seeking such data, it was inevitable that academic historians should renew their interest in local history. Cities, counties, and states were the primary units in which statistical and quantifiable records were compiled.[5] Most of these studies were of the colonial period or the nineteenth century, eras when "society for all but a elite few was bounded by the local community. Only there could the most basic patterns that governed the lives of common folk be traced." Thus in the last fifteen years many books have been written about various social institutions and cultural groups in many cities, towns, and regions of the United States.[6]

Each of these approaches to the study of local history has had its critics. Much of the writing of amateurs lacked any central theme or meaning and made little effort to relate events in the community under study to wider areas or more general conclusions. It also often seemed to lack those critical qualities that academic historians regard as essential to humanistic study. One academic commented in 1940 that most amateur local history "has been so excessively localized as to appear to have no meaning for any community but one." Its pages were characterized by "self-glorification, antiquarianism, and the inability to see his own town as part of a larger community."[7] Finally, amateur historians were often prolific compilers of factual and anecdotal information but showed little imagination or feeling for interpretation in organizing it. Two scholars recently noted: "The jumble of facts often prevented the reader from recognizing the main themes which set a community or state apart."[8]

If the work of amateurs may be faulted for an excessive emphasis upon the locality, most of the recent academic writings have invited the opposite criticism: that they are not really local history, but "national history localized."[9] On the state level, much of the writing has been on issues or periods of national history rather than being based primarily on the characteristics of individual states. Many of the works on towns and cities have been case studies, with the town being selected as an example of such topics as social mobility in the working class.[10]

The use of individual towns as case studies for conclusions on national life has been criticized on several grounds. Some scholars fear this is a misuse of the techniques of quantitative sampling because different localities will vary in the factors that affect the group under study, making conclusions reached in one case not necessarily valid for other localities.[11] Others have noted that historians doing this type of study "found themselves doing history at the local level as an almost incidental by-product of research strategies oriented toward other issues" and were not really creating an academically based field of local history.[12]

Such, then, is the intellectual milieu out of which the Working Together project was born: two very different concepts of what local history is and how it should be studied and written, held by two quite different groups of historians. The main challenge taken up by the Idaho project and reflected in these essays was to bring these two traditions together, to attempt to get each to see the strengths of the other, and thus to build throughout Idaho not only an increased interest in local history but a more enlightened one that would join the university and the historical society as well as encourage a multidisciplinary approach to local history projects.

In this task, the Working Together project and these essays are in accord with some of the most recent writing on local history, which also seeks to promote a union of past local-history studies. Proponents of the uniqueness of individual localities still recognize the need to relate their study to broader patterns and wider areas. National and world affairs have had significant impacts upon the course of events in smaller areas, and the relationship between a locality and larger regions is one of the most important themes in local history.[13] While academic historians have argued that the individual community has lost much of its former significance as a center of the citizen's life and loyalties, there is an increased awareness that local places still retain considerable influence. The community "has determined options available to people and set standards of conduct and belief," and it has served both as "a forger of unifying trends and fosterer of divisive ones."[14] To understand how a locality has served these functions, the place itself, its unique aspects, must be studied along with the national patterns and trends that its history reflects.

There has also been some appreciation of the different modes of writing among local historians. While most nonacademic works are still written in a literary, narrative style, emphasizing the exceptional, the dramatic, and the mystique of place, they are often better organized than were many of the older "mug books" and county histories, and they show greater appreciation of social problems and nondominant groups. Some academic historians, in turn, have recognized the appeal that popular narratives will always have. John Alexander Williams has admonished his colleagues:

> It is unproductive and probably unwise to attempt to change these exceptions. People like stories. They especially like stories in which they can participate, as they can through history that engages their sense of personal identification with their state or community.[15]

Further modifying these contrasting traditions has been the appearance of numerous "public history" studies of cultural resources for public-policy issues in a community, region, or state. The authors are professional historians but are not usually situated in academic institutions; their writings are often under contract to a client and intended to influence public action. As a result, their works embody much of the anlytical methodology of academic local history but tend to present it in a less formal, more narrative style.[16]

This overview of local history as a field of scholarship and practice should provide the reader with a sense of the place of local history within the whole sphere of historical studies. It is a dynamic field, one drawing increasing interest from scholars and amateurs alike, and one in which two long traditions of historical work exist, each with much to offer the other. In order fully to appreciate the value of the history of Idaho, its regions, towns, and sites, however, one must consider some of the more specific qualities embodied in such study.

One of the qualities most often cited is that the study of a community's history can build pride in that community, and this pride, in turn, may be the foundation for civic improvement in many forms. In his essay on industrial history, Allan Comp notes the importance of local history in leading the city of Butte to rebuild part of its downtown area. Some scholars have seen a knowledge of local history as essential to any viable community. Constance Green urged local historians to write for the population of the area they study because "a knowledge of its own past is essential for any community to achieve cultural adulthood."[17]

Local historians have also contended that their field of study can offer the most accurate and complete history of a population. Not only are local historians increasingly interested in the average person, or "history from the bottom up"; they can address that subject without losing sight of the individual. The British historian H. P. R. Finberg has charged that "the national historian, dealing with some vast agglomeration . . . tends to lose sight of the human person." Moreover, national historians often focus on political leaders and figures of success, while "local history brings us face to face with the Englishman at home. By so doing, it restrains the propensity to worship mere power and success."[18] While much recent academic writing in local history has treated local populations in terms of groups, it has often resulted in challenging prior generalizations and stereotypes about those groups. Several essays in this volume reflect this quality of local history. Alan Marshall, in his essay on the Nez Perce, has demonstrated that stereotypes of Native Americans as "savages" who lacked the political and social organization of "civilized society" do not hold up when one tribe is examined carefully.

The study of local history can be equally useful in rectifying broader ideas on the historical developments that shaped the physical or cultural condition of the nation or large parts of it. A striking example of this quality is Kathleen Conzen's study of the location and condition of immigrant groups in nineteenth-century Milwaukee. By showing that they were just as prone to cluster themselves in separate communities there as in eastern cities, she has challenged the "frontier thesis" of Frederick Jackson Turner that the frontier broke down European cultural habits and promoted assimilation and a spirit of democracy.[19]

While none of the essays in this collection attempts such a major challenge to past interpretations, several do offer fascinating challenges to popular beliefs. People often refer to "Mormon settlements" as though the mere presence of persons of that faith gave all areas they settled a homogeneous culture. Yet Jeff Simmonds has demonstrated that technological developments made Mormon communities established in eastern Idaho in the late nineteenth century quite different from earlier counterparts in Idaho or Utah. LeRoy Ashby presents a more complex example of this use of local history. His essay on popular culture first reminds local historians that national phenomena like the advertising and entertainment industries have had tremendous influence over local attitudes in the current century. He then goes on to one of the most local settings, a home in the 1930s, and by reviewing the ads, films, and other forms of culture likely to be seen concludes that the Great Depression may not actually have been so depressing to many American families.

Many other qualities of local history might be mentioned, but it will suffice to note one more, a characteristic very evident among both the staff and the audiences of the conferences on Interpreting Local Culture and History: enthusiasm. Probably the most common reason that so many people participate in various local history projects is the enjoyment they receive from doing so. Finberg admits that he was first drawn to the study of British towns by "the fascination of the subject, the continuous excitement of research" before he had thought out the more intellectual values of such study.[20] Many people find that they are not so much drawn to the study of a local place or area in its totality as they are intrigued with one particular facet of the local scene, or with one technique or resource for its study.[21]

Both the fascination and the focus on particular facets or resources of local history are reflected in the essays in this book. One writer declares that the study of industrial sites and buildings "made me a local history convert; let me discover the fascinating threads that tie our industrial past to the rest of our past, and then experience the excitement of reweaving those threads into patterns that touched people and cultures I never read about. . . ." Others found equal enjoyment in extracting the history of a region from historic photographs, in deciphering the cultural meaning and folk-value of old buildings, in probing the historical messages of folk tales and tall tales, or in the challenge of obtaining oral documentation from local residents that avoids the pitfalls of exaggeration and falsehood.

For other essayists, the most fascinating quality of particular facets of local history is the complexities of life they can reveal. LeRoy Ashby notes that culture "is not a uniform, monolithic entity. It is comprised of clashing, contradictory values and beliefs. Careful examination of popular culture can reveal much about the tensions, the dialogues, the push-and-pulls, the conflicting ideals that comprise American life."

Local history in Idaho, as elsewhere, can be approached in a wide variety of topics and perspectives. As the essays in this book show, it is not only an area for research and writing. It is a field that lends itself to photographic exhibits, site interpretations, oral inverviews, interpretations from fieldwork with buildings and artifacts, and the collection, analysis, and interpretation of an almost limitless array of subjects. Perhaps most important, it is still largely an untapped field, particularly in the West, and one that still offers greater opportunities for the novice historian, the amateur, than perhaps any other area of history. The tools essential to begin its pursuit are still "a respect for historic truth and a capacity for accurate recording."[22] Equipped with these qualities, it is hoped, many readers will gain from these essays further insights on how to interpret, how to give meaning to the written, oral, and physical resources of Idaho's history. It is also hoped that they will better understand how to use various techniques of historical study and, above all, that they will gain further enthusiasm for continuing the fine work of developing local history that the Working Together project and all who have shared in it have thus far carried out.

Notes

1. H. P. R. Finberg, "The Local Historian and His Theme," in Finberg and V. H. T. Skipp, *Local History: Objective and Pursuit* (Newton Abbot, England: David & Charles, 1967), p. 10.

2. John Alexander Williams, "A New Look at an Old Field," *Western Historical Quarterly* (July, 1978), 9:282.

3. These ideas are most fully developed by the Leicester School of British historians, particularly H. P. R. Finberg. See Finberg, "Local History," in Finberg and Skipp, *Local History*, pp. 36-37. A recent work incorporating some of these ideas and particularly stressing multiple resources is David E. Kyvig and Myron A. Marty, *Nearby History: Exploring the Past Around You* (Nashville, Tennessee: American Association for State and Local History, 1982).

4. Donald D. Parker, *Local History: How to Gather It, Write It, and Publish It* (New York: Social Science Research Council, 1944), p. ix.

5. For overviews of recent developments in academic local history, see Kathleen N. Conzen, "Community Studies, Urban History and American Local History," in Michael Kammen, editor, *The Past Before Us: Contemporary Historical Writing in the United States* (Ithaca, New York: Cornell University

Press, 1980), chapter 11, and Alan J. Lichtman and Valerie French, *Historians and the Living Past: The Theory and Practice of Historical Study* (Arlington Heights, Illinois: AHM Press, 1978), chapter VI.

6. Conzen, "Community Studies," p. 275. Much of the recent academic scholarship on local history is summarized in Kyvig and Marty, *Nearby History*, chapter 12.

7. Constance M. Green, "The View of Local History," in Caroline F. Ware, editor, *The Cultural Approach to History* (Port Washington, New York: Kennikat Press, 1940), p. 279.

8. Mark Friedberger and Janice Reiff Webster, "Social Structure and State and Local History" *Western Historical Quarterly* (July, 1978), 9:314.

9. Finberg, "Local History," p. 32.

10. Williams, "New Look," p. 284: Lichtman and French, *Living Past*, pp. 169-171.

11. Lichtman and French, *Living Past*, pp. 172-174.

12. Conzen, "Community Studies," p. 274.

13. Finberg, "Local History," pp. 41-42; Green, "Value," p. 279.

14. Lichtman and French, *Living Past*, p. 168; Conzen, "Community Studies," pp. 289-290.

15. Williams, "New Look," pp. 294-295.

16. For examples of essays in public history, see issues of *The Public Historian* (1978-), sponsored by the National Council on Public History and currently published by the University of California Press.

17. Green, "Value," p. 285.

18. Finberg, "Local Historian and His Theme," pp. 13, 15.

19. Kathleen N. Conzen, *Immigrant Milwaukee, 1836-1860: Accommodation and Community in a Frontier City* (Cambridge, Massachusetts: Harvard University Press, 1976).

20. H. P. R. Finberg, "Preface," in Finberg and Skipp, *Local History*, p. vii.

21. For bibliographies on sources for the use of various materials in local history, see the chapter bibliographies in Kyvig and Marty, *Nearby History*, and a new bibliography, *The Craft of Public History* (Westport, Connecticut: Greenwood Press, 1983). An excellent example of fascination with one aspect of an area is the successful quest of Forest Service archaeology technician Jeff Fee for the "Chinese gardens" near Warrens, Idaho — a quest that resulted in his discovery of nineteenth-century terraced gardens built by Chinese workers in a manner identical to such gardens in China.

22. Finberg, "Local History," p. 43.

Acknowledgments

In the spring of 1981, the National Endowment for the Humanities funded an unusual experiment by the Idaho State Historical Society to bridge the efforts of professional and amateur researchers in Idaho and the Northwest. Over the next three years, this program—"Working Together: A Regional Approach to Community Traditions and History"—sponsored a variety of activities, from publications and conferences to workshops and oral-history depositories. At all times, these projects have been planned with the goal of increasing the quality of the study of local culture and history by making available all potentially useful resources. Although the term "resource" has suffered in the hands of bureaucrats over the past decade, the Working Together staff has used it to connote the techniques of collection, classification, interpretation, presentation, and conservation that together comprise the requirements of local or community studies.

The essays in this volume, with the exception of Lawrence de Graff's introduction, were originally presented at two regional conferences with a focus on Interpreting Local Culture and History. The rationale for these events was that while increased amounts of time and energy were being devoted to the collection of research materials, there was little attention being given to actively interpreting the data collected (which are in themselves passive) to offer more in-depth portraits of community life.

The conferences were held in Boise, Idaho, on September 25 and 26, 1982, and in Coeur d'Alene, Idaho, on November 5 and 6, 1982. Each included a day of public addresses and papers, including the essays presented here. The second day emphasized demonstration and discussion of interpreting local culture and history in public contexts—for example, in photographic exhibits, museum displays, and publications.

Both conferences attracted hundreds of participants from Idaho and neighboring states, and we trust that some of the excitement and stimulation of the events is carried forward through presentation of these essays and comments.

This volume is organized as was the format of each conference, with keynote essays, papers in three major areas, comments on the papers, and responses to comments by presenters. "New Perspectives in Interpretation" is intended to highlight recent efforts both to broaden the base of source materials used in local research and to suggest innovative approaches to traditional sources. "Evaluating Oral Materials" attempts to address some of the difficulties encountered in using oral history or folk narratives in research projects—uses that have certainly increased since the Bicentennial. "Reconsidering Cultural Stereotypes" provides a forum to address particular stereotypes that are found in local research and writing on Idaho and the Northwest. We are interested in not only the scope of these concepts but also how they arise and how interpretation of a particular set of data can help defuse stereotypes.

Many people helped with the conferences and publication; they are truly group efforts. The conferences would not have been possible without the work of Madeline Buckendorf and Keith Petersen of the Working Together project. Also providing valuable time and assistance were Ken Swanson for the Boise conference and Nancy Renk for that in Coeur d'Alene. Boise Public Library and North Idaho College as well as the Idaho State Historical Society graciously provided facilities for conference activities. Kris Ham, of the Idaho Oral History Center, typed the manuscript for this volume.

We are of course grateful to those who made presentations; they shared not only their prepared thoughts but their enthusiasm and expertise throughout the conferences. In particular our thanks go to Allan Comp, who prepared and gave the Boise conference keynote address on few days' notice because of the illness of the scheduled speaker.

Finally, conferences and publications need more than soil, sun, and water to bear fruit. Providing nutrients (mainly funds) for these efforts were the National Endowment for the Humanities, Association for the Humanities in Idaho (now the Idaho Humanities Council), Idaho State Historical Society, and Steele-Reese Foundation.

To all of the individuals and groups listed above, and to all our conference participants, we say a heartfelt "thank you."

Introduction:

History Outside the Historical Museum, or, My Peculiar Torture

T. Allan Comp

Thirty-six hours ago I was on the roof of a building in Pocatello, Idaho, helping to literally peel back layers of history that had been applied to that building. They were layers of a kind of pride, attempts to fix up that building that had been applied at least three different times since the building was first built in 1900. While I was up there I got a message from the organizers of this conference in Boise, Idaho, and was asked to substitute for Tom Schlereth as the keynote speaker. His talk on *History Outside the Historical Museum* was one I could never duplicate and would be foolish to try. Moreover, what I was asked to do as a substitute was to talk about material culture to a group of my own colleagues without slides or notes with which to prepare.

Undaunted, or perhaps crazy, here I am to talk about what you might see outside your historical museum without giving you anything to look at. I should probably elaborate first on how I came to this "peculiar torture," as I have subtitled this presentation. Part of that has to do with where I grew up, part of it has to do with school, and part of it has to do with my experiences since then. I grew up in southern California, probably as ahistorical an upbringing as one could imagine; my interests were largely in hot rods and surfing, certainly not in history. I did manage to finish undergraduate school and, on what might most accurately be described as a dare, I actually got into a graduate school in the East—a place I had never been. That school and its graduate program were probably the most fortuitous accidents this southern California mechanic ever managed. The Hagley program at the University of Delaware is one of those odd combinations of museum and academia. It is neither fish nor fowl; almost a curious kind of purgatory. It has one foot in the world: it is a museum on an industrial site, a rather early industrial site. It has the other foot in academia: a rigorous program in the history of technology and American economic history. With one foot in each, the Hagley fellows are never sure just exactly which one they are standing on. And I am sure that is part of what brought me to my current state of being. What I learned was that one could do serious history about ordinary people and their ordinary work. I also learned that things matter, little pieces of what we call material culture; tools, furniture, buildings—all are valuable historical documents.

After Hagley I taught at Boston University, a kind of standard, academic teaching program that I found was not quite enough to meet the kinds of interests that I had developed at the Hagley program. So my second step was to the Historic American Engineering Record, a part of the National Park Service Office of Archaeology and Historic Preservation in Washington, D.C. For my academic colleagues I was stepping beyond the pale and into the government. Perhaps even worse, I was going to be doing, and did, site-specific history—history about individual places, even individual and rather ordinary buildings. There were no grand theories to work from, no papers on Emerson and his meaning to the twentieth century. In fact, what few grand theories the history of technology or engineering history had managed to develop rarely worked when applied to a specific site.

On the historic preservation side of that effort, I learned very quickly that site-specific history was history that people actually needed; they were waiting to learn about a specific site and they wanted to use that history about that site. I worked in Claremont, New Hampshire, a New England mill town with a million square feet of vacant mill buildings. That town wanted to hold onto the industrial buildings that had helped to create it, and its history became a way of learning how Claremont once used and could again use those mills as both symbols of its past and a promise of its future. I worked in Augusta, Georgia, often called the "Lowell of Georgia," where a power canal system created an industrial town of great vigor that burgeoned after the Civil War and through the early part of the twentieth century. Again, Augusta found in its own history, in an understanding of its own past, a kind of promise for its future. I worked in Lockport, Illinois, a little town on the Illinois-Michigan Canal not far from Chicago. Lockport literally turned its back on the canal that created it—physically lost touch with its own roots. Its history became a way of re-orienting the perspective of a whole town and giving it a great deal more pride in itself.

And I worked in towns in the West. In Butte, Montana, we worked on a history not of mining in Butte, but of commercial life in Butte—"Uptown," as it is called—where the boastful structures built by some of Butte's famous entrepreneurs as well as its small businessmen still speak of a pride and a kind of affluence that Butte can still build toward. In Tacoma, Washington, the railroad station and the buildings around it mark an era like that Tacoma today is again building. And I worked in Lowell, Massachusetts, heartland of industrial America, long before it became a subject for a national park development. In fact, it was the rediscovery of Lowell as a whole system, largely intact, of power canals and textile mills that began to generate the interest that eventually led to a Lowell National Historical Park.

The lesson in all that was one that took me a long time to learn, but one that I find deeply embedded in my own prejudices as I now approach my own work. The history I "did," because of its ties to historic preservation, had a very early judgment placed upon it. If it worked, people could understand what we were presenting. If they could internalize and act on the meaning of that history, then the building or the district in which we were working stayed up. If it did not work, the verdict was uncomfortably clear and my history became an obituary. I also learned an even more important lesson—the real binding power of a shared historical perspective in a community. Working in those towns and others, one learns quickly that people do care about their town's history, and that lots of kinds of people care. I found when you can touch these shared values you tap great power.

Unfortunately, these two perspectives, that of local history and that of the museums, and the appreciation of the potential power that those kinds of perspectives can create, resulted in what I am calling my peculiar torture. That torture is created when you are working in local history, when you know its appeal and its strength, and then must watch local museums and the opportunities of local history pass each other like ships in the night. They may occasionally signal, a short flash of light, a brief exchange from one to the other, but they rarely if ever change course.

Should you now expect a "how to" lesson on bringing better or broader interpretation within your museum, this is the wrong speech. Those inside the museum, at least for this paper, I am assuming are already either convinced or coerced. It is what never gets in, what we never see in local museums, even when it is all around, that creates the peculiar torture I want to talk about. I have carefully studied this torture (at least for the last thirty-six hours), and realize that it actually takes four different, but related, forms; and I have given each of them a title. They are, first, The Torture of the Abandoned Apex; second, The Torture of the Calloused Constituency; third, The Torture of the Forgotten Folk; and fourth, The Torture of the Missed Manuscript.

The Torture of the Abandoned Apex. An apex, at least when driving race cars, is a point in a turn that signals the most important stage in driving through that turn at speed. A driver basically points a rapidly moving car toward that point, dives into the turn, hits that apex, and is able to pull away from that point under full power. Towns, I think, create the same thing. They set up for that turn, set up for their own urban growth, and they hit that apex, create that area of development that sets direction and facilitates a full-power pursuit of whatever destiny they may have defined for themselves. That apex in each town—and I think every town has at least one—may be a business district or an industrial district, but it is always there. It is an area that, once built, sets the direction and viability of that town's historical development for a great many years. Too often we ignore these apex points.

Danville, Virginia, is a tobacco town in southeast Virginia, a town of 40,000 people whose heritage goes back to the brightleaf tobacco industry of the late nineteenth and early twentieth centuries as well as to a large textile industry. I worked with a team of architects, historians, and planners who were asked to study the industrial district created by this effort, looking for ways to redevelop the district and revitalize the local economy. On the first day of our summer there we toured the entire industrial district and stopped, I thought logically, at the local museum to look at the exhibits and to talk with some of the museum staff. After we toured an impressive collection of cigarette packs and textile machinery, we sat down in a classroom to talk with the staff. My first question was, where are we? What can you tell us about the district in which we are located? The answer was not forthcoming; they simply did not know. The museum could literally have been located on another planet and the staff would have known as much about the district within which the museum was located.

For another kind of example, in Pocatello, Idaho, there is no industrial district but there is a commercial core, an apex of remarkable integrity. It is in its building form and architecture eloquent testimony to aspirations and successes, to the architectural and civic pride of the people who built it. Today it is a brand-new historic district. In fact the building I was crawling around on was one of those that is being rehabilitated as part of that historic district. Who created that district? Who was it that pushed in Pocatello to see that district listed in the National Register of Historic Places? It was a tough little planner from Bellevue, Washington, not an old native, not a member of the historical society. Keeping history downtown, as that planner was trying to do, is an appropriate and important role for museums. It may even be a responsibility, because who else ought to speak for the mute artifacts, the buildings that remain from these important apex locations in our own community history? I think too often we save a piece of the building and a photograph and then lament the loss.

The second peculiar torture is *The Torture of the Calloused Constituency,* when we museum folk, the "enlightened" if you will, forget who we are and who we are not. I was in an historical society in a New England town several years ago with a good friend, a Jewish woman with a Ph.D. from New York University who had been born and raised in that same town. She had never been in the local historical society building, and when she came to visit me there she was immediately and totally intimidated. It did not take long to realize that she had learned even as a child that this was not her turf. It was old-line WASP country and not for any newcomer or outsider, yet the institution itself never knew it projected that image. More recently at an historic preservation meeting two professors, one in English and one in geography, gave an impressive discussion with slides about the round barns of the Northwest. It was thorough, caring, and enthusiastic. The scholarship was careful, and the feel for the buildings and their significance that those two professors brought to the topic was most encouraging. After their talk, when the meeting broke for coffee, both of these professors were almost completely ignored. No one walked over to talk to them, no one commented on their paper. I think they also learned that they did not belong, that the community they thought they were a part of was not including them.

There can be a happy ending. When I worked in Michigan we did an inventory of engineering and industrial sites and a publication of that inventory. To get that project through and approved was a long struggle. The staff were disinterested at best; they saw some academic interest in engineering and industrial sites, but as a main-line preservation effort they thought it peripheral. When we finally completed the project and the publication was out, there was a great revelation. There were people out there, other than historians and preservationists, who cared about old things, about old bridges, mills, dams, hydroelectric generating stations, railroads, auto manufacturing plants, and many more kinds of things. And not only were they out there, but there were lots of them. Today, that staff always includes engineering and industrial slides in their talks and they always pick up new constituents for local history. I think the same is possible for the museum world.

The third peculiar torture is *The Torture of the Forgotten Folk* (and, I should probably add, Passed-Over Places). When I talk about folk I mean industrial history, the working history of this country and its exhibit and interpretation. Too often I think the businessman's office and his Victorian home become our image of industrial America. That kind of sanitized industrial history reminds me of the strip of paper I found in my motel bathroom that says "sparkling clean for your protection." Forgotten in this sparkling history of our industrial past are the vastly larger number of men, women, and children who worked hard, short lives in fields and factories to help create the American industrial colossus. It is neither easy nor comfortable to deal with those people, but to leave them forgotten seems to me unforgivable. Passed-over places often suffer the same neglect. I am not talking about the pristine Victorian town or even just a nice town. I mean places that are beat up by history,

Granite Falls started its life as the base camp for the mines of Monte Christo; a more romantic beginning one could hardly imagine. When the mines shut down, timber became a major industry; when timber phased out, the Depression came early to Granite Falls and it never left. Today the town initially appears as a place shattered by the loss of civic pride, shingled in an attempt to cover up its past, and singed often by fires that left gaping holes in the downtown landscape. Fortunately, the local museum might best be characterized as the operating base for a small Sherman tank battalion, a group of bright and determined individuals who will not see their town die. That museum group, working with the chamber of commerce and with the city council and pushing them whenever necessary, brought a team of two architects and an historian to Granite Falls, where they wrote a town history and developed rehabilitation designs for the shingled buildings, the covered architecture of that town's past. The result is a town that has a new sense of pride in itself, largely because it refused to become a Passed-Over Place. It refused to allow the stereotype that we too often attach to small towns to be attached to itself. It took its small-town history as a source of pride and strength, a new source of community identity.

The fourth of the peculiar tortures is *The Torture of the Missed Manuscript,* and here I see buildings and structures as documents or manuscripts. The Salt Lake City Tabernacle is a building that everyone knows, the great turtleback hall, home of the choir, place of incredible acoustics. It seems a very familiar building. When I went to Salt Lake to work with a HAER team documenting that building, I learned that everybody did not know that building. In fact, our study of the building, a careful, detailed study of the structure itself, revealed a whole series of pieces of history that we had never known before: pieces of history about the complex technology transfer from the East coast to the West, about the local resource base, about the communal power that existed in early Mormonism, and about a building that almost did not work. Only because it was artfully reinforced did it become what was then, and remains today, the largest open-span arch in the world.

Another missed manuscript is one that I am working on at present. It is on the Quinault River on the west side of Olympic National Park in a deep glacial valley, a true untouched wilderness. If you go far enough up that valley, thirteen and a half miles on foot to be exact, you find the Enchanted Valley Chalet, a two-and-a-half-story log building never approached by road or railroad. Some of the rangers in that park see Olympic as a wilderness, a place in which no building belongs. My job brings me a different kind of perspective. I see that building as a manuscript and I wanted to know why it is here, so far away from railhead or roadway. What I found is that the building was constructed when speculators hoped to build a trans-Olympic highway. They built ravaged by boom and bust and equally by a loss of civic pride.

I think my favorite example, because I worked there most recently, is a little town called Granite Falls, Washington, with a population of 900. the building in 1930, the highway was never allowed, and from 1930 to 1956 the building functioned as a back-country lodge. It was part of back-country life in Olympic. Today, to me, it is a reminder of man's mark in the wilderness, of how puny in some places our efforts have been and how fortunate we are that they were so. I also see it as a reminder of our capacity to change and perhaps even learn. What the building marks is something we did not do—we did not build a highway—and I think it needs to stand as testimony to our capacity to learn better than to damage important wilderness areas.

I think every building downtown is a missed manuscript. It can become a window on local life, giving us perspectives about ourselves and about our local past that are important parts of what we can talk about in our museums and outside of our museums.

Finally, as a kind of summary of my peculiar torture, let me briefly talk about the Laguna Pueblo. Almost sixty miles west of Albuquerque, Laguna is a special place. Building started there in about 1400; the new church—still there—was built in 1699. It has a very special group of people that opened their village to a team of people I directed for an entire summer. They showed us a new way of life and a fascinating perspective that otherwise would have been unattainable.

What I find in looking back at Laguna is almost all of my peculiar tortures rolled up into one, and a very valuable lesson. Laguna certainly had an Abandoned Apex: the new church of 1699 and the old core village had been largely forgotten. Instead there are clusters of new HUD housing spread around the reservation and new shopping centers where modern people could go. Indeed, the Calloused Constituency presumed that nobody cared for those old areas. The Forgotten Folk were the old villagers and even some of the young who found something lost when they returned to those old buildings and found them slowly dissolving back into the ground. And finally, as a Missed Manuscript, Laguna was eloquent testimony. It had no written history, yet there was a verbal tradition that made it possible for us to help prepare the first written history of that village.

My lesson was one delivered quietly and effectively by the tribal council governor, who I think is my favorite museologist. While we were looking around the village we were standing in the middle of the plaza in front of the church where most of the dances and other ceremonies are held. As a "white eye" I was not really even supposed to be in that plaza, but the governor had asked me to stand there with him to look around at what surrounded this most sacred part of the oldest village on the reservation. When I looked around I could see one old house trailer, falling-down walls, broken windows, buildings that had once been two and three stories reduced to one, and I had to ask the obvious question: "If this place is so important why is it falling apart?" He reminded me that the railroad and the highway and a huge open-pit uranium mine had all come early to Laguna, and that for a long time his own people and their own culture were falling apart. What they saw in the chance to rebuild that old village was a start at rebuilding themselves. Because that old village was part of what they had become, pulling it back together again was a part of pulling themselves and their own culture back together again as well.

I think we are all offered the same challenge the governor offered me. Each of us has an opportunity to pull back the curtains of his own vision. Those who care about a community form the groups that count the most, the groups that can most immediately and effectively touch people's lives, perhaps even expand their own understanding of our shared past and its meaning. They will not be able to do it all, but they can do something now, no matter how seemingly small. It will be one more step in making our field a better one and in helping people understand themselves. And it will be a step in easing my own peculiar torture.

I. *New Perspectives in Interpretation*

The Use of Artifacts in Cultural Research:

A Folkloristic Perspective

Barre Toelken

Hand-produced items from the past and present surround us at virtually all times in our lives. Some of these artifacts are produced by particular people in response to their own artistic interests or to the practical needs of the world in which they live. Others are made according to the accumulated tastes of a whole culture. When we look into oral history, we often find that certain items (family heirlooms, photographs, practical objects, buildings, quilts, and the like) trigger a tremendous range of reminiscence and emotional response and carry a great load of cultural meaning. Archaeologists and anthropologists usually focus their attention on the interpretation of such objects, trying to define not only their uses and their construction but also the roles they may have played in social networks. The folklorist tends to focus attention primarily on the ways in which these objects grow out of the shared values of an entire community, whether that group be defined by family lines, region, ethnicity, occupation, religion, sex, or age. In folklore, the attempt is to find and understand those expressions of all sorts, both material and oral, that are the outgrowth of the group and its values rather than the attitudes of particular single individuals within the group.

A joke, for example, will not circulate very far if it represents only the humorous attitude of the first person who tells it. In fact, when we tell a joke to someone, we are usually doing so because we sense that the joke dramatizes an abstract idea that both the teller and the audience will find funny for some very complex reasons almost never made explicit in the joke itself. Similarly, when someone produces a quilt for someone else, it is usually done according to a set of accepted notions about what a quilt should look like rather than as an expression of the artist's own individualistic vision in fabric design.

There is much more to be said about history and oral history than a folklorist can properly address himself to, but in the compass of this brief essay I would like to concentrate primarily on the ways in which certain objects may reveal to us something far more complex than the content or construction of the object itself might initially suggest. Attitudes, shared values, and cultural perspectives are the dimensions of history on which this talk focuses.

For a beginning point, let us take a fairly common item found across the American scene: the barn. A typical barn in some part of the United States is red with white trim. Very often the farmer himself will insist that the reason for the red paint is that it is the cheapest, and in some cases indeed red barn paint is the cheapest paint available (one often finds out from the local paint store, however, that red barn paint is so cheap because so many local people use it that it can be ordered in great quantities). The farmer will point out that the paint is a preservative for the wood and will go on to say that the design of the barn itself has a mainly practical background. What the farmer may not talk about, but we can assume to be present as part of the total effect of the barn, is whether the barn is well made and whether it is painted according to the codes acceptable in the local community. If purple or pink paint became cheap on the market suddenly, it is safe to say that many farmers would still not immediately switch to those colors. This suggests that there is more than a practical reason behind the fact that barns look the way they do. We know that in some parts of the country barns are connected to farmhouses by a woodshed or some other building that enables the farmer to work with the cows in the winter without leaving the safety of the building. Often referred to as the Vermont or New England connected barn, this kind of building is very traditional and very common in certain parts of New England. But just a few miles away one may find unconnected barns. In other words, a certain design may be widespread, but geographical traditions may not have become entirely binding on everyone in a given geographical area. For this reason, one can conclude that there are certain kinds of traditions about design and color and execution that have become so traditional that barn builders tend toward certain preferences, but not that all barn builders are obliged to follow exactly the same plans. This means that there is both a dynamic situation that allows for local, personal variation and a conservative situation that encourages certain kinds of combinations to be thought of as "normal." Moreover, farmers may be quite unaware of the fact that many of their roof designs go back to comparatively ancient cathedral styles as well as to ship construction. A particular farmer does not need to know all of these historical matters, for usually the barn is built the way it is because that is the way barns have always looked in his district. This is the way Dad built the barn, or this is the way Grandpa thought barns ought to look, or this is how our people normally build barns.

The uses and functions of a barn (or any other practical building) do, of course, dictate much of the floor plan and have a lot to do with the placement of buildings in relation to each other on a farm or ranch. The question of whether wood will be painted, what design the windows will be (some barns in Ohio have a Gothic-style window that looks very much like a church window), what the color or color combination will be, as well as other expressive elements in "barn-ness," are functions not of the practical life of the farmer but of a shared set of aesthetics growing out of culturally acceptable norms. The white trim on many red barns, the intensely detailed shingle work on the sides of barns that are not painted, the delicately recurved roofs, the balance of windows and doors in symmetrical patterns: all testify to a more than practical concern with what might be called shared artistic features, the lack of which or the mismanagement of which can doom the farmer to a reputation for not knowing what he is doing.

Just as some German farmers indicate their wealth and success at farming by placing their manure piles out in front of the barn by the road, American farmers often present their barns, or the front part of the farmhouses, to passersby as a statement—a performance, if you will—about their stability within the local culture and within its economy. Added to that nowdays on many farms and ranches will be implements from the previous generation used as support for mailboxes or newspaper holders; cream separators, hand-held plows, logging chains, and the like are almost always items from the generations that settled and stabilized the farm from homestead into contemporary times. By taking an object from those eras and placing it out in front as the support for a mailbox, the farmer is declaring a kind of pedigree. This always goes far beyond practical necessity, for the post office usually stipulates that a plain post will be used in support of a standard government mailbox. Farmers go far out of their way to use as mailbox supports items from their past that take far more bother to erect and to maintain than would a simple post. Here again, as with the barns, practicality is a part of the function; but the execution, the performance of ideals and values, is as much a part of the item as is its practical dimension.

A good many ranches in the American West are marked off by entry gates made of posts with a crosspiece arranged high enough that a man can ride under it on horseback. Even when the "ranch house" itself is merely a mobile home at the end of the lane, many people today enunciate their sense of being on the land with an ostentatious gateway that proclaims "here is the beginning of my land" to any passerby; it is often decorated further with a sign carrying the name of the family, the cattle brand used on the ranch (if any), skulls of oxen or cattle, ox yokes or singletrees, to name only a few typical additions. To produce gateways like these, the farmer or the rancher needs to go far beyond the practical necessity of providing a gap in the fence through which one may drive or ride. Indeed, it would be difficult to see these ranch entries as anything but symbolic pronouncements of presence and ownership.

Sometimes these aesthetic features become so widely known and accepted by people outside the occupation or the area immediately concerned that they become formally stated expectations of the outsiders. For example, among many who feel that the painted advertisements for tobacco and liver pills on western barns in the 1930s are a part of western culture, there has developed an attitude that farmers ought to keep these signs repainted so that they can *remain* a part of the aesthetic scene. "Motif Number One," a small fish-storage house in Rockport, Massachusetts, is so well known to artists that its owner need only let the rumor get out that he is planning to paint his building and the artist community comes together and paints it for him so that it will remain quaintly old in its "original" colors. Similarly, when the owner of that building decided to provide electrical service to it, the artist community paid for burying the electric lines in the granite pier on which it stands to avoid the unsightly appearance of electrical wires in the pictures of photographers. In this case, the aesthetic judgments are being exercised not by the owner and his fishing community, but by a larger formal aesthetic community of outsiders who want to maintain favorite design elements forever. But in most live cultures, things do not stay the same way forever; they are always changing bit by bit in response to the times. Only someone who is fully conversant with the shared values of his group knows exactly how far a change can be made without allowing his farm, boat, fish house, etc., to be thought of as totally ludicrous or as the property of a lunatic (or, even worse, a outsider).

Sometimes an item is defined one way by its own physical appearance and still another way by oral tradition. In many parts of the desert West the ground is so hard that it is difficult to dig fencepost holes or to drive fence stakes into the ground. In these area, wire fences are often stabilized by "rock jacks," small boxes or bins made with scrap lumber and filled with local rocks to anchor corners and keep wire fences tight. Some of these rock jacks are built as open-sided trangles, and in many parts of the West one hears the local explanation given to tourists that these are in fact rock *traps* which catch the rocks that are being blown across the fields by the high winds. The rock traps act not only to keep blowing missiles off the highways but actually help in so doing to stabilize the fence row itself. Clearly, in these areas there is often a problem of wind, and so to one degree the concept of a rock trap is not a lie but rather a hyperbole. The outsider, of course, does not know this or at least does not know exactly how far the truth actually extends into the story. The insider, secure in his knowledge of his landscape (and probably much to the amusement of his friends who are also insiders), has the opportunity to show humorous differences between himself and the passerby, usually to the embarrassment of the latter. These functioning elements in the daily human lives of the people in a given area are every bit as important to our concept of history as are the artifacts themselves, for they help express the emotional connections of those who share the culture.

Quilts are sometimes dismissed as merely attractive objects that we use to keep warm in the winter. But quilts have also been described by folk-art critics as "unnecessarily beautiful," acknowledging that the warmth of a quilt has very little to do with the tremendous artistic detail of the pattern. Many quilts are the result of collaboration among a number of people, who make the quilt squares separately at home and then come together for the communal piecing of the top and then eventually the quilting of the entire object. The designs of quilts tend to be very regular, symmetrical, linear, just as the way we deal with the land is symmetrical, linear, and regulated. Indeed, one can see from the air many of the same designs plowed into the landscape by ranchers and road-builders. While it is probably too much to suggest that husbands and wives on ranches consult each other for patterns that might make appropriate matches between plowing and decorating the bed, still one cannot help noticing that the culture uses certain recurrent designs to project the idea of stability and regularity in all of life. To this extent, plowing may go far beyond the immediate practical aspect of how to turn over the dirt in a certain area of ground and may have to do with the kinds of symmetry and finesse that demonstrate the capacity of the farmer to handle his machinery in admirably controlled ways. Similarly, the housewife who makes quilts that are extremely geometrical has not had to invent this idea but has picked it up from numerous quilts (in addition to many other things in our culture) that feature symmetry, balance, and geometrical reciprocation.

Moreover, there are some kinds of quilts that "contain" an extra dimension of meaning. It is a fairly common custom, for example, to give a newlywed couple a Wedding Ring or a Log Cabin pattern as a wedding gift. Other patterns such as Drunkard's Path and Turkey Tracks, suggestive of wandering away from the straight and narrow, are usually avoided as gifts for young married couples. Certainly our quiltmakers do not believe there is a magical property within the quilt that gives the design some sort of psychological influence over the person who sleeps under it. At the same time, it is equally certain that the quilters feel there is a definite sense of propriety in giving quilts: some patterns are more appropriate than others in terms of what one wishes for the recipient. In other words, the quilt pattern itself can be seen as a performance of a certain *attitude* that the gift-giver would like to transmit as part of the gift—and who can say but that this is perhaps the most important part of the gift, intensified by the labor, love, and talent required to produce a good quilt?

Still other kinds of quilts, like the Friendship Crazy Quilts, are often stunning examples of inventiveness in stitchery and design. The square blocks that make up such a quilt are arranged in regular, symmetrical rows, but each block itself is made up of materials of all colors and of different shapes. The squares take precedence in the larger pattern; but usually within each square the pieces are stitched together using decorative designs in stitchery that testify to the wide repertoire of needlework skills performed by those who have come together to make an addition to a trousseau or a hope chest. One often finds on such friendship quilts small panels with painted subjects on them (flowers, barns, sport items, and the like) that are reference points to tastes, attitudes, and hobbies of the recipient. Indeed, the heavy load of personal reminiscence (especially when such a quilt is also made out of bits of material from family clothing) is so strong, the intense addition of decorative work by friends so impressive, that one might venture to say that the function of warming someone in a bed is the least important of all the dimensions in a friendship quilt. This means that the quilt itself, in terms of its "content" and execution, is more to be found in the performance of quilting than in the quilt's physical reality.

More strong indications that our physical artifacts are touchstones to more complex beliefs and values are the monuments that we produce for our cemeteries. In Butte, Montana, for example, one sees markers on the graves of Irish people designed to look like Celtic crosses. The design of the stone itself thus testifies to the ethnic and national background of the person buried there and goes far beyond the practical matter of recording name and date. In other parts of the West one finds photographs of the deceased placed on gravestones, especially in cemeteries where many immigrants from central and northern Europe repose. In ranching areas of the West it is common to find ranch motifs such as cattle, horses, lassos, fiddles, and the like, as well as flower containers made of singletrees decorated with ranch brands. Along the coast of the Northwest (for example, at Astoria, Oregon), one finds cemeteries mainly containing nautical designs and motifs, many of them showing exactly which kind of fishing boat was used by the deceased or which local ethnic group he or she belonged to.

Still other kinds of physical expressions of shared values may be found in the ways in which people arrange their yards, both front and back. In many part of the west, Hispanic people have erected small altars to the Virgin Mary in their yards by burying a bathtub on one end as an alcove into which a madonna statue is set. In some areas a fence is more or less expected around the yard, while in other areas it is seen as an offense to neighbors. Even the way one trims the grass or places plants and shrubs in the front yard may be not only a reference to the owner's taste in vegetation but a proclamation to the neighborhood that everything is under control and the neighborhood is a pleasant place to live. Some years ago, when wood-burning stoves were a sign of relative poverty, most people who burned wood left their firewood in stacks behind the house where they were not easily seen from the street. Nowadays, wood-burning devices have become marks of energy conservation and comfortable nostalgia, and one often finds suburban homes with attractive breezeways, porches, and carports stacked neatly with a magnificent display of nicely split wood. Where we put things in our yard says something about our attitudes toward the objects and toward each other, and even in something so practical as our storing of a supply of firewood we can notice some changing values in our society. Going beyond that, however, one notices that certain families in certain regions have particular ways of stacking wood that may depend on the kind of wood being used and how small it is split (which may depend on what kind of device is used to burn the wood).

Just as a neat yard suggests a neat family, a neat and stable woodpile may suggest something, or may at least project an idea for the family who owns it. In some parts of Europe, people in different regions use different shapes of woodpile: some round, some square, some leaning up against buildings, some free standing. In Germany and Austria, it is common to split firewood into fairly small pieces and to stack them so neatly that one can pass his hand over the end of the pile and barely feel a rough surface. Sometimes an entire wall of a huge old farm house will be covered on the outside with a compulsively neat stack of wood which looks so regular that it might have been painted on. One may ask the farmer why so much time is put into the labor of such a neat woodpile when there are so many other things to do on a large farm, and one will often receive the reply: "If one has a messy woodpile, one can't get rid of his daughters." At the same time, the questioner might find out that this particular farmer has no daughters, but he acknowledges living in a village where this value of neatness is an expression of qualities that are deeply valued by other members of the same community.

In some parts of southern Idaho and Utah, as well as a small strip in eastern Oregon, one often sees the so-called Mormon hay derrick, or Jackson fork derrick. Looking like the bones of old dinosaurs on the horizon, these practical machines from the bygone era of loose hay are often allowed to stand on a ranch as testimony to the fact that the rancher has been there since earlier times. One rancher nearly fired a new foreman who as his first act of tidying up the ranch dismantled the hay derrick in a nearby field. This is another indication that objects, when they lose their immediate practical values, may still be highly prized for their symbolic or cultural meaning. Items that tie us together with our family's past or with the vicissitudes of early life in our region are objects that we get rid of only with great hesitation. Indeed, some objects like the Jackson fork hay derrick seem to *gain* meaning with age, in almost direct relation to the speed with which they lose practical value. As with the cream separator or the hand-held plow used as a proclamation at the front driveway of a farmhouse, certain farm implements that testify to age and tenure become more and more symbolic the longer the span of time they represent. They are attachments not only to previous times but to relatives and friends whose actions and values set the stage for our present way of life. We memorialize them and their meaning by using these symbols as more than practical objects.

Artifacts, insofar as they arise from the shared attitudes and usages of closely related people, can be viewed as performances of cultural meaning, as cameos that give physical representation to a wide range of shared abstract feelings and values. Along with our attempt to measure, weigh, photograph, and explain the physical details produced by our culture, we should insure that these human expressive dimensions receive not only attention but a high level of evaluation for the rich and complex way they can reveal our cultural bearings to us.

Technology as a Determinant in Later Mormon Settlement in Eastern Idaho

A.J. Simmonds

In 1931 Walter Prescott Webb postulated in his classic study of the Great Plains that the development of varied technologies made possible the settlement of the American high prairies. Webb maintained that it was the windmill to raise water, the revolver to give protection, and barbed wire to bound the treeless farms that gave pioneer settlers the chance for success on the Great Plains.[1]

While each of the technologies Webb mentions played a role in Mormon settlement in the Great Basin, by no means were all—or even any—of them crucial to Mormon pioneer settlement. Indeed, it is probable that one can isolate but one technology—and that really an adaptation of nature—which played any crucial role in early Mormon settlement.

One looks to theology and sociology, not to technology, to explain Mormon pioneer settlement in the West. Given a stream, Mormons would build a farm village, laid out foursquare with the compass, of wide streets and large lots. Farmyards and residences would be in the village; the farmland would lie beyond it. In a centrally located town square, churches and schools would rise. Beyond the fields, unfarmed land would provide pasturage for domestic animals, and somewhere beyond the unfarmed land—on another creekbank—another village, much like the first, would rise.

If one looks at early Mormon settlement, it is clearly seen as a sociological, a theological phenomenon. Mormons lived predominantly in village clusters surrounded by small watered fields because that was the way they chose to order their society: certainly not for any technological or geographical imperative.

The only adaptive technology that one can discern in early Mormon settlement in the Great Basin was irrigation. And even that was disarmingly simple. Essentially, early Mormon irrigation diverted a creek or river into a ditch that meandered along a hillside in a gently falling grade and supplied water to the fields below it. It was a methodology that quickly—and relatively easily—enabled the settlement of all the hillsides along the Wasatch Mountains from Oxford, Idaho, on the north to St. George and Santa Clara, Utah, on the south.

But as a methodology it had severe limitations. First, it was limited to hillside slopes, a fact which dictated that, though Mormon settlement might stretch for hundreds of miles along the face of the Great Basin's major ranges, it was never more than a few miles in width. In many places a kid with a good arm could have thrown a rock across irrigated Utah; and in virtually all places, a pistol could be shot across the whole width of the irrigated fields. Second, however great the canal, only one side of it could be tapped for water: the other side was uphill. This limited concept of irrigation science restricted the areas open to early Mormon settlement. A valley might be ringed with farm villages and its surplus population urged to emigrate while the flat, fertile valley centers remained uninhabited.

One cannot deprecate the efficiency or the successes of early Mormon colonization. If they did not—as they were wont to claim—make the desert blossom as the rose, they did foster the most extensive agrarian settlement in the early Intermountain West, creating oases that facilitated the occupation and exploitation of other areas. What they did, they did well. But early Mormon colonization in the Intermountain West was limited by more than just the Mormon capacity to man it. It was limited technologically and environmentally to those areas that the Mormons could exploit by the methods they perfected in the Salt Lake Valley in the late 1840s. And those environmental and technological limitations were expressed in several ways:

1) They were limited to those projects that could be accomplished by a labor-intensive cooperative society. Mechanization and—more important—capital for mechanization were largely unavailable.

2) Their colonization was limited to irrigation and to irrigable tracts of land.

3) Since their irrigation techniques were little advanced beyond those of Neolithic farmers in the Fertile Crescent, theirs was a hillside settlement; and while they were very effective at settling sloping terrain, once the Mormons ran out of hillsides, they were stopped. Their technology did not extend to the flats.

In the fall of 1981, in an address on the occasion of the centennial of Preston, Idaho, I compared Preston in northern Cache Valley—settled in 1881—with the earlier Mormon communities in southern Cache Valley that were settled in 1859 and 1860. With the single exception of the necessity for a stream of water large enough to be diverted for irrigation, the answer to every question one can postulate about towns like Mendon, Millville, Hyrum, or Paradise, Utah, can be met by a sociological or a theological answer. On the contrary, virtually every question one can postulate about a town like Preston or Rigby, Idaho, is answerable by reference to some technological factor. And in that dichotomy, in the generation between 1860 and 1890, is to be found substantial and substantive change in the Mormon response to the environment.

What were the changes? What facilitated them? I suggest there were three — three technologies — and I shall discuss each in turn: engineered irrigation; dry farming; and monetary liquidity.

The initial limited concept of the usability of irrigation science in Mormon colonization posed a technological barrier to Mormon settlement, and the pioneers reached it in the late 1860s. Virtually every hillside in Utah was settled by 1870 — settled by the time the transcontinental railroad reached Utah.

Thousands of Utahns (and in 1869 that term included the settlers of Franklin and Bear Lake counties in Idaho) were hired by the Union Pacific and the Central Pacific to build the railroad grade from Evanston, Wyoming, to Wells, Nevada. It was a brutal kind of job, but it taught all sorts of valuable lessons. The workers used all the techniques common to railroad construction: they built a level, elevated grade for the track; they tunneled through mountains; they built trestles over hollows and ravines. And when the transcontinental railroad was completed by the driving of the Golden Spike in 1869, they went on to build the Utah Central Railroad, the Utah Northern Railroad, and — eventually — the Oregon Short Line Railroad. When they were finished with them, they came home to their watered fields and applied what they had learned on the railroad to the problems of irrigation.

They built a railroad grade and dug a ditch down the middle of it and had an irrigation levee. Among the earliest — if not the earliest — in Utah were the canals that carried water from the Logan River to the center of Cache Valley in the early 1870s and the canals from Worm Creek and Cub River that were built between 1870 and 1875 to water Lewiston, Utah, and Fairview and Whitney, Idaho.

They built ditches atop railroad trestles — flumes — and saved miles of construction. They surveyed highline canals and when a mountain intervened, they tunneled through it.

Each of these devices was known in the transportation canals in the Midwest in the 1830s and 1840s. Flumes and tunnels were certainly used in the gold-mining regions of the West from at least the 1850s. But they were not employed for irrigation until the Mormons began their use after the construction of the transcontinental railroad.

Dry farming, the production of crops on land with total annual precipitation of between ten and twenty-two inches, was always intriguing to Mormon pioneers. Could the broad tracts above their canals be farmed? Were there crops that could grow there without the blinding toil of irrigation? For forty years in various degrees and in various places, there were individual and collective experiments with dry farming. John Lamborn's definitive study has traced the tortured course of dry-land agriculture in this region from a concept and a hope in the 1850s to full-fledged science by the turn of the century.[2]

Dry farming required substantial social change for the Mormons. The acreage required for the same sort of yield on dry land that one could achieve on irrigated land (two to three times as much) meant that the farm village could no longer be the basis of Mormon agriculture. The acreage demands of dry farming at last brought the Mormons into the federal land system.

Much has been written about the federal survey of the public domain virtually compelling settlers into physical isolation by placing them on large holdings—from 40 to 640 acres. It may well have been the sheer size of farm holdings that fostered the revolutionary mechanization of much eastern and midwestern agriculture from the 1850s to the 1880s. But in Mormon areas, that was not the case. The Mormon village-and-field system did not readily accomodate itself to the federal survey. Consequently, until the 1870s, the survey was ignored.

No federal land office was opened in Utah until 1869, twenty-two years after settlement. By the time it was opened, the settlement pattern was a fixed one of small land holdings with farmers resident in town, not on their farms. Instead of conforming to the federal land survey, the Mormons made the federal survey conform to their own land system. Patents might be issued for a quarter section, but the patentee then usually deeded parts of the land back to those owners who held it under tenture from the local Mormon bishop. Today, in most counties in Utah, land around the earliest settlements is still described in the lots, blocks, and fields of pioneer surveys rather than by the section, township, and range of the later federal surveys.

But Mormon reliance upon the Homestead and Pre-emption acts for dry farmland in northern Utah in the 1870s and 1880s seems to have conditioned them to the federal survey, conditioned them in such a way that settlement in the Upper Snake River Valley followed traditional American lines.

The third item necessary for later Mormon expansion in eastern Idaho was monetary liquidity: the development of a system of making outside capital in the form of loans and mortgages available to the agricultural community. This was a late development in Utah and Mormon history. In enumerating any list of technologies that facilitated later Mormon colonization, one must consider the role of capital. It may seem out of place to list mortgage banking as a technology, but when one considers the almost separate nationhood of the early Mormon Great Basin, the role of capital becomes crucial to understanding change.

Mormon society was never as closed as its contemporary enemies and some of its modern analysts have suggested. It was certainly open to new technology. Two conditions, however, slowed acceptance: first, the limited land holdings did not provide for the same individual demand for farm mechanization as existed in the Midwest; and the cooperative nature of most Mormon farming actually lessened the need for mechanization. Secondly, there was not the available capital to exploit existing technology. In that regard, pioneer Utah was much like many Third World nations today.

The early Mormon Intermountain West was starved for capital. The overwhelming numbers of immigrants brought little to the area but religious enthusiasm and raw sinew. Even bonanzas like the cross-country California Gold Rush, the sale of Fort Crittenden (home base for Johnston's Army, the Utah Expedition of 1857-1858), or the produce trade with the Idaho or Montana mines were consumed by the demands of a multinational church, spent for religious buildings, or simply lost in a series of ill-founded industrial enterprises. Mormon life in the early Great Basin was too often a dreary litany of barely self-sufficient agriculture.

Outside capital was invested in the mines and railroads of the Great Basin, not in its farms. And the mines and the railroads were not owned by Mormons. Of course, Mormon agriculture was not alone in its dearth of capital resources. The Grangers and Populists are ample evidence that it was a national phenomenon. But Mormon agriculture suffered the added handicap of being so severely limited and circumscribed by its environment: the need for irrigation and the necessity of cooperative endeavor. Early Mormon agriculture in the Intermountain West was locked in a cycle; farms were small at least partially because there was no available capital to mechanize them and make possible a larger operation, and consequently they could not produce enough to foster capital.

That the technology existed to mechanize Utah's farms in the 1860s and 1870s is undeniable. The Midwest was regularly and commonly employing in 1875 agricultural machinery that would not be common on Mormon farms until 1890. Much—maybe most—Cache Valley grain was still being hand-scythed and hand-shocked in 1890 because reapers, binders, and headers were not commonly available to the farmers. The reason seems clear. There was not the available capital to finance the mechanization of Mormon agriculture. In 1890 the total capitalization of all the banks north of Salt Lake City was less than $500,000. Yet a decade later, tax assessment records show that the average farmer possessed a bewildering array of agricultural implements.

The abstract books in the various county recorders' offices seem to indicate why. Cache County, Utah (and until 1872 the county was thought to include all of Cache Valley, including the present Franklin County, Idaho), was established by the Utah Territorial Assembly of 1856. Between 1856 and February, 1890—thirty-four years—mortgages filed with the country recorder filled only two volumes, some 1400 pages. Yet from February, 1890 until February, 1901—eleven years—filed mortgages filled twenty-one books, nearly 13,000 folio pages. Clearly something happened in those years for farm debt in the most important trans-state valley to have increased so astronomically.

What happened in Cache Valley was the availability of a substantial flow of mortgage money from the Midwest. In 1891 George H. Champ, who had been securing right-of-way deeds for the Union Pacific extension from Milford, Utah, to San Pedro, California, visited his sister, who taught school at St. John's in Logan, Utah. Champ had previously been in business in Council Bluffs, Iowa, and Rockford, Illinois, and the financial prospects in Cache Valley interested him. The valley's only bank, Thatcher Brothers, held a virtually monopoly on mortgage money, and short-term loans at interest rates of eighteen percent and more were the norm. Champ seized the opening. He organized Utah Mortgage and Loan (and later First National and Cache Valley Bank) and arranged to invest money from Rockford banks in local mortgages at a lower rate of interest and for a longer period than that of Thatcher Brothers. Success was immediate, and Illinois money handled by George Champ was largely responsible for financing the construction of area canals and for the mechanization of Cache Valley agriculture in the 1890s. From a capital-starved area in the 1880s, Cache Valley and its colonial outposts in eastern Idaho entered the twentieth century with assured access to major money markets in the Midwest.

In his classic study of the nineteenth-century Mormon economy, *Great Basin Kingdom,* Leonard J. Arrington wrote: "The prime economic problem of Mormon Country in the late 1870s and early 1880s was overpopulation. In every valley there were signs that the continued flow of immigration, and the natural increase in population, had filled up the land. Young married couples were not able to find farms; older people found themselves under-employed."[3]

But even the agricultural population of most Mormon areas is today much greater than it was in the 1880s. Arrington's claim must be redacted to stress that in the 1880s, given the available technology, the Mormon colonies had reached a point of saturation beyond which there was no clear way to increase land utilization to accomodate the increasing population. But new areas were found: in the center of Utah's valleys and—most important—in the Upper Snake River Valley of eastern Idaho. And the new areas were opened and exploited by recourse to the technologies mentioned above. Because of those technologies, Mormon colonization changed—changed dramatically enough that a Mormon area in Madison County bore much more resemblance to a Protestant area in Gem or Payette or Canyon County that it did to early Mormon centers in Utah.

Early Mormon settlement was village settlement. Maps of the earlier settled valleys in Utah show numerous towns close together. The farmers lived in the village, and the villages were but a few miles apart. Later Mormon colonization—that in most of eastern Idaho—was made independently of the farm village. Indeed, villages as anything more than neighborhood or crossroads hamlets are virtually nonexistent in the Upper Snake River Valley. Later Mormon settlement did not often employ the village; but it did give rise to towns. And the towns that are born from the later colonies differ in few ways from the towns that developed in the Midwest. Preston, Rigby, St. Anthony, Ashton, even Driggs and Victor, are essentially farm towns whose only difference from other farm towns in the Midwest or the Northwest or anywhere else in the republic is that they are largely inhabited by Mormons. There is a fundamental difference between this kind of Mormon town and a Mormon village of the 1850s.

In 1860 one cannot separate the town of Franklin from the settlement of that part of Franklin County. They are synonymous. But in 1900 it is clearly possible to separate Driggs from the settlement of the Teton Basin. The relationship between land and town has become a symbiotic role, not an exclusive one.

It was in large part the practicality (because of new techniques of irrigation and the new practice of dry farming and the access to long-term mortgage money for mechanization or canal construction) of utilizing larger farm units that also brought Mormon settlement into compliance with federal land laws.

The map of Madison or Fremont or Bonneville or Bingham County shows numerous placenames. But most of the dots are those for crossroads villages, for schools, for post offices. They are with few exceptions the names of places that grew upon the land in response to the settlement of the land. They are not towns surveyed and staked and occupied as a prelude to land settlement.

There was no compelling reason why Rexburg could not have been settled like Smithfield or scores of other early Utah towns as the Mormons themselves were doing in the 1880s in northern Mexico. The fact that it was not suggests that the pioneer settlement pattern was a response to the environment as much as to a sociological or theological tenet; and that once new technologies made possible different environmental responses, the Mormon population was willing to embrace them.

Mormon settlement in the Upper Snake River Valley occurred largely on isolated homesteads watered by huge feeder canals capable of irrigating vast tracts of land—vast tracts of level land, not the hillsides of early Utah, and not the limited canal systems of early Utah.

But, of course, the three technologies that facilitated the later Mormon colonization of Idaho also facilitated the settlement of non-Mormons in Idaho; they, and others, were employed along the whole extent of the Snake River Valley. And that is the point. It took these technologies to settle the major parts, the richest agricultural parts, of the Intermountain West. They are the technologies we must look at to understand the settlement of most of southern Idaho. Most of southern Idaho is the product of these technologies, and in their employ the state's farmlands enjoy a unifying theme. However many cultural differences might separate Teton County from Payette County or Fremont from Camas, the way the land was settled is not one of them. However much the eastern Idaho counties might feel themselves an extension of Utah, only in their religious origins is that true. Later Mormon colonies in Idaho—whether in the Boise and Payette, the Little Wood, or the Upper Snake River valleys—represented as much a break with Utah antecedents as Utah represented with the Midwest.

Notes

1. Walter Prescott Webb, *The Great Plains* (Boston: Ginn and Company, 1931; reissued, New York: Grosset and Dunlap, [1957]), pp. 510-511.

2. John Lamborn, "A History of the Development of Dry-Farming in Utah and Southern Idaho" (master's thesis, Utah State University, 1978).

3. Leonard J. Arrington, *Great Basin Kingdom* (Cambridge, Massachusetts: Harvard University Press, 1958), p. 354.

Interpreting Eastern Washington through the Camera of a Seattle Photographer

G. Thomas Edwards

How many times have you heard the assertion that a picture is worth a thousand words? Do you believe it? But does not this commonplace saying assume that a viewer understands what he sees? Poignant Civil War photographs and spectacular views of enormous trees prompt considerable interpretation; such pictures support those voicing the assertion. But many photographs are not worth even a hundred words because the viewer lacks experience or knowledge for intelligent interpretation. It is the historian's task to provide informed and interpretive captions that will make photographs significant. To make any photograph more rewarding—perhaps even worth a thousand words to some viewers—the interpreter must value an old adage: "seek and ye shall find."

When asked to prepare this essay, I was told: "We have found that while there is a good deal of information on identifying, cataloging, and preserving photographs, there is little discussion of interpreting historic photographs." I was asked to provide "a chance to learn about the interpretive process and view it at work in relation to a specific research question." I hope to fulfill my obligation by summarizing an interpretation of photographer Asahel Curtis' early work in eastern Washington. I shall outline my research methods and interpret some photographs. Fortunately, I shall not show how each is worth a thousand words.

Curtis, a skilled Seattle photographer, took approximately 60,000 pictures from 1897 until his death in 1941. He made a good living through selling prints of buildings, plants, machines, mines, mills, and farms. As a commercial photographer he focused on "the products, process, and prospects" of Washington.[1] Like other boosters, he stressed economic growth. But his work can be used as effectively by social historians as by those studying economic themes. The political, economic, cultural, or social questions historians ask about photographs, like those they ask about written documents, provide interpretations.

In the summer of 1980 the Washington State Historical Society asked me to be among the consultants who would, under the direction of librarian Jeanne Engerman, study the Curtis collection. The Society holds his negatives and wanted to prepare a traveling exhibit; thus consultants would help choose and interpret photographs. While examining several hundred prints, I became curious about those depicting agricultural conditions along the state's arid river valleys. I formulated basic questions: Why would a Seattle cameraman in the years between 1906 and 1911 have traveled east of the Cascades and taken numerous shots of farms, homes, crops, and rural landscapes? Why had Curtis made contracts for irrigation subjects with railroad corporations, commercial clubs, and land companies with investments in the Yakima, Snake, and Columbia river valleys?

From studying regional history, I was aware of the economic boom that occurred along these river valleys in the early 1900s; historical geographer D. W. Meinig, for example, stated that "there was a continuing influx of people and considerable speculation in land; an expansive optimism pervaded the . . . major irrigation districts."[2] Curtis' camera had recorded much of this significant story. I decided to demonstrate this by interpreting appealing and representative photographs; obviously the pictures and Curtis' business records must be supplemented by facts discovered through traditional research methods. Jeanne Engerman expressed enthusiasm for such a study because she favored these rural scenes over urban ones. Historians always welcome moral support.

I must digress to admit that I came to this historical task with little experience. I had been reared and educated in Portland, Taft, and Eugene; in these places mud puddles, not irrigation ditches, filled annually. For about sixteen years I had made numerous automobile trips through and airplane rides over the arid valleys of eastern Washington and had posed very few historical questions about the irrigation systems operating on the barren landscape. I more frequently inquired of my wife about how many more miles until we were out of sage and into trees. The reason I mention my lack of background prior to 1980 is to emphasize that the historian's interest and technique, not his experience, are crucial factors in interpreting photographs. The researcher does not need to have served as a Civil War infantryman to describe Gettysburg or to have been an orchardist to write irrigation history.

After concluding that I had a worthwhile research topic, I decided that my first task was to discover how boosters had used the Curtis photographs. A search for eastern Washington's promotional literature was rewarding: I found dozens of appropriate brochures, pamphlets, and booklets in Tacoma, Eugene, Portland, and Seattle libraries. Although the Whitman College Library was initially of little use, a coincidence quickly changed things. A retired railroader offered the library about fifty promotional publications that would serve as a starting point.

Pamphlets trumpeting the advantages of Yakima, Ellensburg, Spokane, Kennewick, Sunnyside, or Walla Walla were anticipated, but I was surprised to find that such hamlets—some of which have died—as Two Rivers, Attalia, Burbank, Beverly, and Hanford had champions. These Washington towns and villages contended with each other for immigrants and investments; furthermore, they competed with such other communities in the region as Boise, American Falls, Hailey, The Dalles, Mosier, Stanfield, and Baker.

Many handsome eastern Washington publications contained Curtis photographs; sometimes his illustrations received interpretation. But the boosters did not usually provide enough information for either potential immigrants or historians. For example, they enthused over irrigation—a ten-acre farm would provide its owner with "the salary of the average bank president"—but generally glossed over its techniques and difficulties.[3] A study of promotional literature prompted additional questions about illustrations; for example, why were such subjects as farm homes frequently included and why were graphic shots of land preparation generally ignored?

To find answers to questions about early irrigation techniques, I sought to interview those who had practiced or observed them. I found such authorities by asking Frances Hare of the Yakima Valley Museum to arrange a meeting with knowledgeable men and women. She graciously assembled five Yakimans; they sat around a table, examining my xeroxed copies of photographs. I recorded their wide-ranging responses. These authorities voiced details and interpretations that could not be found in any printed source. Some photographs *were* worth a thousand words to them: Curtis linked them with their adolescence. William Gray, superintendent of the United States Bureau of Reclamation office in Yakima, patiently explained irrigation techniques past and present. Pasco historian Walter A. Oberst provided insights and led me to the Franklin County Courthouse, where I found legal records of irrigation companies. The process of interpretation is never complete; every time I show slides the audience provides additional details, ideas, and names of informed individuals. I would encourage everyone analyzing twentieth-century photographs to consult with local authorities; librarians and members of local historical societies often recommend those who can help interpret.

Although interviews were very beneficial, it was still necessary to use such traditional sources as books, articles, newspapers, government documents, city directories, manuscripts, maps, and other photographic collections. Fortunately Curtis dated most photographs; therefore, I did not have great difficulty, as many researchers do, with dates. It was necessary to compare Curtis with other cameramen. I was able to place him in historical context by consulting with University of Washington librarian Dennis Andersen, an authority on regional photography. During a trip to Riverside, California, my wife and I gathered materials that provided a comparison of Curtis' promotional photographs with those made by other talented professionals working for the citrus industry.

This, in brief, was the method I followed in accumulating information. I shall interpret some Curtis photographs that document the economic boom that occurred in the arid valleys between 1906 and 1911. Many of these scenes were published in attractive promotional pamphlets. Obviously agricultural centers in the thinly populated arid region lacked the resources to publish such literature. Thus urban professionals prepared them, and the best came from Portlander William B. Wells. Having acquired editorial and advertising experience with *The Pacific Monthly* and *Sunset*, Wells was a resourceful booster employed by the Harriman railroads. Wells devised a community plan whereby local commercial clubs and Harriman's various Pacific Northwest railroads signed contracts for the publication of promotional materials. He dispatched photographs, artists, and writers to more than sixty towns and claimed that between 1907 and 1911 his office arranged for "the whole burden of community publicity [to] be taken from the shoulders of the community and placed on the great Harriman system."[4] About ninety Oregon, Washington, and Idaho communities worked out agreements for the production of what Wells called "community literature." The Portland executive boasted that over 12,000,000 copies were published and that the $750,000 expended on the community plan—the railroads put far more money into it than did the towns—was of tremendous regional benefit.[5]

Several cameramen, including Curtis, worked for Harriman's railroads. Some of the requirements imposed by Wells helped me interpret Curtis' work. The Portlander expected the Seattleite, like others in his craft, to "produce . . . work which would represent the community to best advantage and induce settlement."[6] Specific instructions read:

> If apple orchard, give boxes grown per tree, cost of production per box, selling price, cost of land, cost of planting, net profits per acre, etc. Where unusual records are made in any line, secure them. Human interest stories are especially wanted. These details are as important as the photograph itself, and the photographer is relied upon to dig out the information desired.[7]

The photographs published here help document two very different irrigation histories: the unsuccessful attempt to develop a part of the

Columbia River Valley and the prosperous transformation of the Yakima River Valley. In 1909 the Burbank Land Company, struggling against severe physical obstacles in an effort to transform Columbia River sagelands into orchards, paid Curtis to photograph their accomplishments. This resulted in valuable pictures of the Burbank Project that stretched south of the Snake River.

Sited five miles above the mouth of the river, a pumping station lifted water into a main canal (fig. 1). The company maintained that by bringing water to the land an acre increased in value from $20 to $500. The main canal ran thirteen miles southeasterly toward Two Rivers, a new town in the Burbank Project. A county map helped me to identify most of the buildings. From the sandy intersection of Sixth and Broadway, Curtis captured in one exposure nearly all of the town and much of its traffic (fig. 2). The buildings on the left facing Broadway are a store, an unidentified structure that may have provided office space for the local dentist and lawyer, and the Two River Hotel. Across Seventh Street is a livery stable. On the right is the Pioneer Cash Store, a business that advertised hay, grain, and feed, and next door is a building that probably divided its space between the post office and the Two Rivers Investment Company, sellers of real estate. The only other building in town housed the office of the telephone company and the *Two Rivers Tribune*, a newspaper serving 100 local inhabitants who hoped that prosperity based upon irrigation would mean improved streets, sidewalks, shade trees, lawns, a bank, and more business. While citizens predicted that by 1912 some 10,000 people would prosper in adjacent irrigation districts and that Two Rivers had a brighter future than either local competitors (such as Attalia and Burbank) or the new lands opened in the Yakima Valley, the town dozed amid heat, sand, dust, and sage.

Curtis posed a teacher and her ten pupils in front of a one-room school house (fig. 3). Promoters rejected this bleak photograph but used a small print of one that shows the main flume carrying water to a new alfalfa field. Below the cedar flume is an irrigation ditch or settling basin; pipes or tubes carried the water from this source to the maze of furrows. Although my Yakima authorities recalled many such scenes, boosters rarely selected such stark pictures.

Curtis took a series of remarkable shots that demonstrated the way that the land was prepared for irrigation, including a primitive way to grub sage (fig. 4). Following the grubbing and burning of sage, the land was, if necessary, plowed, then graded to provide for the flow of water, and finally ditched. All of these preparations could be done within two weeks at costs ranging from $20 to $50 per acre.

The primitive conditions of the Burbank Project contrasted with the older Yakima Valley irrigation districts whose boosters wanted Curtis to record both their general prosperity and the promise of small irrigated

Fig. 1. Pumping station on the Burbank Project. This and the following photographs are from the collection of the Washington State Historical Society and are used with its permisson. WSHS #13383.

Fig. 2. The town of Two Rivers, Washington, nine miles southwest of Pasco—on neither the Columbia nor the Snake rivers. WHSH #13364.

Fig. 3. Teacher and students at a one-room school in the Yakima Valley. WSHS #13389.

Fig. 4. Grubbing sagebrush in Walla Walla County. WSHS, unnumbered.

farms. Thus dozens of his pictures show the economic boom. He captured many irrigation techniques, including intercropping. While waiting for fruit trees to grow, orchardists practiced intercropping, the growing of fruits, vegetables, and forage between the rows of young trees. Photographed in the spring of 1910, one young orchard is cultivated so that "a dust mulch is formed, which acts as a non-conductor of moisture";[8] in fact, about three inches below the surface the dirt is "so moist that it will form a ball in the hand." This technique prevented the roots from drying out. The farmer will soon dig irrigation rows. This typical two-year-old orchard contains apple trees and peach-tree fillers. The larger peach trees will provide a crop in their third year; the apple trees will take nearly twice as long to produce commercially. Sometime after the trees are twelve years old, the orchardist will cut out his peach trees in favor of his more valuable apple trees.

This illustration can be used to do more than explain intercropping; an economic historian, for example, could use it in discussing the market problem. Too many such orchards had been planted; overproduction meant ruinous prices in 1912.

Two panoramic views, taken in 1908 from a hillside overlooking the productive Upper Naches Valley, were proof of the wonders of irrigation (fig. 5). Although Curtis took many photographs from elevated sites, they were less important than his harvest pictures because the latter supported the argument that good—even sensational—profits could be made in orcharding. Promoters glowingly described a variety of crops, especially alfalfa and apples. One scene showing the harvest of alfalfa—a profitable forage—appeared in color (fig. 6). All of my five consultants complained that one winesap tree needed pruning. No doubt it would have improved the tree, but it would not have improved the photograph.

Two views of the 1910 peach harvest were designed to show nature's bounty (fig. 7). But an interpreter can also emphasize harvest techniques and working conditions; farm laborers, for example, received about $2.50 a day. Farmers hiring harvest hands recognized that they should be well trained, but one employer complained: "All labor seems to be daffy about amusements. The men would rather work in town for fifty cents a day where they can have a glass of beer after supper and see a ten-cent show. Jobs are too plentiful now for labor to stick."[9] In the late summer numerous exhibits of fruits and vegetables competed in fairs or were shown in cities in an attempt to broaden markets.

To attract attention, all the irrigated districts published photographs of trees, harvests, and exhibits. But there was one factor that only a few of the regional competitors enjoyed: the work conducted by engineers employed by the United States Reclamation Service (later the Bureau of Reclamation). The Service's projects, including the construction of dams and ditches, gave Yakimans an upper hand over Columbia Valley

Fig. 5. The Upper Naches Valley. WSHS #11313-1.

Fig. 6. Stacking alfalfa after harvest near Grandview, Washington. WSHS #21210.

Fig. 7. A "stone boat" hauling freshly harvested peaches in W. I. Huxtable's orchard.

Fig. 8 A Bucyrus dredge enlarging the Sunnyside Canal near Zillah, Washington. WSHS #21277.

developers who lacked federal assistance. In listing local advantages, Yakima boosters made certain that potential investors and immigrants understood the importance of the Reclamation Service. An example of its assistance was a Bucyrus dredge that slowly enlarged the Sunnyside Canal (fig. 8). A 1911 photograph shows the dredge's stern as its endless buckets chew the banks near Zillah.

Although no single photograph may be worth a thousand words, they collectively demonstrate developments in irrigated districts and neatly supplement the historian's prose. There is a timelessness about photographs; in 1982, as in 1910, a picture of a bearing apple tree or a child in an orchard can be more effective than several paragraphs. The work of Curtis and other cameramen makes us more aware of a significant boom in eastern Washington's arid river valleys. In the early 1900s, promoters used remarkable photographs to tell a story; the historian can also use them to advantage.

Notes

1. David Sucher, editor, *The Asahel Curtis Sampler* (Seattle: Puget Sound Access, 1973), n.p.
2. D. W. Meinig, *The Great Columbia Plain: A Historical Geography, 1805-1910* (Seattle: University of Washington Press, 1968), p. 442.
3. *Richland* (Seattle, n.d.), p. 39.
4. William Bittle Wells to Thomas Vaughan, November 11, 1957, William Bittle Wells Papers, University of Oregon Library, Eugene.
5. Wells praised his scheme: "As for the results produced by the Community Plan, judging by increased population, bank deposits, postal receipts, the laying out of new streets and sidewalks, the development of farming areas, and in every other aspect of community progress, the results were sensational." Wells, "The Story of My Life," unpublished manuscript, p. 125, Wells Papers.
6. Wells, "Outline of Co-Operative Plans," p. 1, Wells Papers.
7. "Record of Subject Photographed" (a form required of photographers working for the Harriman railroad lines), Wells Papers.
8. *Zillah Washington* (Zillah, n.d.), p. 14.
9. *Seventh Biennial Report of the Bureau of Labor Statistics and Factory Inspection, 1909-1910* (Olympia: State of Washington, 1910), p. 145.

Comment:
Understanding Ourselves

Judith Austin

Both Jeff Simmonds' essay on the impact of technology on settlement patterns and Tom Edwards' on promotional photography provide some sound ideas for looking at the history and development of our own communities. At a time when so much of Idaho is planning anniversary observances—the centennial of the state itself in 1990, that of a number of towns in this decade, and a great many 75th-anniversary celebrations—such ideas may be of special value to those working in local history.

How did a community get where it is? It is easy to say, if you live in a town that has been created or shaped by irrigation, that the crucial question is "when did water come?" But that may be true only in the most immediate sense. Where did the technology come from that made the canals and headgates and dams possible? Was it shaped by previous experience in Utah? Was it the dream of a mining engineer who wanted to try something different? Was it the expertise of highly trained hydraulic engineers who had built dams and irrigation works before?

Where did the capital come from to build the irrigation works? Was it human capital, provided by Mormon colonizers? Was it venture capital, provided by developers under the Carey Act—more successful in Idaho than in any other state in the West, as residents of the North Side system in south-central Idaho can attest? Was it federal capital, necessary when the size and complexity of the systems (and perhaps the need for fairness to settlers as well) required far greater funding than any private source could provide—as in the Boise and Minidoka projects, early creations of the federal government's reclamation program?

Once settlers came, how did they know how to farm on irrigated lands? How did they know what crops to plant, how much water to apply to them? Or *did* the first settlers on irrigated lands know much at all about how to use the land? Are the farmers in the area now the descendants of those first settlers, or did the first move on in failure and did it take another series—or more—of farmers and more assistance from experts to make a success of the land?

The same sorts of questions can, of course, be asked of other kinds of communities. Was the lumber town a "company town"? Are its community services built on company-provided facilities (are they *still* company-provided?)? What shaped the mining community? Were the buildings occupied by its residents and shopkeepers built on a standard set of plans provided from an office elsewhere? Were their plans the creations of local builders? Were they bought from catalogues?

In other words: how do we happen to know how to do what we do? Why are our communities laid out as they are—and why are the buildings in them designed as they are? What factors have shaped where we are?

Those who live in southwestern Idaho tend to assume that south eastern Idaho towns are like Utah towns—at least when they are know to be distinctly Mormon. There has been little cross-state research—little looking, for example, at how Congregationalist New Plymouth (as much a planned community as any in the state) compares with communities in the Mormon Upper Snake River Valley.

Nor have we looked closely at the difference agricultural technology makes in development. We are often asked why Boise grew so tremendously between the 1900 and 1910 censuses. The answer is relatively simple: the Reclamation (or Newlands) Act of 1902, which established the U.S. Reclamation Service, now the Bureau of Reclamation; and the development of the Boise Project, which created a large agricultural area for which Boise is the chief market and supply point. This is a step beyond the coming of technology and capital to southeastern Idaho that is described in Simmonds' essay. What—if anything—is different about the town that grew from this later technological development? Is there the same amount of difference between the towns of the 1870s and those of the 1910s as there is between those of the 1850s and 1870s—towns, that is, that perform essentially the same functions in their regions?

The basic data for answering these questions, for learning what has shaped our communities, are available largely within the communities themselves. Early bank records—as Simmonds' essay demonstrates so well—are major indicators of the capital available to "do things." The dates of founding of established businesses, the dates on which land was taken up and houses were built within the community, the dates on which businesses *closed* or industrial operations moved away: all these may give a sense of how the community has been shaped. They also need to be linked with external factors: technological development, the coming of the railroad (or the highway or air service), the impact of a war—be it Indian or worldwide—the spread of a religious doctrine. No community grows in a vacuum, and any community will be better understood when compared and contrasted with others.

The materials that Tom Edwards has analyzed are the sorts of materials that need to be studied to understand any community. But he has gone one step further: he has looked at how a community chooses to present itself to the world. Each community makes such presentations, whether consciously or unconsciously, in a variety of ways. The name of the local newspaper, the tone of its editorial pages and its advertisements at various stages of the community's growth (or decline), the presence of a chamber of commerce or commercial club or merchants' association and that organization's activities: all indicate a community's view of itself. So do the issues and speeches in campaign for mayor or city council, and the ways in which a municipal government controls (or does not) the growth of the community. So do commencement speeches and even sermons.

And so—as Edwards has so well demonstrated—do publications produced by any or all of those groups. Indeed, the books in the public library or the objects and photographs collected by the local historical society may themselves reveal what a community and its residents thought important enough to buy, to keep, to read and look at.

The study of any community, whether for an anniversary or as a matter of ongoing interest, must be based on more than recollections and obviously "historical" data. It must include both the perspective of outside influences—economic and technological and political—and the picture the community has presented of itself over time. Those factors, too, as Simmonds and Edwards have demonstrated, can be examined relatively easily by the researcher. And they can provide as much color, as much liveliness to the story, as any other sources.

Industrial History and the Local Museum:

Three Case Studies

T. Allan Comp

Before I discuss industrial history and its application in local history, it is only fair to warn that I might be accurately described as an industrial history junkie. I discovered it in undergraduate school, specialized in economic history and the history of technology in graduate schools, and then found a job that for seven years let me work on local industrial sites all over the United States. It was that last experience that made me a local history convert: let me discover the fascinating threads that tie our industrial past to the rest of our past, and then experience the excitement of reweaving those threads into patterns that touched people and cultures I never read about in graduate school. That kind of discovery takes the researcher out of the library and into working places, reading buildings like manuscripts, talking with folks who spent their working lives in the very places you seek to study, and then back to the library to fit it all together. The effort, for me, is a delight, and I hope I can communicate some of the joy as well as some of the perspectives of industrial history.

In the following essay three kinds of industrial sites are discussed as case studies in local history and local understanding. In the notes following the text, the kinds of sources used in researching each are described. Because no one paper could ever address all of industrial history, I have tried to use three widely divergent examples: a copper and lead smelter, a social hall, and some Idaho bridges. Each is only an example of a much larger type, but each should serve as a generic introduction for the interested researcher.

Buildings—especially industrial buildings—can sometimes testify to remarkable chapters in our social history, chapters no better written than in the structures themselves. In 1973, this historian was asked to prepare a brief history of the Tooele Smelter, the "last custom smelter in the Mountain West" (apparently its only claim to fame). When I arrived at the plant it was already shut down, a massive site in which abandoned buildings stood mute in the Utah summer. A few curious discrepancies between what I thought would be there and what was actually there led me back to more research. That research, corroborated and enhanced by the record of the site itself, revealed a much larger sense of significance for the plant and for the people and cultures of the Salt Lake Valley as well.

In the early years of the twentieth century, the Salt Lake Valley of Utah contained eight large smelters, and their heavy smoke blanketed the area. In 1908, a group of private citizens, most of them farmers, brought suit against these smelters, claiming the industry was ruining their lands. The court decided in favor of the farmers and ordered the smelters to either stop polluting the land or stop operation. All but one smelter closed; that one simply bought all the farms that surrounded it.

There remained a high demand for smelting, but the new public policy established by the court required new technologies if the smelters were to remain open and free from court suit or closure. Studies of wind and weather patterns, vegetation, and livestock were completed before smelter sites were chosen. Smelter design included new processing methods, new ways to handle ore and other materials, and, most important, new ways to reduce emissions—especially dust. This included a variety of innovative approaches, all aimed at eliminating the toxic flue dust that brought the original court suit.

Fig. 1. The Tooele smelter in 1914. Photograph courtesy of the author.

The Tooele Smelter of the International Smelting and Refining Company was the second copper smelter and the first lead smelter constructed after the Utah court decision and, eventually, the last custom smelter in the Mountain West (fig. 1). (A "custom" smelter accepted ores and concentrates from a variety of shippers, rather than from just a single mine or ore body. Variation in the chemical compositions of different ores required maximum flexibility and attention from Tooele and its managers.) Tooele was actually two smelters in one; both copper and lead plants existed on the same site, and both were completed between 1910 and 1915. Over three million dollars went into construction, with almost 100 different departments or divisions represented in the budget. The plant became famous for its low manual-labor requirements, yet it still employed 500 to 600 men throughout the year. Operations continued without major modification until January, 1972, when rising maintenance costs forced the old plant to shut down.

The copper smelter was originally the only plant anticipated, and the general plan called for extensive storage bins, a sampling and grinding mill, a calcining or roasting plant, and numerous smaller departments. Plant construction required 10,000 tons of structural steel, 200,000 cubic yards of excavation by steam shovel and mule team, and over 26,000 cubic yards of plain and reinforced concrete. The 350-foot main stack alone required 1.75 million bricks for its construction. Ten miles of industrial railroad track within the yard were required to facilitate the movement of an anticipated ore flow of over 4,000 tons per day. Severe winter weather and steel shortages delayed construction somewhat, but working crews of from 350 to 600 men helped to speed the process.

The copper-smelting process has four steps, and the main problem is to keep tons of ore and intermediate products moving smoothly from one step to the next (fig. 2). Most smelters at the time relied heavily on manual labor to accomplish this movement and, if contemporary reports can be accepted, Tooele instituted several innovations in an attempt to cut down on manual-labor requirements. Ore arrived in railroad cars and went into storage bins. From the bins, it went by conveyor belt to the sampler and crushers, then on another conveyor to the roaster bins. The thirty-two MacDougall roasters received supplies of ore, coke, and flux automatically as required (fig. 3). Roasted ore or "calcine" emptied automatically into storage bins. From the bins, small rail cars carried the calcine to the reverberatory furnaces. It was the reverberatory that actually melted the ore, which then separated into slag and matte. Converters then purified the matte, dumping slag into slag cars and almost pure blister copper into ingots ready for shipment to the refinery. Virtually the entire process moved without the aid of human hands, and visiting engineers consistently commented on the ease of materials movement and the absence of the usual dust created by less efficient methods.

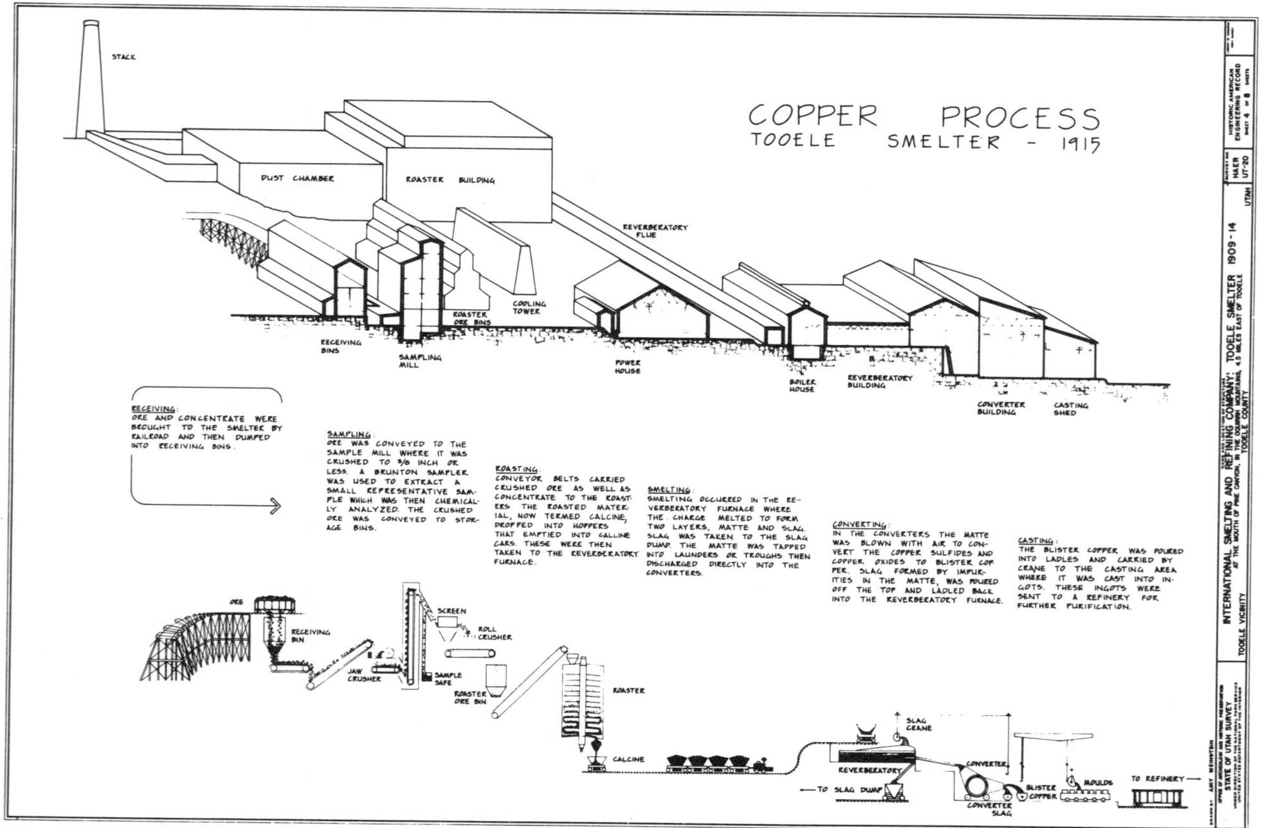

Fig. 2. A modern diagram of the copper-smelting process.

Unfortunately, the Utah Consolidated Mine, main supplier to Tooele, ran out of its good copper ore, and production figures at Tooele fell far below capacity. The *Copper Handbook,* the primary journal-encyclopedia for the copper industry, reported the smelter was "most excellently designed and equipped," "technically a masterpiece," but, judging from production figures, "scarcely . . . a commercial success, as yet."

With 2.5 million dollars invested in a safe site, extensive transportation facilities, and a relatively clean smelter, the International Smelting and Refining Company was not inclined to give up. Smelters were generally expected to last at least five years and sometimes ten before ore ran out; one year of less-than-full-capacity operation was too great a loss even for a company as big as International. Instead of closing, the company took advantage of several new ore discoveries, spent an additional half-million dollars, and opened a lead smelter on the same site while it continued copper smelting. This decision was a brave one considering the dangerous and visible pollutants created by most lead smelters, especially when the hills around the smelter were already turning brown from the sulphuric acid released into the air by copper processing. Copper smelting continued at Tooele until 1946; but it was the newer lead smelter that turned Tooele into a paying venture, one that lasted far longer than originally expected.

Fig. 3. Copper roasters. Photograph courtesy of the author.

Construction on the lead plant started March 1, 1911, and the first lead blast furnace was blown in exactly one year later. This construction of a lead plant by a company primarily engaged in copper smelting produced a number of innovations, largely the result of borrowing from copper techniques. Much like copper ores, lead ores were first sampled and milled or crushed, then roasted, melted, and poured into ingots for shipment to the refinery. Milling and sampling machinery paralleled that used on copper ores, but the last three steps were quite different. Instead of the multiple-hearth MacDougall furnace used to roast copper ores, the Tooele lead smelter took advantage of a new development in roasting, the Dwight-Lloyd sintering machine. The Dwight-Lloyd machine changed sintering into a continuous process in which ore was spread on a moving belt, ignited by a gas flame, burned as it passed along the belt over a forced draft, and then automatically dumped into railroad hopper cars. Savings in labor and time with the continuous machine are obvious and, in fact, sintering remains the basic roasting method in lead smelting today. The ten machines installed at Tooele in 1911 operated until the plant shut down in 1972.

Blast furnaces substituted for the copper reverberatory furnaces, melting the sintered ore and thus separating it into layers, and here Tooele broke new ground in materials handling. Charging a lead blast furnace usually required the frantic work of between thirty and forty men; at Tooele, it took four. Sinter and other materials arrived on railroad cars that dumped directly into storage bins located above the furnaces. To charge the furnace, one simply opened a bin and the charge dropped through two heavy trap doors and into the furnaces.

Lead smelting produces some rather toxic byproducts, products traditionally allowed to escape into the atmosphere. Tooele, unwilling to take chances on damage suits, took every available precaution (fig. 4). The sintering plant produced large volumes of fine dust high in lead content. To catch this dust, sintering fumes ran first through a 450-foot baffled flue, six feet wide and ten feet high. Inside this flue, the company hung 32,000 steel wires to accelerate the dust-settling process. After leaving the flue, the sinter fumes went to a Cottrell treater, one of the major innovations responding to the court decisions and one of the first electrostatic precipitators. The Cottrell consisted of a large number of long metal tubes with an electrical wire hung in the center of each. When the wire received an electrical charge, current passed from the wire to the tube, negatively charging the dust particles in the gas and causing them to adhere to the sides of the tube. To clean the Cottrell, one simply turned the electricity off and hit the tube; the collected dust fell to the hoppers below.

Blast furnaces used a different form of filtration. After passing through a 600-foot flue again filled with thousands of wire to slow air currents

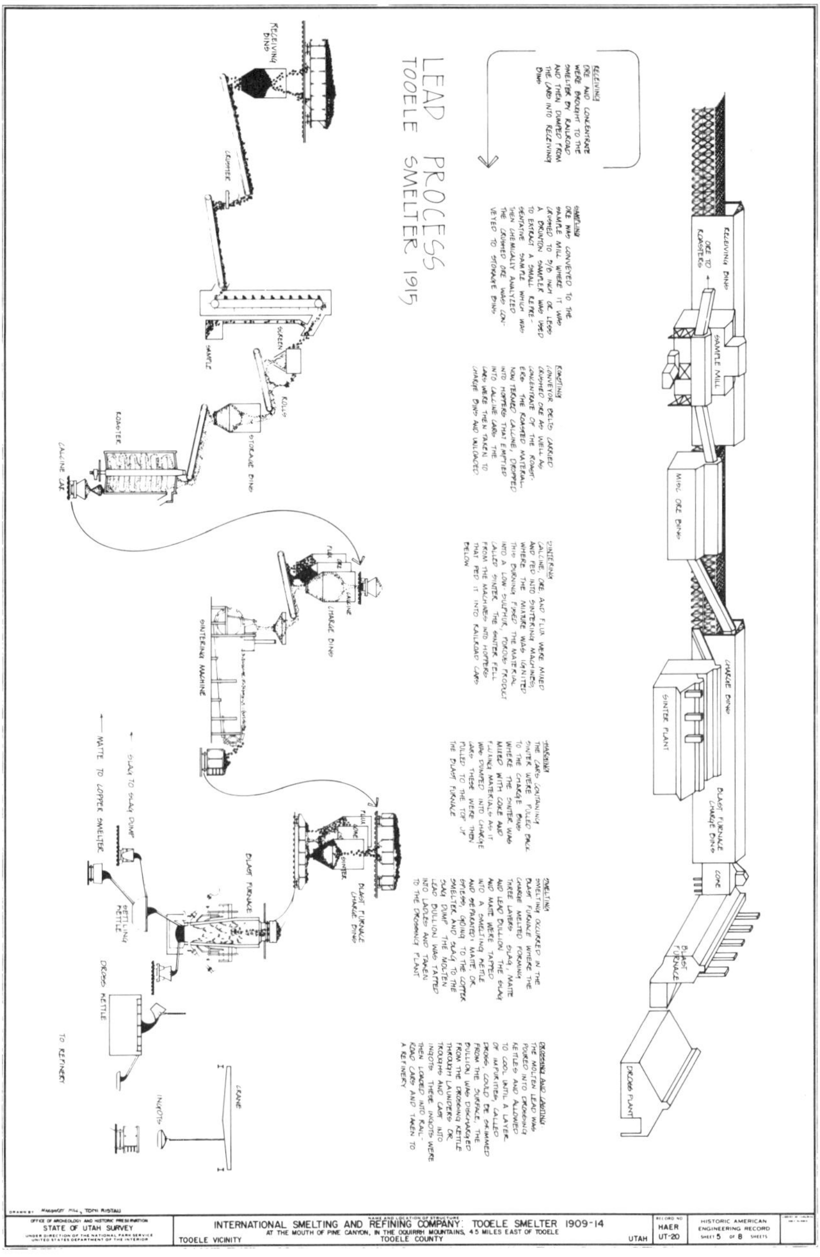

Fig. 4. A modern diagram of the lead-smelting process.

and accelerate dust settlement, blast-furnace gases went to what was appropriately named a bag house. One hundred sixty feet long and fifty-four feet wide, the bag house contained 1,400 tubular cotton bags. Furnace gases, forced by a fan, filtered through these bags and then up a 200-foot stack. To clean the bags, Tooele developed a remote method by simply reversing the air flow several times in succession, thus expanding and collapsing the bags and shaking the dust into hoppers below. Gases from the copper converters went through a similar bag house.

A decade after its construction, the Tooele Smelter contributed about 20 million dollars annually to the Utah economy, paid one-sixth of the county taxes, and supported five-eighths of the county population. Treating an annual average of three-quarters of a million tons of ore, the smelter produced 72,000 tons of lead, 10,000 tons of copper, and several valuable byproducts, including 9 million ounces of silver.

As a first reaction to anti-pollution decisions, the Tooele plant demonstrates both the successes and the failures of this early action. It can be asserted that several significant improvements in smelter practice came in response to the threat posed by damage suits from nearby residents. None of the filtration devices was specifically required by law. Their installation and development sprang from a company decision to protect itself from suspicious or even hostile neighbors, neighbors that included the state supreme court. The Cottrell treater, improved bag-house filtration, better dust settlement in the flues, and cleaner, safer, mechanized materials handling all received favorable comment in the contemporary engineering press. The automatic movement of materials cut down on labor costs and isolated workers from many of the more dangerous smelter jobs, especially in the lead plant. At the same time, the smelter went to great lengths to make sure local farmers either would not, or could not, sue for damages. Weather stations, agricultural surveys, land options, and outright purchase all helped to protect the plant from what smelter men called the "smoke farmers."

Although this site is now totally demolished, the records allow us to explore the conflict between a communitarian-agrarian culture and a newer capitalist smelting industry. The results of that conflict took the form of specific technological developments, each a response to a court-enforced public policy. This new policy of accountability for capitalist enterprise forced the development of new technologies and provides a unique opportunity to study the interplay between technology and culture.

The communitarian interests that forced the technological change were neither political nor economic. The court decision against polluters carried the force of Mormon social/religious tradition, and it ruled against the interests of both the capitalist-owners *and* a state anxious for economic development. Culture thus set the rules, and technology met them.

A second and much earlier "industrial" building benefitted from this same social/religious tradition, but its most remarkable record is found only within the structure itself. In April of 1863, Daniel H. Wells, the Mormon church's superintendent of public works, announced plans for a new Salt Lake City tabernacle. The plans and the idea were the work of Brigham Young, the spiritual and temporal leader of the new Mormon settlement. President Young wanted a large building free of interior columns in which to conduct public meetings. Although the construction was nominally under the direction of the public works department, because of its size and importance, the tabernacle became the special concern of Brigham Young. It was he who chose the builder, Henry Grow, and he who consulted almost daily with the church architect, first William Folsom and later Truman Angell.

Building materials came from the local area. Pine timbers for the roof were cut in the Wasatch Mountain range, east of the city. Hardwood for the pegs came from the more arid western mountains, just across the valley. Stone for the piers came from the sandstone cliffs of Red Butte Canyon, a natural cut in the Wasatch Range. Carried down the mountains on ox carts and horse-drawn wagons, these materials were assembled by local craftsmen under the supervision of two local builders.

Henry Grow came to Utah from Pennsylvania, where he claimed to have worked on the construction of bridges and culverts on the Norristown and Germantown railroads. Converted to Mormonism in 1842, he moved to Nauvoo and later to Utah, arriving there in October, 1851. He settled first in Ogden; but in 1852, Brigham Young called him to Salt Lake City, and he moved there to supervise the building of bridges and mills. Although his most spectacular project was the roof over the Tabernacle, Grow earlier used the lattice truss in building two timber bridges in the Salt Lake Valley. Brigham Young, familiar with Grow's use of the lattice truss, asked the builder to supervise the roof truss.

Grow worked under the general supervision of the church architect. From 1861 to the spring of 1867, that position was filled by William Folsom, a man who, like Grow, received his training (as a contractor/builder) in the East and came west only after converting to Mormonism. Folsom arrived in Salt Lake City in 1860, and in 1861 he was called to replace an ailing Truman Angell as church architect. Folsom held that position until Angell resumed the post in the spring of 1867, when the tabernacle was only partially finished. It was his duty, and later Angell's, to supervise the general construction of the tabernacle. While Grow directed the building of the roof, the architect was responsible for both the finishing work and the interior design.

The tabernacle is an auditorium, 150 feet wide and 250 feet long, with no interior columns. Constructed from local materials, it was designed and built by local craftsmen. Yet it has been called "the most masterful piece of timber construction in the United States," and today, more than a hundred years after its completion, it remains the only structure of its kind in the United States.

It is the roof structure that makes the building a significant chapter in the history of wood technology (fig. 5). Nine lattice trusses, fifteen inches thick and nine feet deep, with a clear interior span of 132 feet between piers, form the center section. Thirteen smaller half trusses, converging on the midpoints of the first and ninth, or end, full spans, complete the semicircular ends of the building. Each truss consists of four parallel timber bents or ribs, each a composite of four 2½-by-12-inch timbers bent to the arc of the roof. These four ribs are connected by a lattice of web members each 2½ by 12 inches to form the truss.

The tabernacle was built in three stages that took four years to complete: first the foundations for the piers; then the piers; finally, the roof truss. Daniel Wells announced plans for the tabernacle in April of 1863. By June 3, the *Deseret News* was able to report that the foundations for all the piers were almost completed. The piers themselves were raised in late 1864. At that point, Brigham Young advised the builders to stop work so the piers could settle before the massive roof truss was begun. Early the next year, lumber for the roof was cut, but it was not until September 1, 1865, that the wood was sufficiently cured to be used in construction.

Henry Grow had learned his technique building timber bridges, tall Town trusses, and lattice trusses. He was able to transfer this experience to the tabernacle, at the same time taking what was normally a flat web of timbers and arching the structure to create the great domed roof.

With the piers completed, scaffolding was erected for the first four main spans. Using the scaffolding for support (much like the construction of a masonry-arch bridge) the lower bents were put into place, the web members laced between these bents, and then the upper bents connected. Purlins and rafters for the roof sheathing were placed as soon as possible and by June, 1866, less than a year after work on the roof began, sheeting was in place over the main spans. By August, 1866, work on the west end was begun; and while the west end was being framed scaffolding was extended for the east end. The last construction photo shows the last open section of the roof truss and in the foreground the steam plant used in shaping the timbers used in the bents. The half spans used on each end are complete, the rafters for the roof cover all but four spaces between the end trusses, and the original wood-shingle roof covers all but this last section.

The roof truss is actually a three-centered span in which the radius of the two outside curves is considerably smaller than that of the center of the span (fig. 6). This lattice of timbers is made up of timber web

Fig. 5. The tabernacle under construction. Photograph courtesy of the Church Archives, Church of Jesus Christ of Latter-day Saints.

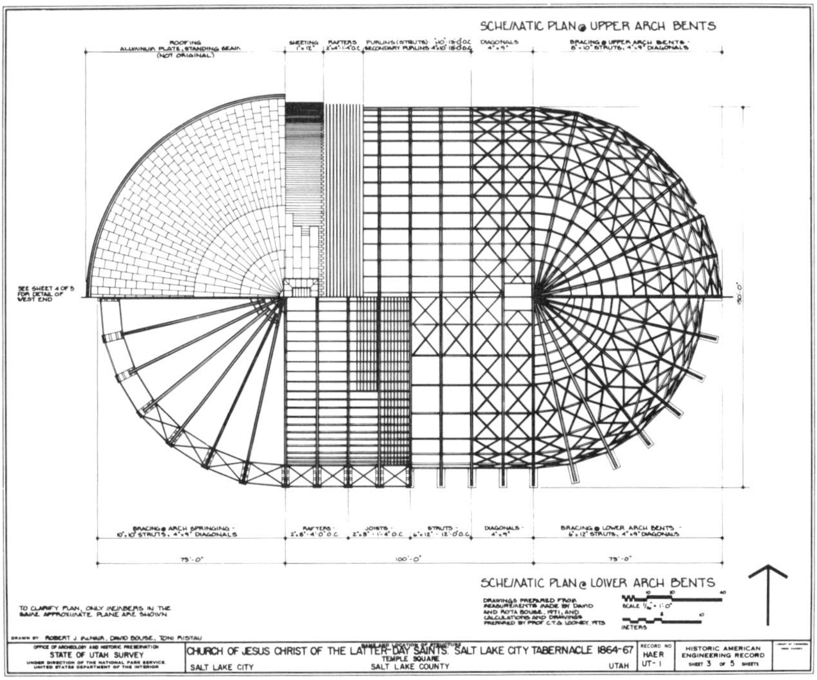

Fig. 6. A modern schematic drawing of the tabernacle arches.

members that serve to weave together the four bents. These bent or rib members are spliced and joined with iron bolts to make them continuous over their entire length, and they were actually bent to the proper curve. (Cutting the members to form would have greatly reduced the fiber strength of these members.) Each connection between the web and the bents is made with four 1¾-inch hardwood pegs, each driven through all the members and then wedged from both ends. The use of four pegs instead of one eliminates the possibility of rotation at these connections and renders the structure indeterminate. Where each truss meets the stone pier, it sits on a bed of heavy timbers a foot square; there is no actual connection between truss and pier.

Other timbers add to the overall rigidity of the entire structure. As each separate truss was completed, it was joined to those on each side of it by a series of heavy cross-timbers in both planes of the truss. The result might be loosely termed a square tube in which the sides are formed by the large trusses and the top and bottom by the cross timbers. What this created, once all nine major trusses were erected, was a solid center section little affected by lateral loadings, an important consideration for the builders for the later addition of the two ends.

The builders took extraordinary pains to insure the tightness and rigidity of each connection. The double wedging of the wooden pegs has already been mentioned, but there are also wedges at the mortise-and-tenon joints connecting all timbers, especially the cross timbers connecting the top and bottom bents of each span and the X bracing between these spans. At each of these points, the timbers were first joined and pegged and then a hardwood wedge was driven into the joint to spread and stiffen the connection. These wedges will not be found in ordinary wooden truss bridges and were apparently used by the builders to help insure the rigidity of the total framework.

Creating the half-round ends of the building posed one major problem: how to join the many half arches at the center of the last full span. From the photos and the evidence in the building, it seems that the builder was apparently uncertain as to just how to accomplish this as well. What he did was to bring the center half arch up to the center of the main span and then bring the other short spans up to as close as they would fit. At that point, they were simply butted into supporting cross braces and terminated. Although both ends are constructed in essentially the same manner, the fitting and butting of the shorter spans on the second (east) end is considerably better than of the first (west).

How does it all work? The great arched roof structure is not in fact an arch; it is an indeterminate truss so rigid it works like a beam. If it did work like an arch the lateral or outward forces exerted by the weight of the arch would be carried to the piers. The resultant of these forces would fall outside the piers and they would overturn, bringing the

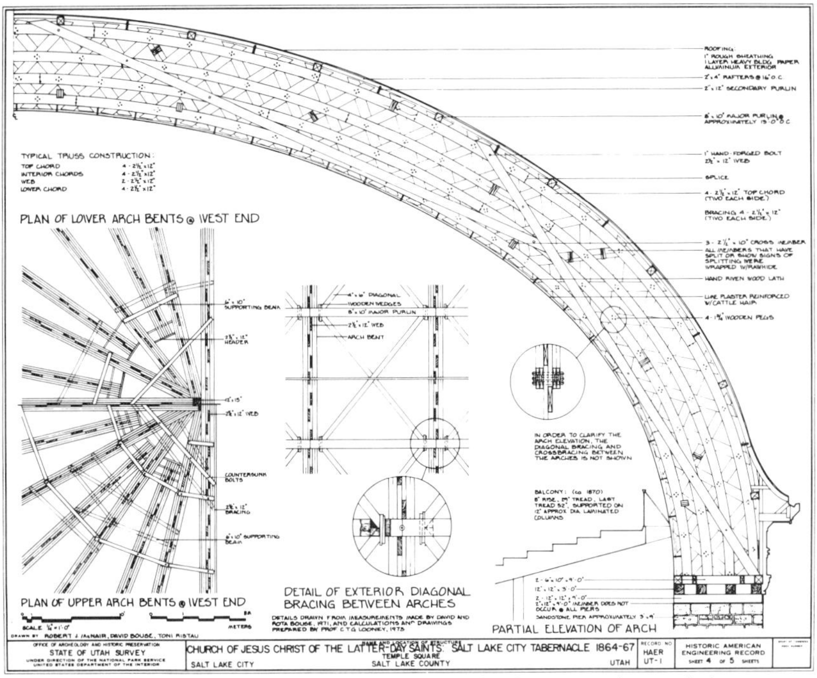

Fig. 7. Straight diagonal braces were applied across the arch bents.

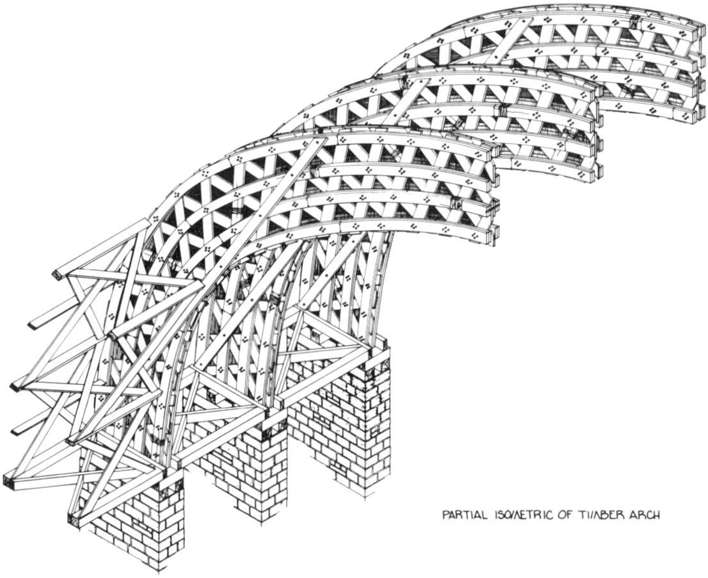

Fig. 8. The added braces reach to the top portions of the arches.

building down with them. In fact, the roof structure is so rigid, the complex of web, bents, and bracing members so stiff, that the entire structure sits atop the piers exerting no significant lateral force on these piers.

At the same time that the east end was being framed, the roof over both the west end and the center section was being completed—that is, it was covered with a final layer of wood shingles.

In July of 1867, with the interior work of the plasterers and the roofing of the carpenters, two sections of the roof were completed and covered. Work on the east end continued and on October 7, 1867, the building opened to the public in time for the annual October conference.

The important thing the construction photos do not show, and what the literature examined to date does not discuss, is that this giant lattice truss, even with all the builder's special attention to rigidity, apparently did not work. At some point between the time the building was sufficiently completed to begin removing the supporting scaffolding and the time the truss was completely enclosed by interior lath and plaster and exterior roof, one or more of the great trusses started to spread. The dead load of over one million board feet of timber was more than the truss could hold without distorting, once the scaffolding was removed. The only indication of this problem—or at least the solution to it—can be found in the truss itself; it does not appear in any of the photos nor is it mentioned in the printed material. Here the structure is the document, the only document, and an elegant one at that.

To correct this terrible threat on both sides of every full span, the builders added long timber braces and connected them with iron bolts at every point the brace intersected the bents (fig. 7). These braces were installed across the small radius on every full span and across the larger upper radius of several of the main spans as well. By thus tying together those parts of the trusses most susceptible to distortion, the builders solved their problem. And the solution worked—after more than a century there is no evidence of spread in the trusses. It is clear that the intuitive design of the great arched lattice truss, once the bracing timbers spanning the arc of the span were added, worked—quite possibly better, or at least longer, than the builders ever dreamed.

According to tradition, Brigham Young, when asked what kind of building he wanted, answered by opening his umbrella and pointing to its arched ribs (fig. 8). Wherever the idea originated, the tabernacle's shape was sufficiently unique to generate public interest. As a result, the newspaper published weekly progress reports. Likewise, the church disseminated information in both foreign and domestic journals.

But the historian must realize that these published reports address a concerned church. Seeking to reassure its brethren, and to encourage converts, the church anxiously followed the physical progress of the tabernacle, visible proof of triumph over the desert. *Scientific American*

(June 8, 1867) described the structure as "a monument" to the "zeal and unparalled unity of purpose and labor on the part of the Mormon people." The written record, mindful of this unity and its critical role in the taming of the wilderness, ignores any of the problems encountered or the techniques applied in the construction of this "monument." As a result, the building today speaks more clearly of its own history than does the written record.

The lattice truss of the tabernacle was a common technology utilized in an unprecedented form and scale, an example of genuine innovation, a known technique modified to meet new demands. It is a structure that indicates its own resource base—both of materials and of skills—and it reveals as well its own construction difficulties. Other contemporary roof trusses relied heavily on iron components; iron was scarce and expensive in Utah, and it is used sparingly. Utah did have both the skills and the manpower to do the job: there was only one minor accident during the entire construction process. When it was time to plaster the interior, 250 men answered the call from Brigham Young and they left, finished, sixteen days later.

A single site can thus be a microcosm revealing both its context and its own unreported history. The cohesiveness and resourcefulness of early Mormon culture, the limitations of the Utah resource base and the way this could be overcome, even a quick and effective response to a potential disaster, are all here. We need only look.

Bridges are a final example—and this time a local one—of the revealing nature of industrial history. And here the pattern somewhat expands itself, asking us not only to "read" the structure but to use its very presence as a constant reminder of our industrial culture—and a great excuse for some interesting historical research. Bridges, especially the iron and steel structures of the late nineteenth and early twentieth centuries, are pure industrial expressions. Both their form and their function are visible, yet they are often and sadly ignored in our search for local history. Deriving their structural form from earlier wooden precedents, these "truss" bridges were built with materials that could withstand the elements and that provided a strong, safe structure within the financial capability of many small communities.

Every one of those local bridges has at least a small story to reveal about public decisions, anticipated economic and transportation developments, or actual community achievements. Each also has its own technological story as well, a separate story of load characteristics and the specific engineering of the ways in which those loads would be carried to the bridge supports, length of span, truss type, and occasionally a contribution to bridge engineering history. Thus these industrial structures not only serve as gateways or links in a transportation network, they also serve as gateways to historical understanding and visible links with the aspirations of our past.

The Kamiah railroad bridge over the Clearwater River is one such link (fig. 9). During the 1890s, the Camas Prairie region was rapidly becoming an important agricultural producer, and the Northern Pacific extended a branch from its Clearwater Short Line eighteen miles along the river to Stites. Steamboats were also expected to be important transportation on the Clearwater, so when the railroad crossed the near near Kamiah in 1900 it built a "swing" bridge, a bridge that could pivot on a center point to allow steamboat passage on the river. Although large grain warehouses were constructed at Spalding, Big Eddy, Peck, and Kamiah, the steamboat traffic never really materialized. Today that swing bridge is one of the few signs of the way we carried eastern and midwestern ideas about river transportation into the Mountain West.

The second story is the bridge itself, a hybrid creation originally built as two spans at some unknown location much further east in about the 1880s. The railroad brought these used bridge spans to Kamiah and actually suspended the entire weight of the spans from a new central tower, thus allowing the outer ends of the two trusses to swing free of support when the bridge pivoted to open the river for traffic. The old spans are constructed of cast-iron Phoenix columns, a particular form patented by the Phoenix Iron Company of Philadelphia. The Kamiah bridge is the only cast-iron bridge in Idaho (largely because western railroad development post-dated the use of cast iron), and one of only two swing bridges still remaining in the state. Far from being "just a bridge," it is a remarkable cast-iron survivor far from its original home and a fascinating early chapter in the Camas Prairie region as well as in the reuse of truss bridges.

A second remarkable survivor was a timber railroad bridge built in 1906 over the Kootenai River at Bonners Ferry (fig. 10). The bridge is part of the Spokane International Railway built by D. C. Corbin, a colorful entrepreneur in the logging and mining regions of both the United States and Canada. The line was intended to provide an alternative to the Great Northern Railroad's hegemony in northern Idaho, and the actual work was carried out by the Canadian Pacific Railroad. The 900-foot bridge, the longest on the Spokane International, was completed in 1906. The line was acquired by the Canadian Pacific in 1917, reorganized under private ownership in 1941, sold to the Union Pacific in 1958; through it all the bridge remained unchanged — until it collapsed in 1985.

The Bonners Ferry railroad bridge was a Howe timber truss, once a common form on western railroads, which utilizes massive timbers to take the compressive loads and ties them all together with thin steel rods or bars working in tension. Few Howe trusses survive today, and Bonners Ferry's was one of the longest spans to survive so long. Thus in one

Fig. 9. The railroad bridge at Kamiah. Photograph courtesy of the author.

Fig. 10. The SIRR bridge, which collapsed in 1985. Photograph courtesy of the author.

Fig. 11. The Owsley bridge. Photograph courtesy of the author.

Fig. 12. The Manning Crevasse bridge. Photograph courtesy of the author.

old wood bridge were an early Howe truss, a fascinating entrepreneur, railroad completion that crossed both a continent and international borders, and the most important reason for the continued existence of Bonners Ferry.

Later steel truss bridges appear more familiar, but their historical and structural significance may still be great. The Owsley bridge (1920-1921) over the Snake River near Hagerman seems familiar in its Warren truss configuration, but historical investigation opens a broader perception (fig. 11). Designed and built by the Idaho Bureau of Highways as a link on the old Idaho Pacific State Highway, it was the first major bridge designed by the year-old bureau. Because of deep water, the bridge had to span the river with a single unsupported span. State Bridge Engineer Charles A. Kyle developed a continuous through cantilever truss that carried the roadway over a 264-foot clear center span. Instead of a series of separate spans, Kyle's design made the entire length of the bridge a single structural element. As the only continuous through truss remaining in Idaho, the bridge not only merits its decorative end posts and name proudly stamped across its portal, it merits our historical understanding. More than an end to a slow ferry crossing and a symbol of the rapid increase in highway transportation, the Owsley bridge is Idaho's first attempt at developing its own design—and a success shared by all its citizens.

Finally, because failures may be just as interesting as successes, let us look at the Manning Crevasse bridge over the Salmon River near Riggins (fig. 12). Constructed by the Civilian Conservation Corps (a response to another form of industrial failure) in 1938, the bridge was part of a road intended to connect Riggins with Shoup but never completed. Heroic effort went into its construction—it is a timber suspension bridge 240 feet long—but it stands on a road to nowhere. Once the most common bridge type used to cross the main Salmon River, the Manning Crevasse bridge is today one of four remaining timber suspension bridges in the state and a proud chapter in the history of CCC building in Idaho.

Each of these industrial structures, be it a massive smelter, an astounding tabernacle, or a simple bridge, is really an unwritten chapter in local, regional, or national history waiting for our attention. The sources of this history are as varied as industrial history itself, but they are neither secret nor hidden. The real challenge of local industrial history is not finding adequate sources but in seeing with adequate eyes and minds. Industrial structures are initially mute, and their appearance is rarely as inviting as the pioneer home or the business office. But once our historical vision pulls us beyond an apparent contemporary reality, new worlds await. As an exploration of our past in its fullest dimension and as a central aspect of our present situation, industrial history offers a great treasure. For the local museum as well as the local historian, that treasure is a vein of ore rich in context, texture, humanity, and pure delight.

A Note on Sources

Idaho has two distinct advantages to offer the researcher, the Idaho State Historical Society, with its excellent staff, and Dr. Merle Wells, retired State Historic Preservation Officer and an institution in himself. Both set standards of scholarship, collegial generosity, and interest in local history that are matched by few other institutions or individuals in the West. There is no better place to start. For general reading, a book by Kenneth Hudson titled *World Industrial Archaeology* is the best introduction, and reading the Society for Industrial Archaeology's *Newsletter* and *Journal* will give the beginner a good understanding of the field and its practitioners. The most scholarly source is *Technology and Culture,* the journal of the Society for the History of Technology.

In working on Tooele or any other similar site, contemporary professional journals are some of the best resources. These include *The Engineering and Mining Journal, Salt Lake Mining Review, The Mining World,* and *The Copper Handbook.* Information on major persons came from contemporary volumes of *Who's Who in Engineering;* an evaluation of the various filtration processes was in a textbook, *The Principles of Metallurgy* by John L. Bray; and finally there were oral interviews with the former superintendent and several of his staff. All that, along with help from a student metallurgist and a lot of patience walking around that vast site, finally produced a sense that is really was possible to follow processes and understand materials flows.

The Salt Lake City Tabernacle research depended on traditional local history sources for its written information. The *Deseret News, Salt Lake Tribune,* and *Salt Lake Telegraph* all carried articles. There were a master's thesis, a collection of data by the Daughters of the Utah Pioneers, and a host of articles beginning with the *Scientific American* in 1867. None of these directly addressed the structure of the roof truss, and there were several frustrating dead ends. Henry Grow, the eastern bridge builder responsible for the roof, was impossible to find in Pennsylvania (where he claimed to have worked) in spite of an exhaustive search through railroad histories and pamphlets as well as Philadelphia directories from 1825 to 1850. In the case of the tabernacle, one could only read in historical sources around the site. Specific historical data on its construction could only be extrapolated from the structure itself.

Bridges tap the full range of historical sources. The Manning Crevasse bridge is mentioned in the *Engineering-News Record,* the most important national engineering journal. More local sources included titles such as *Pioneer People, Pioneer Days in Idaho County, History of the Canadian Pacific Railway,* and the Idaho Department of Public Works biennial reports. Finally—and predictably—local newspapers like the *Idaho County Free Press, Bonners Ferry Herald, The Spokesman Review,* and the *Gooding Leader* proved useful sources.

Finally, do not ever hesitate to call a fellow industrial history junkie. We are all missionaries anxious to spread the good news of industrial history at the local level and are always delighted to aid in its discovery.

Popular Culture and Historical Research

LeRoy Ashby

"*I* got a hot rod Ford and a two-dollar bill. Know a spot just over the hill." So sang country-western recording star Hank Williams around 1950. He announced in another tune that his new-found love had him "Howlin' at the Moon." At about the same time, Grand Ole Opry celebrity Kitty Wells crooned sadly that "It wasn't God who made honky tonk angels."

What is the historian to make of such material products of the world of popular culture? The answer, many would say flatly, is "nothing" – or at most "as little as possible." Nonetheless, over the past several decades the subject of popular culture has increasingly received scholarly attention, and its defenders warn more skeptical colleagues that the serious study of the past should include an examination of such cultural artifacts as comic books, Harlequin romances, Elvis Presley and the Beatles, sports, how-to-do-it books (from how to repair a toilet to how to make love), advertising, movies, television soap operas, radio serials, Big Mac hamburgers, shopping malls, ethnic jokes, and *Playboy* magazine.

Not surprisingly, the willingness of historians to consider mass culture as a suitable field for scholarly research became especially noticeable in the 1960s. During that frenzied decade, a kind of revolution occurred within the historical profession. "Revisionist" historians raised new questions and drew more than they had in the past on research methods and models from other disciples. The various social movements of the sixties encouraged an unprecedented scholarly interest in the history of non-elite groups: blacks and other racial and ethnic minorities, women, the working class – the masses of "anonymous Americans" who traditionally had not held political office, managed wealthy corporations, negotiated with foreign leaders, or received mention in city social registers. The "new social history" used census records, studied communities and neighborhoods, probed the world of the slave quarters, focused on rank-and-file workers, reexamined the role of mobs, and scrutinized family relationships over time. Books and articles devoted growing attention to "inarticulate" Americans, those who traditionally represented the "underside of American history." While the census records, tax rolls, parish rosters, and legal files illuminated important aspects of the lives of common Americans—where they lived, how much property they owned, how socially and geographically mobile they were, what their fertility rates were—they were less informative regarding the world that people carried in their heads: their thoughts, values, aspirations, expectations, and frustrations. Popular culture seemed in this respect an invaluable source.[1]

Insights that mass culture can provide into the past have been particularly evident in recent interpretations of the Great Depression, a subject that scholars have traditionally examined primarily in economic and political terms. Warren Susman, Richard Pells, Andrew Bergman, and J. Fred MacDonald, for example, have shown how extremely important the messages of movies, best-selling books, popular magazines, and radio were for Americans trying to make sense of their troubled times.[2] As Susman argues provocatively, the 1930s was the "age of Mickey Mouse" as well as Franklin Roosevelt. The cultural equivalent of FDR's declaration that Americans needed to fear only fear itself was Walt Disney's Oscar-winning song in 1933, "Who's Afraid of the Big Bad Wolf." Viewed on this level, the thirties were as much an era of faith and reaffirmation as a time of anxiety and doubt. Certainly the more positive side was apparent in popular culture where, despite enormous economic stress and failure, the Parker Brothers' game "Monopoly" found a huge audience and Dale Carnegie's *How to Win Friends and Influence People* shook the publishing world in 1936. Carnegie's message was simple and reassuring: individual success was still possible if one developed a magnetic and persuasive personality. (In another sense, Carnegie's book also helped to chart a major, ongoing social and economic transformation. The earlier Ben Franklin emphasis on character increasingly gave way to a cult of personality, which emphasized external impressions and projected images of self rather than internal values. This shift symbolized the transition from a producer-oriented to a consumer-oriented society, in which people identify themselves largely in terms of what they and others buy. Thus, by the 1980s, advertising made it clear that common folk might not play golf as well as Arnie Palmer, but they, like that famous linkster at his boyhood home in Latrobe, Pennsylvania, could also use Pennzoil.)[3]

While Carnegie's book served as a towering cultural landmark, so too did *Life* magazine, which first appeared that same year. For many people, *Life* documented and defined nothing less than the American way of life. Publisher Henry Luce ordered his photographers to capture on film America's grass roots, and he jammed his new journal with material about common citizens. As one photographer recalled, the idea was that "here, set down for all time, you may look at the average 1937 American as he really is" and "take stock of some of the abiding things which are magnificently *right* about America."[4]

In *Life* and elsewhere, popular culture during the Depression celebrated the tenacity and moral fiber of the plain folk—from Grant Wood's famous painting "American Gothic" to radio soap operas such as *Ma Perkins* and *Just Plain Bill* (with its theme song of "Polly, Wolly, Doodle"); from Frank Capra films such as *Mr. Smith Goes to Washington* to the reassuring ending of Margaret Mitchell's phenomenal best-seller, *Gone With the Wind*, that "After all, tomorrow is another day," and to Ma Joad's comment at the conclusion of John Ford's film rendition of *The Grapes of Wrath:* "We're the people that live. Can't nobody wipe us out. Can't nobody lick us. We'll go on forever, Pa, 'cause we're the people." Even monster movies, so popular in the thirties, were reassuring, despite the eerie settings and terrifying creatures. In the end the monster—whether Dracula, the Werewolf, the Mummy, or Dr. Frankenstein's creation—was eliminated and the village was able to return to normal. Contrast the 1930 horror film with those of the late 1970s and early 1980s when, as in *Halloween*, it turns out that humans really cannot kill the boogeyman.[5]

Hollywood's treatment of gangsters in the Depression era may be a historical barometer of changing public attitudes on authority, crime, and government. Gangster films were extremely popular at the box office in the early 1930s (some fifty films were made in 1931 alone) but gave way in the mid-1930s to movies that championed law enforcement agencies. Early Depression films such as *Little Caesar* and *Public Enemy* tended to show the police as corrupt and unsympathetic—resembling the callous "flatfoot" officers who used nightsticks to drive unemployed Americans off park benches. In constrast to the dull, unimaginative cops, cinematic gangsters as portrayed by James Cagney were tough, romantic, adventurous characters. The public, after all, did not go to the theater to watch Cagney's honest but boring brother work his way through night school in *Public Enemy*. In the mid-thirties, however, law and order made a comeback, largely in the form of federal agents. Significantly, these movies often starred actors who had earlier been famous in gangster roles: Cagney and Edward G. Robinson were now on the side of authority. Hollywood advertising and local editors made much of the fact that in the 1935 film *G-Men*, Cagney was "battling crime. . . . " A *Time* magazine reviewer lauded the 1936 movie *Bullets or Ballots* because it brought "Edward G. Robinson . . . back into the crime fold, this time on the side of the law." Historian Andrew Bergman believes that the shift in the gangster formula during the Depression was not accidental. It reflected an evolution from the cynicism and despair of the Hoover years, when government was perceived as offering a billy club instead of relief, to the hope that came with the New Deal, when government offered a friendly hand.[6]

Students of the recent cinema could easily find evidence of another transition in Hollywood's treatment of crime and justice. During the late 1960s and early 1970s, a period seething with social protest, many popular films showed heavy-handed cops and corrupt government officials misusing authority and betraying the public trust. In contrast, convicts and people in trouble with the law often emerged as martyrs. *Easy Rider, Cool Hand Luke, Bonnie and Clyde, Butch Cassidy and the Sundance Kid, The Getaway, Papillon,* and *Charlie Varrick* were prime examples. But a notable transformation was clearly under way by the mid-seventies, as a much-publicized conservative backlash against the forces of change took place. By 1981 the shift was symbolically complete, not only following the national elections but in American theaters as well. A two-page advertisement in *Newsweek* showed Paul Newman in police uniform and announced: "He's Been Breaking the Law for Years. A con man in 'The Sting.' An outlaw in 'Butch Cassidy and the Sundance Kid.' A smuggler in 'Exodus.' A pool shark in 'The Hustler.' A convict in 'Cool Hand Luke.' Now PAUL NEWMAN has gone straight . . . to the most commanding role of his career in FORT APACHE, THE BRONX."[7]

Some scholars suspect that it is possible to make too much of all this, at least in terms of values, aspirations, and expectations of rank-and-file citizens. Indeed, for historians seeking insights into the world of the average citizen (or something similar), popular culture may be an interpretive trap. It may tell less about the grass roots than about yet another elite group: promoters and entrepreneurs. It may say less about consumers than about marketing. Unlike folk culture, which swells up informally within all groups, popular culture is managed. Because profits are at stake, the fare of the mass media tends to be safe, predictable, noncontroversial. It focuses on the familiar; it soothes rather than disrupts. Like a Holiday Inn, it offers the best surprise: no surprise.

Moreover, because media capitalists prefer to rework successful formulas, it is a "retread culture." Famous personalities show up again and again—precisely because they are well known—in advertisements, on talk shows, in programs that show celebrities doing even banal things (like one focusing on Johnny Carson's trip back to his hometown in Nebraska), and in gossip sheets with stories about celebrities doing things that are . . . well . . . not so banal. And when the famous personalities die, the media provide the public with screen biographies in which celebrities play celebrities: Loni Anderson as Jayne Mansfield and Kurt Russell as Elvis Presley, for example.[8]

Because of the commercial aspects of popular culture, television programs such as *The Jeffersons* hardly offer real insights into contemporary black life. Instead, as black scholar Leslie Owens has written, such TV shows "tell us more about the profit motive and how it shapes American perceptions of life than about black Americans."[9]

If one believes that popular culture is an entrepreneurial creation, then it is possible to see it as essentially a modern opiate of the people—one of the means by which a commercial culture trivializes everything. In the world of mass advertising, religion, for example, thus becomes just another product. A poem circulated in a Methodist newsletter in Illinois in the early 1970s dramatized this very effectively:

GOD IS . . .

1. God is like Coke—He's the real thing.
2. God is like GM—He's got the mark of excellence.
3. God is like Ford—He's got the better idea.
4. God is like Gillette—He's the closest to you yet.
5. God is like Illinois Bell—There's more to him than meets the ear.
6. God is like Reader's Digest—He's always renewable.
7. God is like Hunt's New Snack Pack—He goes everywhere with you.
8. God is like Cream of Wheat—He sticks with you.
9. God is like Pepsi Cola—You've got a lot to live and He's got a lot to give.
10. God is like Bayer Aspirin—He works wonders.
11. God is like Nationwide—He's on your side.
12. God is like Right Guard—He gives you 24-hour protection.
13. God is like Campbell Soup—You and He go together.
14. God is like Pan Am—He makes the going great.[10]

By the late twentieth century, God had become the equivalent of a deodorant. Even television's revivalist preachers of the 1980s sometimes resembled Sunday morning editions of the Merv Griffin show, combining talk-show settings (comfortable chairs and indoor plants included) with slick musical productions in which striking women ("like variations on Charlie's Angels in discreet gowns") and men ("all Bruce Jenner look-alikes in J. C. Penney vested suits") sang "God is greater than anyone can tell."[11] A programmer for the Christian Broadcasting Network candidly admitted, "Johnny Carson has set us a standard."[12] Little if any difference separated such a statement from the graffiti scrawled on the wall at Elvis Presley's Graceland mansion: "Elvis is not dead—he's just on tour with God."[13]

On this level, some social critics have stressed the enormous co-optive powers of modern capitalism. In America, they argue, a prime way of dealing with dissenters has been not to send them packing to some gulag but instead to turn them into "Famous People," advertising their books and interviewing them on the Mike Douglas show. Sixties radical Abbie Hoffman thus complained that "Warner Brothers and Columbia Records have taken over the counter-culture. . . ."[14] But Hoffman proved as susceptible as anyone to the lure of media fame. By 1980 he was the subject of a film, *My Name is Abbie, Orphan of America.* According to the promotional literature, "Here is a film which captures Abbie 20 years later, a bit more subdued, but still witty, perceptive, and provocative."[15]

Even individuals who, unlike Hoffman, spurned media attention found that their works were like putty in the hands of a commercial culture. In mid-1969, for example, an advertisement in *The New York Times Magazine* included a picture of Paul Goodman's *Like a Conquered Province,* a book that vigorously criticized America as an "empty society" in which, among other things, middle-class people wandered aimlessly across the barren terrain of a consumer world. The advertisement, however, was not for the purpose of publicizing Goodman's book. Instead it urged readers to buy a particular brand of women's beach attire. The book was merely a prop in the hands of a leggy model wearing a $32 swimsuit. The work of a well-known social critic had become part of a come-on for beach wear.[16] In 1982 the title "Reds" may have evoked memories of Warren Beatty's recent movie extravaganza about John Reed, a founder of the American Communist Party, the man whom Leon Trotsky appointed as the first Soviet consul to the United States, and one of two Americans whose ashes are buried in the Kremlin wall. But the "Fall '82 Reds!" were different, at least as they were advertised in *Family Circle.* The focus was not on Karl Marx, but on marks left by different shades of Cover Girl Lipsticks. "The Cover Girl Reds" included famous models Cheryl Tiegs and Christie Brinkley, a far cry from Emma Goldman.[17]

Even if popular culture ultimately tells us more about the people who produce it—about mass merchandising and social control in a commercial society—than it does about the so-called "inarticulate majority" of Americans, it is far from useless as social history. A major question is why particular books, movies, fads, sports, music, and other mass media creations are popular at particular times. How does one account for the huge popularity of Timothy Shay Arthur's *Ten Nights in a Barroom* in the middle 1800s or Charles Sheldon's *In His Steps* at the turn of the century, or rock 'n' roll in the 1950s, or the television mini-series *Roots?*[17]

Culture, moreover, is not a uniform, monolithic entity. It is comprised of clashing, contradictory values and beliefs. Careful examination of popular culture can reveal much about the tensions, the dialogues, the push-and-pulls, the conflicting ideals that comprise American life.

Examples of competing ideals and myths that have shaped the American experience are abundant. For instance, Americans have typically celebrated progress and change. The Ford Motor Company thus claims always to have a better idea. At General Electric, progress is the most important product. Bendix, "helps to create the future." Alcoa Aluminum "can't wait for tomorrow." Yet, resting uneasily alongside the fascination with the new and the different has always been a strong sense of nostalgia and loss. Hence the lure of "Marlboro Country" or the "high country" of Coors. ("It's no downstream beer. It's no city beer. It's Coors.")[19] Expensive coffee table collections of Currier and Ives prints and "moldy oldie" record albums also indicate a large fascination with "the good old days."

Another source of cultural tension in America derives from the ideal of "a government of laws, not of men." Certainly that goal is basic to the nation's revolutionary heritage. Yet at the same time, one of the most popular heroes in the United States has been the lone gunfighter who imposes personal justice and works outside normal legal channels. The Clint Eastwood character in the Spaghetti westerns of the 1960s and Mickey Spillane's tough private eye, Mike Hammer, have personified such tendencies. Ironically, one of Richard Nixon's favorite films, which he showed several times in the White House, was *Chisum*; the president, occupying the nation's top governmental position, applauded the John Wayne character who stepped outside the established legal authorities to establish his own brand of law and order. The 1974 movie *Death Wish* elicited thundering approval from urban audiences when Charles Bronson singlehandedly gunned down muggers and killers following the rape and murder of his wife and the rape and psychological destruction of his daughter. "Fill your hand," Bronson instructed one terrified and confused punk, thereby showing the relevance of the legendary Old West shootout to modern urban problems. Such movies confirm historian Michael Feldberg's statement: "The conflicting ideologies of lawful procedure and frontier action—the Perry Mason image versus the Lone Ranger image—seem constantly to war with each other."[20]

Another cultural battle has pitted the love of individual freedom and mobility against the desire for roots and family. "Don't tread on me" was a famous revolutionary era slogan. More recently, Burger King has said, "Have it your way." Or as the Schlitz Brewing Company reminds people, "You only go around once in life, so you need to grab all the gusto you can." The suggestion is that individuals should look out for their own happiness: they owe it to themselves. One result has been a "no deposit, no return" mentality in which Americans flee responsibilities, hitting the road in pursuit of new starts.[21] "'Scuse our dust" has been a popular slogan and the Open Road a compelling attraction. "I only feel at home when I'm gone" is the message of a country-western song. "What's a mile in America?" asked an old riddle. "It's something you put behind you." A familiar plot in cowboy movies has portrayed the solitary gunslinger saving the little town. Yet he subsequently pushes on, unwilling to make permanent commitments. The town was worth rescuing, but apparently did not offer enough to settle into for the rest of his life.[22] Literary critic Leslie Fiedler has argued that the theme of flight in American culture has been largely a male phenomenon. Whether it is Jiggs, of the comic strip "Bringing up Father," lighting out for Dinty Moore's saloon, or Rip Van Winkle with his gun and dog Wolf fleeing "the drab duties of home and town," the plot is familiar: "a man on the run, harried into the forest and out to sea, down the river or into combat—anywhere to avoid 'civilization'. . . ."[23]

But uneasily juxtaposed against the theme of flight are contrasting images: "Home, Sweet Home"; Thanksgiving and Christmas holidays with families reverently gathered around the dinner table; trips to Grandma's place; and the popularity of Norman Rockwell's illustrations. Here is the world of predictability and stability. Even modern tourists who light out for wide-open towns such as Reno and Las Vegas—frontier country, where the action never stops—usually seek only brief flings, temporary escapes. After all that fast life they head back to Cedar Falls, Iowa, or Niceville, Florida, where life is less chancy, roots presumably deeper.[24] The Open Road has gone full circle to bring its occupants home again. As someone recently said, eating "a lonely Whopper in a deserted Burger King is the pervasive fear-fantasy" that haunts Americans. Some of the most successful television programs—*Happy Days, Little House on the Prairie, The Waltons,* and *Gunsmoke* (where Doc, Kitty, Festus, and Matt gather at the Long Branch)—emphasize neighborly life, close ties, obligations, trust, and friendship. In *M*A*S*H, Hill Street Blues,* and *Lou Grant,* the army hospital unit, police precinct, and urban newspaper room stand as island communities of comradeship and affection. When the Pittsburgh Pirates won the National League pennant and World Series in 1979, they and the media made much of the "We Are Family" motif.

With allowances for such extended families as the Pirates, the presumed family norm in American popular culture has been one that is stable, intact, and economically self-sufficient, and includes two parents with the husband as the breadwinner. Such has been true, for instance, in *The Danny Thomas Show, Leave It to Beaver,* the Hardy family of the 1930s and 1940s movies starring Mickey Rooney, the comic strip "Blondie," and the 1978 McDonald's Restaurant suggestions for things "the whole family can have fun doing together." (The McDonald's format includes evenings during which family members—Mom, Dad, and their young son and daughter—draw a "family portrait"; or get "in touch with [their] roots" by looking at old slides, home movies, or family photos; or jointly watch and then critique a movie; or have a "family game night" which can include Musical Chairs and even Blind Man's Bluff: "Can you recognize the other members of your family just by touch? If you can't you'll end up helping with the dusting and vacuuming.")[25]

But while popular culture has been a mythic bastion for the stereotypical nuclear family, it has also made notable accommodations with the real world of rapidly growing divorce rates and expanding numbers of single-parent families and working women. Examples range from radio and television soap operas to television programs such as *One Day at a Time,* movies such as *Kramer vs. Kramer,* and a host of country-western songs: "If You Want to Keep the Beer Real Cold, Put It Next to My Ex-Wife's Heart," "For Better or for Worse, but Not for Long," "Your Love Left a Ring Around My Finger," "Married, But Not to Each Other," "Sleeping Single in a Double Bed," "I'm Gonna Have a Wino Decorate Our Home," and "I Gave Her a Ring, and She Gave Me the Finger."

Numerous other "clusters of worries,"[26] contradictions, and tensions within American culture abound in the mass media. While Americans have traditionally expounded values of hard work and pulling oneself up by one's own bootstraps (a staple plot of popular fiction and films ranging from Ragged Dick to Rocky Balboa), many cheered several years ago when Johnny Paycheck sang "Take This Job and Shove It." While demonstrations of faith in the "system"—in the basic fairness and effectiveness of the American way of life—have been abundant (in the 1941 Frank Capra film, *Meet John Doe,* a reporter defiantly tells the villain: "There you are Norton—the people. Try and lick that."), common wisdom holds that it's not what you know, it's who you know. Many comedians poke fun at political innocence: "A real patriot is the fellow who gets a parking ticket and rejoices that the system works." "The only thing better than four aces is a Colt .45." "The lion and the sheep may lie down together, but the sheep won't get much rest." And while Americans certainly like to cheer for winners and heroes (hence the popularity of John Wayne, Sugar Ray Leonard, the 1980 Olympic hockey team, Sergeant York, or more recently Lenny Skutnik, who pulled a woman from the icy Potomac following a January, 1982, Air Florida plane crash), an exceptionally popular comic strip is "Peanuts," in which the hapless Charlie Brown simply perseveres. At one point when Lucy enjoins him to push his "grocery cart of life," he replies, "I think I have six items or less." On another occasion when Linus asks him what he is doing, Charlie Brown says, "I just thought I'd stand here and watch the world go by . . . . It never came by."[27] One of the most successful comedians has been Woody Allen, a study in frustration and ineptitude: "I was breast-fed through falsies," he says. When wrestling with life's Big Questions, the clearly overpowered Allen concludes "that death is an acquired trait."[28]

Even the blandest and most banal examples of popular culture can often, on close examination, reveal a society wrestling with itself, trying to reconcile its own competing ideals, sometimes holding them in delicate balance, momentarily soothing social tensions but not always with predictable results. The early history of amusement parks (such as Coney Island), resorts (such as Atlantic City), and movies illustrates this very well. In the troubled 1890s, when class conflict was much in evidence from Coeur d'Alene to Chicago and elsewhere, promotional literature at Atlantic City affirmed the ideal of class harmony. One reportedly claimed that the young man who earned $4 a week could enjoy his vacation alongside "the pompous millionaire" and could in fact probably flirt "with the millionaire's daughter right before the old man's eyes." In a nation shifting from its traditional rural roots to an urban setting, Atlantic City claimed to offer both worlds: "The City by the Sea," a serene place with open air, the ocean, *and* the excitement of the Boardwalk, attractive young women in bathing suits on a crowded beach, and urban variety. "If you don't see what you want, it is because you haven't asked for it," announced one handbook.[29] At both Atlantic City and Coney Island, during a period still much under the influence of Victorian dating standards, there was also the opportunity to enjoy a kind of moral holiday, to have fun, to abandon self control, however briefly. There were even picture postcards to which the sender had to apply only a signature: "I AM HAVING A H . . . OF A GOOD TIME AT CONEY ISLAND." One of the carnival rides asked, "WILL SHE THROW HER ARMS AROUND YOUR NECK AND YELL? WELL, I GUESS, YES!" And at a time when industrial machinery was intimidating, dangerous, and ruthlessly efficient, the recreational machinery at Coney Island and Atlantic City (the Ferris wheel, roller coaster, and other rides) demonstrated that the modern world of driving gears could also offer pleasure and amusement. In subtle ways such amusements helped citizens adjust to twentieth century technology.[30]

If an Atlantic City or Coney Island helped to ease the transition from one era to another, so did they also point directly to something else: managed environments. As historian John Kasson has said, beneath that "illusion of anarchic freedom" was "the ability to coordinate mass activity through technology." Despite the aura of danger on rides such as the Loop-the-Loop, riders knew they were safe. The sign itself said: "The Greatest Sensation of the Age . . . No danger whatever." Standardized rides elicited standardized responses. The world was ready for Walt Disney.[31]

Historian Lary May has argued that on the eve of World War I movies also helped to bring about a major cultural re-orientation. Hollywood, for the record, endorsed Victorian morals of respectability and virtue. But numerous films offered peeks at alternative lifestyles. In a 1913 film, for example, Theda Bara, having lost her memory during a kidnapping, for a while abandoned her upper-class, proper background and became a cabaret woman, donning a revealing dress and whirling wildly in the savage "Apache" dance. Later, her memory restored, she returned to the world of decorum. A common formula in Mary Pickford's films between 1914 and 1918 was for her to play a respectable genteel female whom foreigners snatched from her Victorian world and forced to live, until her rescue, with gypsies, Italians, or other reputedly hot-blooded people. Pickford and Theda Bara invariably ended up back within the boundaries of home and Victorian values; meanwhile, middle-class audiences had vicariously experienced lives that were excitingly and alluringly different from what they knew.[32]

While such silent films may have dramatized the collision of old and new values and facilitated accommodation to changing mores, popular culture of the superficially placed post-World War II era prepared the way for the tumultuous sixties— and did so on several levels. Although Hollywood certainly confirmed in numerous ways the conventional view of the postwar period as one that celebrated American virtues and reflected Cold War paranoia, a number of movies cast doubt on the success ethic, materialism, and the idea of a comfortable world in which the system worked. Audiences learned from movies such as *Double Indemnity* and *The Treasure of Sierra Madre* that the pursuit of money could produce treachery and betrayal. In other films, such as *Laura* and *The Big Clock,* wealthy individuals emerged as crazy and murderous parasites. More than a handful of movies portrayed the struggle to preserve integrity against greed. In *The Hustler,* Paul Newman as Fast Eddie Felson tells his female friend what he really like to do: not hustle bucks or even win, but instead simply play pool well. She replies that in his own way he is thus a real winner because most people never find satisfaction in what they do. At the movie's end, Fast Eddie and Minnesota Fats (Jackie Gleason) pay each other the highest of compliments: "You shoot a great game of pool." The Oscar-winning *On the Waterfront* echoed McCarthyite themes (by justifying informing, and thereby implicity condoning as patriotic the testimony of "friendly witnesses" before government investigating committee); yet it also indicted a culture that too often sacrificed honor for success. Hence when the Marlon Brando character recalled that he once was a boxing contender, that he had class and was not just a bum, he took viewers into "the heart of the national experience that transcended the postwar years: the yearning to have class and be somebody without surrendering one's honor or integrity in the process."[33]

The 1950s were undoubtedly the age of the organization man,[34] but one of the smash movies (based on a best-selling novel) was *From Here to Eternity.* The character Robert E. Lee Prewitt points up a compelling dilemma: as an arch individualist, he says, "If a man don't go his own way, he's nothing"; yet Prewitt at the same time is "in love" with the highly regimented army. Sergeant Warden (Burt Lancaster) emerges as "the classic survivor," someone who is an organization man, yet who shrewdly manipulates the system. Insofar as the modern organizational world rests upon predictability and rules, it faced even deeper trouble in a series of Alfred Hitchcock's best films. In *Rear Window, The Man Who Knew Too Much, North by Northwest, The Wrong Man, Psycho,* and *The Birds,* evil and irrationality stalked the everyday world, ready at any moment to ambush innocent people, turning their worlds inside out, or making the most normal activity—such as taking a shower—the occasion for horror. For good reason Richard Pells contends that "the media had examined skeptically the very quality of life in postwar America." Affluence, wealth, success, normality, respectability, and corporate organization had all passed before the jaundiced eye of the camera; individual integrity and even personal rebellion had received sympathetic treatment. In this sense, Pells argues "the popular culture of the 1940s and 1950s helped shape the consciousness of a new generation that would seek to redefine the American dream in the 1960s and 1970s."[35]

Even the most jejune affirmations of the American dream, such as those on much of television in the 1950s, supplied images crucial to the expanding cultural conflicts and social criticism of the 1960s. Landon Jones, in his book on the Baby Boom generation, has emphasized the influence of TV on the sixties youth culture. Youths who came of age in the mid-1960s had learned to sing "Pepsi Cola hits the spot/12 full ounces, that's a lot" before they knew the national anthem. They had seen violence on television, but rarely blood or pain—the foolishly persistent Wily Coyote invariably survived despite the punishment that the Road Runner inflicted upon him. Family dramas had seldom suggested anything about poverty or marital unhappiness. Ozzie Nelson had never talked about unemployment, and Beaver Cleaver's problems had not included separated parents, even on a trial basis. Television's lessons had been reassuring. Life was fair. America's history was one of freedom and fair play (as in *Death Valley Days, Zane Grey Theater,* and *Bonanza*); police officers and federal agents were friendly folks (as in *Highway Patrol, Dragnet,* and *The FBI*); justice prevailed (as in *Perry Mason* and *The Defenders*). Consumption was the key to life's challenges, and the big choice was between Colgate and Crest. Such a view of the world shattered during the sixties. James Simon Kunen, student at Columbia University during the strike in 1968 that closed the school for weeks and ended in violence, wrote "I realize that my conception of the philosophy of law comes not so much from Rousseau as from Fess Parker as Davy Crockett." Or as Yippie leader Jerry Rubin proclaimed: "To be a yippie you got to watch color television at least two hours a day, especially the news."[36]

In a way, then, moral censors have historically had good reason to worry about "sinful" theaters, amusement parks, and television. Such forms of popular culture have often short-circuited in substantial ways the advice of traditional cultural arbiters. A common theme has been that of respectable representatives of genteel culture—ministers and educators, for example—watching in dismay the spreading popularity of dime novels, movies, comic books, and television. One basic component of the conflict in defining American culture has been that of class. Historian Robert Sklar has maintained that movies swelled up from the ranks of immigrant workers at the turn of the century. Guardians of "respectable" culture fought back through censorship, trying to dictate what was morally acceptable in American society.[37]

Class has also influenced country-western music. For poor working-class whites, country-western music filled the same needs as the blues did for blacks. Indeed, some observers have labeled it "white soul music." Country music often dwells on failure, ruined crops, lost loves, lonely nights in grubby bars—the underside of the American dream where one finds dead ends, not open roads, vulnerability instead of power.[38] Resentment and resignation often seethe in country songs. Lefty Frizzell, for example, conveyed the bitterness and frustration of many marginal Americans when he sang about the son of a Saginaw fisherman supposedly not "good enough" for the woman he loves. And in the late 1960s and early 1970s, substantial numbers of people who believed they stood for bedrock American values cheered wildly when Merle Haggard stridently claimed to be an "Okie from Muskogee." By the early 1980s, as some commentators compared working-class Americans to a loose cannon crashing about unpredictably on the ship of state, the words of Hank Williams, Jr.—"A Country Boy Can Survive"—or Merle Haggard—"Are the Good Times Really Over"—were no less political than an incumbent senator's stump speech.[39]

While the element of social class has provided considerable tension within popular culture, so also has race. On numerous occasions, whites have critiqued their culture by "crossing over" into the perceived worlds of blacks and Indians. In minstrel shows, whites in blackface poked fun at their culture and white audiences guffawed, releasing their disappointments and frustations more easily than if the attack had been more direct and thus more threatening.[40] In the 1920s wealthy whites went on "slumming" parties to Harlem to let loose their own inhibitions in an atmosphere that was supposedly more primitive.[41] Similarly, the romantic image of the American Indian has provided a convenient yardstick against which whites have periodically criticized the values of an Anglo, middle-class society. Films such as *Billy Jack* and advertisements showing the aging but noble warrier shedding a tear as he surveys a ravaged landscape, littered with refuse and pollution, are prominent recent examples.[42]

Certainly the theme of race is basic to the history of rock-'n'-roll music. As popular culture critic Mark Miller has humorously observed, Elvis Presley "was the first white person in America to get a hysterical white mob to approach a black phenomenon without violating the Bill of Rights."[43] Presley certainly supplied what Sam Phillips of Sun Records had looked for: "A white boy who can sing colored." As Phillips reasoned, "If I could find a white man who had the Negro sound, the Negro feel, I could make a billion dollars." Elvis' first hit, "That's Alright Mama," came directly out of the world of black singers. Arthur "Big Boy" Crudup, a black man from Mississippi farm country, had recorded a version that Presley had obviously heard. The similarities between Crudup's recording and Presley's were striking. In Memphis, a local disc jockey who kept getting requests to play Presley's record also received questions about Presley's race. Presley later recalled, "Made a record and when the record came out a lot of people liked it and you would hear folks around town saying, 'Is he, is he?' and I'm going, 'Am I, am I?' "

But according to Greil Marcus' brilliant analysis, Presley did not simply echo the sounds of black blues music. Marcus, who makes much of the ongoing tensions and contradictions in American culture, has argued convincingly that Presley blended various competing values and ideals into his own unique concoction. White soul music and black blues, the Open Road and dead ends, Saturday night (when the white South exploded in local bars and brothels) and Sunday morning (when hangovers and guilt from Saturday's excesses matched up with evangelical church services) provided a volatile combination which Presley ignited in his own explosive way. Imagine, writes Marcus, the 19-year-old Elvis in a tacky recording studio in the mid-1950s working with a song, "Milk Cow Blues Boogie," that dozens of black artists had sung. A little way into the song, Presley suddenly says, "This don't move me." "Let's milk it," he shouts exuberantly as he transforms the song, galvanizing it with new energy. The young Presley, from this view, was a cultural rebel and innovator, the cultural counterpart to the Supreme Court's monumental *Brown* decision.[44]

Not only do various kinds of popular culture illuminate social trends, but also they have become increasingly important as means by which Americans view events and themselves. A wounded marine in Vietnam, awaiting a helicopter to pick him up as snipers' bullets hit the dirt around him, moaned, "I *hate* this movie."[45] And unquestionably, as the influence of photography, newsreels, and television has grown, politicians have fretted more than ever about the images they present.[46] Lyndon Johnson in the 1960s told an aide to "sell the Johnson image as one of a big, tall, tough Texan"; and Secretary of State Henry Kissinger styled himself as "the cowboy entering a village or city alone on his horse"—right out of "a wild West tale, if you like."[47]

This fascination with one's appearance in the media has in several instances helped to inspire acts of violence against nationally known figures. In 1972 Arthur H. Bremer was obsessed with how he would look on the television news. At one point Bremer spurned a well-positioned shot at President Richard Nixon in order to return to his hotel room to don clothes that would enhance his appearance on television. Shortly thereafter, Bremer, presumably dressed appropriately, shot George Wallace in a Maryland shopping mall as TV cameras dutifully recorded the event for posterity. The failed assassin of Ronald Reagan, John W. Hinckley, Jr., viewed the movie *Taxi Driver* fifteen times, shaping a fantasy world in which he, like the Robert DeNiro character Travis Bickle, stalked a politician and fell in love with Jodie Foster. Lee Harvey Oswald, John F. Kennedy's killer, anticipated that he would receive the kind of reception awarded Will Cain in the Gary Cooper movie *High Noon*. The murderer of John Lennon wrote an essay about his own death in which he parodied a Beatles' song: "John Lennon died a couple of weeks ago and I died too. Bang, Bang, we're all dead." As journalist Priscilla Johnson McMillan has written, Americans are becoming all too familiar with "the lone assassin . . . who, lacking a sense of who he is, shops among artifacts of our culture—books, movies, TV programs, song lyrics, newspaper clippings—to fashion a character."[48] If George Wallace, John Kennedy, John Lennon, and others were victims of individuals who fabricated themselves out of "the bits and pieces of popular culture,"[49] so too might the Vietnamese and Cambodians have shuddered at national leaders who saw themselves as Matt Dillons and Lone Rangers. Similarly, critics of Richard Nixon—a football fan whose presidential codename was "Quarterback," whose bombing strikes against North Vietnam in late 1972 carried the label "Operation Linebacker," whose anti-inflationary program was his "game plan," and whose black case containing America's nuclear strike capabilities was his "football"[50]—might well have wished that he were more enthusiastic about bird-watching than about the glories of the gridiron.[51]

What has all this to do with local history? One of the overwhelming trends in America over several centuries has been the erosion of local and regional culture by nationalizing forces. "Island communities"[52] have been continually on the defensive—against mail order businesses, franchises, big-city (and usually eastern) publishing firms, movies, and television. Social critics have fretted about an homogenized nation that has become "two coasts connected by United Airlines."[53] Parents in small towns have staged numerous battles to protect their children from the intrusion of outsiders who, through such factors as changing fashion, movies, New York-published textbooks, rock-'n'-roll records, and television, have allegedly undermined family authority and exposed sons and daughters to different, ostensibly risque and immoral life styles. Passions over such matters have sometimes fueled local politics in combustible ways. In the 1920s, the 1950s, and even more recently communities have heatedly debated school dress codes. Similar controversies have raged around comic books, the contents of television programs, and—as in Kanawha County, West Virginia—local control of public schoolbooks.

Columnist George Will, writing about the steady encroachments of a nationally oriented culture upon village America, has recalled the 1954 move *Shane* in which the boy tells his sodbuster father: "Somebody's comin', Pa." The father replies grimly, "Well, let 'em come." And come they did, as Will has observed; by the 1980s those Westerners who prided themselves on their distance from eastern dudes usually did so while watching on their SONY the same programs that played in the Bronx. "If we really want to preserve regional identities," Will argues, not altogether facetiously, "we should make it a crime to broadcast 'Three's Company' across state lines."[54]

But while resistance to outside messages and influences has been a notable part of local history, so too has accommodation, however tentative. In the 1920s, for example, some small-town editors reasoned that movies might in fact slow the population shift from farms to cities by providing vicarious escape to urban excitement, thereby "removing the desire to experience [cities] in person." The Farm Bureau made several films aimed at propagandizing in behalf of the virtues of both traditional rural life and the Bureau. And village ministers gradually shifted their opposition to movies from "Never!" to "Never on Sunday!"[55] In 1978, a fundamentalist church in Lewiston, Idaho, tried to compete with Super Bowl Sunday on sporting turf: it offered a football for everyone that "attend[ed] Morning Worship" and a "Stuffed Animal or Football signed by O. J. Simpson for the one bringing the most people."[56]

If such instances reveal a grudging recognition of social and cultural realities, other examples have shown numerous local groups enthusiastically trying to hasten the pace of change in their communities. They have embraced outside trends, often from a booster's perspective, trying to "pep up" and widen the appeal of their areas. From this perspective, the opening of a McDonald's franchise can signal a community's or neighborhood's arrival. The golden arches in effect suggest an external stamp of approval: locals have presumably passed muster and received outside recognition, thus affirming their place on the national map.

In Pekin, Illinois, in the 1970s and 1980s, this quest for outside acceptance and respectability clashed jarringly with a desire to protect local tradition. For at least half a century Pekin high school athletes had competed under the nickname of "Chinks." Ultimately, however, proud local custom collided with emerging social priorities. Embarrassed school authorities concluded that the traditional nickname was a racial slur against Chinese-Americans and incongruous in a nation that formally extolled the virtues of tolerance. When school officials changed the name of the athletic teams to "Dragons" in 1980, some 100 students demonstrated, carrying signs such as "Pekin Chinks, Dragons Stink." According to one student who claimed that his parents wholeheartedly backed the protest: "My dad was a Chink and doesn't want to see it changed either." A graduate of Pekin High, vowing to battle to restore the old name, said: "It brought spirit to the community. It made people feel good. Now everything is going down the drain."[57] (One can imagine similar showdowns elsewhere—for example, in Orofino, Idaho, location of one of the state's mental hospitals, as custom bumps into new sensibilities and the nickname "Maniacs" hangs in the balance.)

The very stuff of local history, then, has been a dialogue—a dialectic—vital to American culture at large, and thus evident in popular culture. Ways in which communities have presented themselves (the "City by the Sea," for example), the rituals of sporting events, the flux of censorship campaigns, the impact of national fads, and the means by which citizens have adjusted to or resisted nationalizing trends provide some of the most important themes of local history. In recent years, cries of "We're number one!" have echoed across the landscape, as ardent fans feverishly waved their index fingers in the air, all trying to distinguish their communities, regions, neighborhoods, or schools from others, all ironically looking the same, participating in common rituals taken increasingly from the mass media. In a sense, it is as impossible for the local historian to ignore popular culture as for the corner service station owner to disregard changing gasoline prices. As George Will said, the boy was correct: "Somebody's comin', Pa."

Notes

1. As historian Russel B. Nye said in his pioneering overview of the subject, "Popular art confirms the experience of the majority, in contrast to elite art. . . . For this reason, popular art has been an unusually sensitive and accurate reflector of the attitudes and concerns of the society for which it is produced." Nye, *The Unembarrassed Muse: The Popular Arts in America* (New York: Dial Press, 1970), p. 4. For useful summaries and analyses of the major shift in American historiography in the 1960s and after see, for example, Gordon Wood, "Star-Spangled History," *New York Review of Books,* August 12, 1982, pp. 4-9; Herbert Gutman, "Whatever Happened to History?", *The Nation* (November 21, 1981), 233:521, 533-554; C. Vann Woodward, "A Short History of American History," *The New York Times Book Review,* August 8, 1982, pp. 3, 14; Tamara Hareven, editor, *Anonymous Americans: Explorations in Nineteenth Century Social History* (Englewood Cliffs, New Jersey: Prentice-Hall, 1971), pp. vii-x. Essays in the Hareven book provide good examples of ways in which historians

are probing the lives of "anonymous Americans"; see particularly Lawrence Levine's article on slave songs and David Grimsted's on melodrama. Other examples are in Thomas Frazier, *The Underside of American History*, 2 vols. (New York: Harcourt Brace Jovanovich, 1982). For a two-volume anthology that specifically uses popular culture as a way of understanding the past, see David Burner, Robert Marcus, and Torj Tilson, editors, *America through the Looking Glass: A Historical Reader in Popular Culture* (Englewood Cliffs, New Jersey: Prentice-Hall, 1974). As the editors point out, viewed historically, popular culture means "any form of expression or custom that achieves popularity among a large group of people." It gives meaning to the daily lives of a large audience and ranges from marriage rituals and childbearing techniques to humor, etiquette books, fashions, and domestic architecture (pp. 3-4).

2. Warren Susman, editor, *Culture and Commitment, 1929-1945* (New York: George Braziller, 1973), pp. 1-24; Susman, "The Thirties," in Stanley Coben and Lorman Ratner, editors, *The Development of an American Culture* (Englewood Cliffs, New Jersey: Prentice-Hall, 1970), pp. 179-218; Richard Pells, *Radical Visions and American Dreams* (New York: Harper & Row, 1973); Andrew Bergman, *We're in the Money: Hollywood Films and the Depression* (New York: New York University Press, 1971); J. Fred Mac Donald, *Don't Touch That Dial! Radio Programming in American Life from 1920 to 1960* (Chicago: Nelson-Hall, 1979).

3. Susman, *Culture and Commitment*, up. 13-17, and "The Thirties," pp. 197-198. On the cultural shift, see Richard Huber, *The American Idea of Success* (New York: McGraw-Hill Book Co., 1971), and Paul Carter, *The Twenties in America* (New York: Thomas Y. Crowell Co., 1968), pp. 27-33, 72-73.

4. William Stott, *Documentary Expression and Thirties America* (New York: Oxford University Press, 1973), pp. 129-130. Warren Susman, during the "Teaching a Decade" workshop at the Sixth Biennial Convention of the American Studies Association (Boston, October 28, 1977), again emphasized the usefulness of *Life* as a research source for the 1930s.

5. Pells, *Radical Visions and American Dreams*, pp. 269-270, includes a thoughtful discussion of thirties horror films. On more recent trends, see Ron Rosenbaum, "Gooseflesh," *Harper's* (September, 1979), 259:86-92. On 1930s soap operas, see MacDonald, *Don't Touch That Dial!*, pp. 234-236, 239-257.

6. Bergman, *We're in the Money*, pp. 3-17, 83-91.

7. *Newsweek* (January 26, 1981), 97:58-59.

8. Robert Brustein, "The Retread Culture," *The New York Times Magazine*, October 26, 1975, pp. 38-54, discusses this phenomenon.

9. Leslie Owen, "Dialogue: Is popular culture social history?" *Humanities* (January/February, 1980), 1:15.

10. "Wee Chatter" (weekly publication of the Methodist church in Normal, Illinois), January 30-February 5, 1972, p. 1.

11. John Mariani, "Television Evangelism: Milking the Flock," *Saturday Review* (February 3, 1979), 6:22-25.

12. Henry Fairlie, "Born Again Bland," *The New Republic* (August 2 & 9, 1980), 185:17.

13. Mariani, "Television Evangelism," p. 25.

14. "The straight word on Abbie Hoffman's hair," *Life* (October 11, 1971),

71:77. See also Robert Brustein, "Revolution as Theater," *The New Republic* (March 14, 1970), 162:13-17.

15. Promotional letter, Jonathan Miller (Icarus Films) to Dear Friend, September, 1982.

16. *The New York Times Magazine,* January 4, 1980, p. 25.

17. *Family Circle* (September 16, 1982), p. 95. For other discussions of the cooptive powers of popular culture, see Stanley Aronowitz, *False Promises: The Shaping of American Working Class Consciousness* (New York: McGraw-Hill Book Co., 1973), pp. 51-134, and Jeffrey Schrank, *Snap, Crackle, and Popular Taste: The Illusion of Free Choice in America* (New York: Dell Publishing Co., 1977). Schrank believes, for example, that "it is more realistic to consider television in terms of a social control device than as a communication medium" (p. 34).

18. See, e.g., Janice Radway, "Dialogue: Is popular culture social history?" *Humanities* (January/February, 1980), 1:14.

19. For an interesting analysis of Marlboro Country as "a merchandised metaphor," see Bruce Lohoff, "The Higher Meaning of Marlboro Cigarettes," *Journal of Popular Culture* (Winter, 1969), 3:441-450.

20. Michael Feldberg, *The Turbulent Era: Riot and Disorder in Jacksonian America* (New York: Oxford University Press, 1980), p. 89.

21. See, e.g., Sheldon Wolin, "Carter and the New Constitution," *New York Review of Books,* June 1, 1978, p. 18. "We leave the central city to the poor, deposit the elderly in nursing homes, entrust the dying to thanatologists: no deposit, no return," Wolin writes.

22. The "discrepancy between the demands of society and the heroic individual's honor and freedom has always been near the surface of the Western," writes John Cawelti. The result is "the Lone Ranger, a hero who fights to bring law and order to the West yet who continually flees the very communities he has helped to found." Cawelti, *The Six-Gun Mystique* (Bowling Green, Ohio: Bowling Green University Popular Press, 1970), p. 79. Cawelti's little book is splendid on its subject.

23. Leslie A. Fiedler, *Love and Death in the American Novel* (revised edition; New York: Dell Publishing Co., 1966), pp. 25-26, 339-341.

24. John Cawelti is good on the appeal of Las Vegas in "The Frontier and the Native American," in Joshua C. Taylor, *America as Art* (New York: Harper & Row, 1976), pp. 174-179.

25. See the fifteen "family activities" cards that McDonald's made available at restaurants in 1978.

26. Michael Wood, *America in the Movies* (paperback edition; New York: Dell Publishing Co., 1976), p. 21.

27. "Peanuts," July 18, 1982, and November 29, 1980.

28. On Allen, see Michael Wood, "Allen's Alley," *New York Review of Books,* June 29, 1978, pp. 14-16, and Jack Kroll, "Woody," *Newsweek* (April 24, 1978), 91:62-66.

29. Charles Funnell, *By the Beautiful Sea: The Rise and High Times of That Great American Resort, Atlantic City* (New York: Alfred A. Knopf, 1975), especially pp. 24-55.

30. Funnell, *By the Beautiful Sea,* pp. 56-158, and John F. Kasson, *Amusing*

The Million: Coney Island at the Turn of the Century (New York: Hill & Wang, 1978), especially pp. 40-50, 70-82. In the 1980s, Pac-Man and other electronic games may play a similar role in aiding the adjustment of rank-and-file Americans to the computer revolution—a revolution in technology as important to the national experience as were the railroad and autombile in earlier times.

31. Kasson, *Amusing the Million,* pp. 81-82, 105-106. As Michael Harrington has written, Disney World is "a reactionary and very modern future in the fantastic costume of a dead past. In our 1984, perhaps Cinderella's Castle will look down on us rather than a portrait of Big Brother. Our national model will be a small town fraudulently concocted by a huge corporation; a celebration of free enterprise within the confines of a perfect monopoly; a homely, reverential, authoritarian and corporate-dominated place . . . George Orwell's Mickey Mouse." *The Next America: The Decline and Rise of the United States* (New York: Holt, Rinehart & Winston, 1981), pp. 151-152. See also "Cyclops," "Sentiment Every Sunday," *Life* (May 19, 1972), 72:18, for a discussion of Disneyland as a "controlled environment," and Peter Schrag, *The Decline of the WASP* (New York: Simon & Schuster, 1971), pp. 194-202.

32. Lary May, *Screening Out the Past: The Birth of Mass Culture and the Motion Picture Industry* (New York: Oxford University Press, 1980), especially pp. 96-196 and 200-236, on the "cultural reorientation"; on Bara, pp. 106-107; on Pickford, pp. 118-144.

33. Richard H. Pells, "Images of the Past: Popular Culture and Postwar America," in Jack Salzman, editor, *Prospects: An Annual of American Studies,* No. 5 (New York: Burt Franklin, 1980), pp. 439-455. See also Wood, *America in the Movies,* for a discussion of *The Hustler* and other postwar films. Wood and Pells provide examples of ways in which scholars can agree and disagree over interpretations of movies.

34. Scholarly works such as William H. Whyte, Jr., *The Organization Man* (New York: Simon & Schuster, 1956), and David Riesman, *The Lonely Crowd* (New Haven: Yale University Press, 1950), dealt with this theme as did fiction such as Sloan Wilson's best-seller—made into a movie starring Gregory Peck—*The Man in the Gray Flannel Suit* (New York: Simon & Schuster, 1955).

35. Pells, "Images of the Past," pp. 448-449, 452-455.

36. Landon Jones, *Great Expectations: America and the Baby Boom Generation* (paper edition; New York: Ballantine Books, 1980), pp. 47-49, 139-148; also, Mark Crispin Miller, "What happened to the Sixties," *New York Review of Books,* August 4, 1977, p. 18.

37. Robert Sklar, *Movie-Made America: A Social History of American Movies* (New York: Random House, 1975), especially pp. 3-157. See also Kathleen McCarthy, "Nickel Vice and Virtue: Movie Censorship in Chicago, 1907-1915," *Journal of Popular Film* (1976), 5:37-55.

38. See, e.g., Greil Marcus, *Mystery Train: Images of America in Rock 'n' Roll Music* (New York: E. P. Dutton, 1975), pp. 19, 150-153, 158; Christopher S. Wren, "The Great White Soul Sound: Country Music," *Look* (July 13, 1971), 35:11-39; David Halberstam, "Hank Williams Reconsidered," *ibid.*, p. 42.

39. For one discussion of the growing discontent in country-western music, see Florence King, "Red Necks, White Socks, and Blue Ribbon Fear," *Harper's* (July, 1974), 249:30-34. For a provocative interpretation of recent "Middle American

Radicalism" see Kevin P. Phillips, *Post-Conservative America: People, Politics, and Ideology in a Time of Crisis* (New York: Random House, 1982), pp. 193-204.

40. Robert Toll, *Blacking Up: The Minstrel Show in Nineteenth-Century America* (New York: Oxford University Press, 1974), especially pp. 65-71.

41. Nathan Huggins, *Harlem Renaissance* (New York: Oxford University Press, 1971), especially pp. 84-136, and Gilbert Osofsky, "Symbols of the Jazz Age; The New Negro and Harlem Discovered," *American Quarterly* (Summer, 1965), 117:229-239.

42. Robert Berkhofer, Jr., *The White Man's Indian: Images of the American Indian from Columbus to the Present* (New York: Random House, 1978), pp. 27-29, 107-108, 110-111.

43. Mark Crispin Miller, "The King," *New York Review of Books*, December 8, 1977, p. 38.

44. Marcus, *Mystery Train*, pp. 137-205. Luc Sante is among others who have noted "the dichotomy that was to inform [Presley's] whole life: rebellion and assimilation," a "failure to acknowledge apparent contradictions. This was most fruitfully put to use in this early music, with its inspired marriage of white country and black rhythm and blues, a previously taboo coupling." "Relic," *New York Review of Books*, December 17, 1981, p. 22. See also Lucian F. Truscott IV, "Elvis Presley's Deep-Fried Demise," *New Times* (September 2, 1977), 9:68.

45. Michael Herr, *Dispatches* (paper edition; New York: Avon Books, 1978), pp. 188-189.

46. David Halberstam has written, not altogether facetiously, regarding the 1960 presidential debates between John F. Kennedy and Richard Nixon: "On such decisions—Max Factor Creme Puff instead of Shavestick—rode the future leadership of the United States." "President Video," *Esquire* (June, 1976), 85:94-97. Television's impact on the relationships between national politicians and the grass roots has been profound. The old whistle-stop campaigns that took presidents and their challengers into small towns have given way to the staged media events: brief appearances at a flood site, a dedication, or a particular event, all duly recorded on tape for the evening news while the individuals promptly catch the next airplane flights to distant destinations.

47. Johnson's quote is in Ronnie Dugger, *The Politician: The Life and Times of Lyndon Johnson* (New York: W. W. Norton & Co., 1982), p. 140. In this respect, Dugger's chapter titles are illuminating: "From the Alamo to Khe Sanh," "Indians and Communists," "From Deer Creek to Pleiku," "The Politician as Western Hero." For the Kissinger quote, see Garry Wills, "Kissinger," *Playboy* (December, 1974), 21:122. Wills adds that Kissinger hopes "not only to play Hoot Gibson but to catalog the kinds of audience response this wild West tale will inspire."

48. Priscilla Johnson McMillan, "An Assassin's Portrait," *The New Republic* (July 12, 1982), 187:16-18.

49. *Ibid.*, p. 17.

50. Walter LaFeber and Richard Polenberg, *The American Century* (New York: John Wiley & Sons, 1975), p. 430, and Harry Jebsen, Jr., *Sports: A Microcosm of Twentieth-Century America* (St. Louis: Forum Press, 1978), p. 2.

51. Similarly, when President John Kennedy explained why it was essential for America to land human beings on the moon, he asked: "Why does Rice play

Texas?" Quoted in James Barber, *The Presidential Character* (Englewood Cliffs, New Jersey: Prentice-Hall, 1972), p. 326.

52. Robert Wiebe, *The Search for Order, 1877-1920* (New York: Hill & Wang, 1967), chapter 1, uses this term in his superb discussion of challenges that small-town America faced in the late nineteenth century.

53. Michael Novak, "White Ethnic," *Harper's* (September, 1971), 243:48.

54. George Will, "Wagons in a Circle," *Newsweek* (September 17, 1979), 94:116.

55. Don Kirschner, *City and Country: Rural Responses to Urbanization in the 1920s* (Westport, Connecticut: Greenwood Press, 1970), pp. 68-70, 250.

56. Advertisement, First Assembly of God Church, *Lewiston Tribune*, January 14, 1978.

57. *Lewiston Tribune*, September 5, 1980.

Comment: *New Perspectives in Interpretation*

John R. Jameson

There are still some who long for the more simple days when history concerned the study of power as exercised by military and political elites. What transpired in smoke-filled rooms and command tents occupied the energies of most historians as they concentrated on kings, presidents, and generals—the "great men" whose decisions and actions shaped the world. Accordingly, one had only to analyze and interpret their papers to gain an understanding of what was important over time in the human experience. The powerless—racial and ethnic minorities, children, most women,[1] and other "have nots" in an increasingly urban, industrialized, and impersonal society—consequently received scant attention from the chroniclers of an elitist past.[2]

Fortunately, largely since the 1960s, these neglected groups more and more have become the objects of "expanding fields of inquiry."[3] A sophisticated use of nontraditional sources (for example, census data, photographs, oral histories, material culture) has provided the documentation necessary for writing histories of the so-called inarticulate.[4] A related development has been the study of the nontraditional sources themselves to help gain a broader understanding of the multidimensional human experience. Industrial history and popular culture are two examples of the latter.

T. Allan Comp advises the researcher in industrial history to go "into working places, reading buildings like manuscripts, talking with folks who spent their working lives in the very places you seek to study, and then back to the library to fit it all together." According to LeRoy Ashby, the researcher of popular culture faces a similar task, studying a wide variety of cultural artifacts from comic books to television soap operas, Big Mac hamburgers, and shopping malls. Obviously, both industrial history and popular culture rely heavily on interdisciplinary techniques and nontraditional sources, two characteristics of the "new interpretation."[5]

Comp's discussion of the construction of the Salt Lake City Tabernacle illustrates well why industrial historians as well as others have turned to nontraditional sources to complement published and manuscript materials. The tabernacle is an unusual case, for there were no photographs, plans, or other paper documents, primary or secondary, on the interior construction. In fact, only through an analysis of the structure itself could one learn of the potential disaster faced by the Mormon builders or the innovative techniques they used to solve the dangerous problem of the timber trusses.

Comp's case studies of a Utah smelter and the Idaho bridges demonstrate that technological, cultural, political, and social developments at the local level, when placed in a regional and national context, provide substance and sometimes new dimensions to what otherwise would only be unsupported historical generalizations. For example, the Progressive Era's penchant for overall efficiency and improved working conditions for factory laborers takes on added meaning in view of what took place at the Tooele smelter. Here the mechanization of the plant and the introduction of anti-pollution devices resulted in a safe working environment. Yet none of these measures was taken out of altruistic concern for the smelter's employees. Rather, the anti-pollution innovations were implemented to avoid lawsuits filed by neighboring farmers angered by the sulphur dust that blanketed the countryside. And the reason the company mechanized the plant's operation was not for the safety of the employees but to reduce labor costs: where it had previously taken thirty to forty men to charge a lead blast furnace, four did the task at Tooele.[6]

Whereas industrial history's principal contribution to interpretation is the case study, LeRoy Ashby's analysis of films, advertisements, songs, and even games indicates that popular culture offers several interpretive perspectives. For one, it reveals the values, aspirations, and fears of ordinary Americans as they responded to change and crisis—despression, war, the shift from a producer to a consumer society—and as they tried to reconcile competing and conflicting ideals—progress versus nostalgia; government of laws versus the lone gunfighter; individual freedom and mobility versus the security and identity found in a job with a Fortune 500 corporation and belonging to a family, neighborhood, and community.

Yet Ashby points out that "popular culture may be an interpretive trap," for it "may tell less about the grass roots than about yet another elite group: promoters and entrepreneurs." In other words, the study of popular culture could disclose more about the merchandiser than it does about American consumers, the so-called inarticulate majority. Nevertheless, Ashby contends that popular culture is "far from useless as social history. A major question is why particular books, movies, fads, sports, music, and other mass media creations are popular at particular times." The answer to this difficult question brings one full circle back to the grass-roots consumer.

So far, we have seen that industrial history and popular culture both offer new perspectives in interpretation; but what, if anything, is their contribution to local history?

In his case study of the Idaho bridges, Comp succinctly states the tie between industrial and local history: "Every one of those local bridges has at least a small story to reveal about public decisions, anticipated economic and transportation developments, or actual community achievements." He concludes that "these industrial structures not only serve as gateways or links in a transportation network, they also serve as gateways to historical understanding and visible links with the aspirations of our past."

Popular culture, on the other hand, challenges the assumed uniqueness of the local environment and shows that national trends and products had more of an influence on the culture, socio-economic institutions, and popular attitudes and values than did local ones. Nevertheless, local history has an important function in relation to popular culture, for the former provides an arena for an in-depth study of the effect of these trends and their accompanying material culture on a specific locale.

Actually, popular culture and industrial history have both contributed to the erosion of local and regional culture through such nationalizing forces as the railroad, the automobile, mail-order catalogues, Hollywood films, and the sameness of Holiday Inns or Burger Kings. Yet there has also been a pride in becoming part of this homogenizing process, whether a town acquired the "Golden Arches" of McDonald's or a smelter plant, for these were the outward signs of a progressive community. Concurrent with the effort to attract these nationalizing elements, there was also a drive to protect local traditions and environments—as shown by the Pekin, Illinois, boosters protesting having to change the school teams from "Chinks" to "Dragons" or the Utah farmers going to court to stop "progress" if it meant a polluted landscape and lifestyle.

In conclusion, then, industrial history, popular culture, and the new interpretation in general emphasize the complexity, diversity, and richness of human experience at all levels of place (local, regional, national, world) and personality (grass roots, elite). The days of simple, one-dimensional "great men" interpretation are no more. Long live the New Interpretation!

Notes

1. Occasionally the deeds of a Queen Elizabeth I or a Joan of Arc demanded the historians' attention; nevertheless, women were only regarded as worthy of

study when they thought and acted like "great men."

2. A well-done analysis of American historians' preoccupation in textbooks with an elitist past and their gradual inclusion of "have nots" in the national experience is Frances FitzGerald, *America Revised: History Schoolbooks in the Twentieth Century* (Boston: Little Brown & Co., 1979).

3. Michael Kammen, editor, *The Past before Us: Contemporary Historical Writing in the United States* (Ithaca, New York: Cornell University Press, 1980), has three parts—Units of Time and Areas of Study; Expanding Fields of Inquiry; and Modes of Gathering and Assessing Historical Materials. The essays in the second and third parts and Kammen's introduction provide a veritable state-of-the-art overview of the new interpretations, including social, poltical, and labor history; community studies and urban and local history; blacks, women, and the family; oral history; psychohistory; quantification; and comparative history.

4. The American Association for State and Local History has published several excellent books for lay and professional readers on the use and interpretation of nontraditional sources. A representative sample of recent publications includes Barbara Allen and Lynwood Montell, *From Memory to History: Using Oral Sources for Historical Research* (1981); David E. Kyvig and Myron A. Marty, *Nearby History: Exploring the Past around You* (1982); and Thomas J. Schlereth, editor, *Material Culture Studies in America* (1982).

5. Common to both papers are the use and anlysis of sources in material culture. Archaeologist James Deetz offers a broad definition of material culture that relates well to our essays. For Deetz it includes not only tangible artifacts from the most simple—a straight pin—to the most complex—a space vehicle—but also processes and "human motions" such as butchering livestock, parades, and dancing. Deetz does not limit his definition to the solid state, either. "Fountains are liquid examples, as are lily ponds, and material that is partly gas includes hot-air balloons and neon signs"—and human speech. James Deetz, *In Small Things Forgotten: The Archaeology of Early American Life* (Garden City, New York: Anchor Press/Doubleday, 1977), p. 24.

6. Unfortunately, the Tooele case study does not shed light on why only one company out of eight responded and the others closed down. Also, Comp fails to place developments at the smelter in a larger historical context. While he does mention the clash over goals and values at the local, state, and church levels, not once does he discuss the Progressive Era as such.

II. *Evaluating Oral Materials*

True Tales and Tall Tales

Jan Harold Brunvand

I would like to begin with a partial quotation from the first paragraph of my book on urban legends, *The Vanishing Hitchhiker:*

> We are not aware of our own folklore any more than we are of the grammatical rules of our language . . . [for] we do not concentrate on the form or content of our folklore; instead, we simply listen to information that others tell us and then pass it on—more or less accurately—ot other listeners.[1]

The pronoun "we" in that question refers to all of us as *folk*—carriers and transmitters of folklore. But what I want to discuss here is "we" as *folklorists*—collectors and students of folklore—and some ways that we may increase our awareness of what folklore is, how it evolves, and especially what it might tell us about local culture and history.

Oral folklore comprises the person-to-person word-of-mouth communication that becomes structured and stylized as it passes from mouth to ear across time and space. Not all oral communication is folklore, nor is all folklore oral; but the examples here are oral folklore, and specifically of spoken narratives.

The stories I have in mind are those people tell—which occasionally get printed—that seem to be reasonably true accounts of actual happenings from the relatively recent past, but which often prove to be traveling semi-fictional tales localized to a particular setting, such as the Intermountain West.

In general terms, folklorists strive to collect, classify, and carefully to compare these stories in order to understand their peculiar style, structure, function, and meaning in the contexts in which they are told. Often such stories are referred to as "legends," or more particularly as "historical legends," "personal legends" (including "anecdotes"), or "local legends." Some specific ways that we folklorists gather and analyze legends will be illustrated in my discussion of a few typical examples.

In Austin and Alta Fife's book on Mormon folklore, *Saints of Sage and Saddle* (1956), a remarkable experience involving a pioneer child and a rattlesnake is described in a section on the settlement of the town of Manti:

> Upon arriving at the present site of Manti in central Utah the Saints camped on the side of the hill where the temple now stands. Little did they know until the warm days of spring that they had selected for their camp a prodigious den of rattlesnakes. On the first warm day thousands of the poisonous reptiles crept into the dugouts, the tents, the wagons, the beds, everywhere. It was estimated that from five hundred to fifteen hundred were killed in a single day. As many as a hundred and fifty serpents were found hibernating in a single ball. One woman noticed that her child was sickly. She could not account for this until one day she saw him take his bread and milk out on the side of the hill and feed a rattlesnake some of it with his own spoon. As soon as this practice was stopped, the child got better.[2]

What we have here is not the ideal of folklore fieldwork — the verbatim words of a storyteller, and the variations that oral circulation produces. Instead we have a secondary level of field data — that is, a summary of the story's background, and a paraphrase of one typical version.

The historical facts behind the incident serve as a prologue: the Saints *did* settle Manti early in their occupation of Utah, rattlesnakes *did indeed* infest the first campsites, and a temple *was* later built there. The references to varying numbers of snakes that were seen and killed suggest the workings of oral tradition as these accounts passed down through generations. But starting with the line "One woman noticed that her child was sickly," we get the gist of a story that the Fifes were told five different times. Thus we have the criteria of multiple existence and probably also of variation to validate this story as genuine folklore. In its structure we see that the essential plot for any retelling of the story would contain the elements: 1) sickly child, 2) feeds a snake, 3) parent intervenes, and 4) child recovers health.

This is a curious narrative but not a totally fantastic one, and we might accept it as describing an actual pioneer experience. However, we find that some Utah people tell variations of it. For example, in 1967 a student collected a version in which a little boy in Manti feeds part of his sandwich to a rattlesnake, saying "Some for you and some for me"; in 1971 I was told that it was a little girl sharing her glass of milk with the snake.[3]

When we look for further versions of the child-and-snake story, another picture emerges. *The Motif-Index of Folk Literature*, a standard comparative reference work, assigns the number B1765.6. to the theme

"Snake eats milk and bread with child."[4] Pursuing this motif in the satellite index for Anglo-American folk narratives,[5] we can locate versions of the story in published folklore collections from the Ozarks, German Pennsylvania, New England, and Virginia, and from blacks in southern Michigan. In each case the incident is treated as if true; the particulars of the story vary somewhat, but the basic pattern remains constant. Beyond the American series of child-and-snake stories, the *Motif-Index* cross-references the theme to the listing of international folktale types, where we encounter "The Child and the Snake" as Tale Type number 285, a story known throughout middle and northern Europe and somewhat less commonly in eastern and southern Europe with a possible prototype among the folk stories of India.[6] (The distribution patterns that can be sketched for such stories depend upon where folklore has been best collected: a story known this widely is probably also told in many other regions as well, but it may not yet have been collected elsewhere.)

Eventually we leave these esoteric byways of bibliography for a more familiar source—the famous Grimm brothers' fairy tales. The Child and the Snake is to be found even there (first published in 1812) in a readily recognizable form; a little girl shares her bowl of bread and milk with a snake while singing a song to it; the mother rescues her child by killing the snake. The conclusion is somewhat different. Instead of the child being sick and then recovering, in Grimm the child was happy with her reptile friend, but she sickened and died after it was destroyed, perhaps suggesting a spiritual connection to the animal companion.[7]

To briefly summarize this first example: the Manti, Utah, story initially appears to be a Western pioneer-experience narrative reshaped by oral tradition, but after some investigation it proves to be a widespread American settlers' tale. Further comparative study shows that it is ultimately a European narrative, relocalized and adapted to become part of American folklore. One interpretation that follows from study of the child-and-snake story is that the Manti folk were not consciously spreading fiction disguised as fact in order to glorify their past; rather, Americans in several different places accepted the same story as true because it was plausible. The story probably survives in oral tradition because it says something memorable about how our ancestors might have come to terms with one of the dangers that were part of the task of taming the wilderness.

Different in style and content from such "true" tales in oral narrative tradition are the "tall" tales (also called "lies," "windies," or "whoppers") that western storytellers relate. Often these cluster around a particular local character—"the biggest liar in seven counties" or the like. This may be someone like Len Henry, a squawman among the Nez Perce, about whom I gathered stories in northern Idaho in the early 1960s.[8] People told me their own variations of the tall tales Len was famous for (he had died some fourteen years earlier), and these fell into the familiar patterns of traditional exaggeration found in such books as Vance Randolph's *We Always Lie to Strangers* and Roger Welsch's *Shingling the Fog and Other Plains Lies.*[4]

They said Len Henry claimed that he stuck his buggy whip into a snowbank and forgot it, and in the spring it had sprouted, taken root, and become an apple tree.

He said he popped some popcorn one day and his little dog saw it in a big bowl, thought it was snow, and lay down and froze to death.

He started to jump across a deep canyon one time, saw that he wasn't going to make it, so he just turned around in midair and jumped back.

After a string of Len Henry tall tales, people sometimes told me "true" tales, or anecdotes, about the kind of man Len Henry was. They said that one time he was watching some men work on a car engine, and the hood was up with the engine running when old Len (who knew about horses but not about cars) reached in, touched a spark plug, and then quickly jerked his hand back again. "Did it shock you, Len?" someone asked. "Nope," Len replied. "I was too quick for it."[10]

For years I accepted this anecdote as an apt illustration of the witty storyteller coming up with a snappy response when caught looking foolish. It was only through serendipity, not skillful folklore research, that I came to realize that this anecdote is traditional, perhaps even a story Len told on himself. A student told me a story (and later I found a published version) about a blacksmith who had frequently been bothered by a curious boy hanging around the shop and picking up anything that wasn't nailed down to inspect it. One day the blacksmith, seeing the boy ambling over, heated up a horseshoe and laid it on the anvil; sure enough the boy picked it up, then really quickly he put it down again. "Did you burn yourself, son?" the blacksmith asked. "Nope," the boy replied, "it just don't take me long to look at a horseshoe."[11] This lad was obviously a future master storyteller, and the story is a nice illustration of how a narrative—whether true or not—can so well illustrate a particular personality type.

Local characters—liars, skinflints, drunks, eccentrics, and so on—are frequently subjects of traditional stories. A special dimension in the performance style of local-character anecdotes is found in the stories about immigrants and their difficulties with English. The storyteller, whether of the same group or not, is obliged to render an imitation of the dialect as best he can.

I collected a number of Norwegian dialect stories in Alberta one summer, several of them dealing with the very common problem of a newcomer trying to buy something from a storekeeper who spoke only

English. In the following text transcribed from a tape, the storyteller himself has slight difficulties with English:

> There was a Norwegian lady, had just come from Norway, and she needed some matches, and she couldn't speak a word of English. She went to the store thinking that the storekeeper wouldn't be able to speak Norwegian. She went into the store and thought a monologue [he meant a pantomine] would be a good way to explain what she wanted. So she illustrated that she put a pipe into her mouth, and then she very deliberately took a match—she just pretended that she took a match. She took it out of a box or something, and then put it in her fingers, just the way that you would hold a match when you're going to stroke it on the side of your pants leg and light it. And she made a good stroke on her pants leg and pulled it up, and it looked like the match lit, and she put it over to her pipe to light it, and then she held the match out. And the storekeeper said, *"O, er det fyrestykker du vil ha?"* She answered, *"Nei, kan du snakke Norsk? Og her starr jeg og snakker Engelsk!;;* [Transition: "Oh, is it matches you want to buy?" "No! do you speak Norwegian? And here I stand speaking English."][12]

Such an anecdote, whether literally true or not (and I have not found an analogue for this one yet), shows us typical problems of newly arrived foreign settlers in the West. The story also provides in its language a bit of the flavor of the immigrant experience.

Sometimes a slight touch of dialect just spices up an anecdote about a local character. Here is such a story that rambles around somewhat before coming to its point. It was collected by a student from Cedar City, Utah.

> Oscar Larsen was an interesting character. As a small boy he came to this country from Sweden. Arriving in New York City he worked there for some time with an uncle in a blacksmith shop. While working in this shop, a spark from the anvil caused the loss of one eye. He came to Cedar City where two of his boyhood friends, Albert Lundale and Charlie Lundgren, were engaged in the sheep business. At the age of fifty, Oscar was one of Cedar City's more well-to-do citizens and a director in the Bank of Southern Utah. Some years ago the Las Vegas Chamber of Commerce hosted the Cedar City Chamber of Commerce and among the group was Oscar Larsen and William R. Palmer, who at that time was president of the Cedar Stake. President Palmer had also lost one eye as a small boy. As the group was shown around Las Vegas, they came to the old red light district. As the driver of the bus started down the street, Oscar turned to Will and said: "Vell, vell, Vill. I vill risk one eye if you vill!"[13]

The names, places, ages, and specific events mentioned here all bespeak a local tradition based on actual fact. One wonders a little about the coincidence that two old one-eyed Mormons, one Swedish, would end up in such a situation, but the storyteller related this one as pure fact before a Cedar City audience that presumably would have challenged him if they had not known or heard of these characters. The fact is that the "risk one eye" punchline shows up in two other American folklore collections, one from North Carolina, the other from the Ozarks.[14] Possibly Oscar Larsen and his friend "Vill" both knew the traditional story and were alluding to it in their conversation. At any rate, Vance Randolph in annotating the Ozark version traces printed sources for the story back to the 1920s. Perhaps the lesson here is that an apt anecdote may become attached to local characters whenever it fits, whatever the odds are that such a perfect fit will occur. Incidentally, the older variants of this story set the incident in a church: a woman's dress gets pulled up above her waist during her possession by the Holy Spirit in a revival service, and the minister warns that any man who peeks will be struck blind by the Lord. One says to another, "I think I'll risk one eye." In the Utah text the religious theme applies to the characters themselves (as Mormons) rather than to the situation. The risk of any eye is only an implied curse for peeking at the shady ladies of Vegas, and the phrase "one eye" now refers to their having only one eye each.

The next story is truly a factual family anecdote, preserved essentially correctly over a considerable time, in both oral and printed form. A student told it to me first just as she had often heard it from members of her family:

> My grandmother was a teacher at a schoolhouse in a mining camp and has to tend to all the problems of barest essentials in the schoolhouse. There's this one little kid all of a sudden starts screaming bloody murder and starts jumping up and down holding his rear end. My grandmother goes over and blood is spurting out. My grandmother pulls his pants down and sees a big splinter sticking out of his behind. There is no school nurse or tweezers on the premises. She pulls the kid toward her and puts him across her lap, gives the splinter a jerk with her teeth and pulls it out.

Notable in the style of this version is the quick shift from past tense to historical present tense: "My grandmother *was* a teacher . . . and *has to* tend to all the problems . . . *There's this* one little kid . . . " etc. Another interesting touch is the almost punning term "barest essentials" in the first sentence, and the contemporary reference "There is no school nurse or tweezers on the premises." The emphasis here is strictly upon the situation—the time grandma, a resourceful old gal on the frontier, got to the seat of a problem with her teeth.

When my student mentioned to me that her grandmother had included the anecdote in a little pamphlet of reminiscences, I requested that she bring it in and let me read the published version. It went like this:

> Something happened in school that day . . . An eight year old girl, sliding from one end of the rough plank seat to the other let out a horrible scream. I picked her up, laid her face down on the desk plank, flipped up her skirts and pushed down her pants. Yes, there it was, a terrifying big sliver of dirty wood sinking fast into her little fat bottom. It was too far in to grasp with my fingers, and the flesh was closing over it rapidly. Since my fingers were of no use, I forced the flesh back with my lips, then clamped my teeth over the protruding end and drew out the sliver. All during this her little sister stood near, jumping up and down, frantically screaming, "The teacher's biting Sally's ass. The teacher's biting Sally's ass."

This time the emphasis is upon the reaction rather than the event itself, and the changes in the story are significant. Two generations of repetition (evidently without reference to the printed source) have altered the character from a girl to a boy, abbreviated the detailed description of the accident, and toned down the language of the punchline, which gets a special punch in grandma's version from repetition. The twentieth-century family is willing to preserve its ancestor's funny experience, but "The teacher's biting Sally's ass" is evidently too strong stuff for them to repeat anymore.[15]

A somewhat similar anecdote complete with another naughty word in the punchline was reported in the family folklore tradition of another student. He did a fine paper on a series of anecdotes concerning his great-grandfather, William Wood—an Englishman and the first Mormon in the Wood family.[16] Here is a portion of the student's paper concerning the story in question:

> A few months ago Grandma Wood, Uncle Jim, Aunt Imogene, were all over to my dad's home. After we finished off a delicious dinner, we all moved to the family room. Soon the topic turned to William Wood. Eighty-eight year old Grandma said she knew a story about him but didn't think it would be proper to tell. Uncle Jim jumped up and said, "Mother, that's a true story that took place in church; now, what could be wrong with that?" This is the story that Uncle Jim told:
>
> When William Wood got old, he started to lose his hearing so he got himself a horn which he carried around and put in his ear when he needed to hear something. In his butcher shop he had another contraption which he kept on his counter. It was a tube with an earpiece he put in his ear and a microphone type end for people to talk into. When customers would come into the shop, he would point this end at them,

> lean over the counter, and say, "What do you want? What do you want?"
>
> When William Wood went to church, he would move a chair right underneath the pulpit so he could direct the horn toward the speaker. He lost a milk cow one Sunday and so he asked the bishop to announce it in church and ask if anyone knew its whereabouts. Well, in those days you didn't have to buy a marriage license, but to get married legally, your marriage had to be announced three times publicly. That Sunday the bishop got up and announced the forthcoming marriage of a young couple, then he described the virtues of the bride to be. After he finished William stood up from his place in front of the pulpit and said, "If you're not sure which one she is, brothers and sisters, she's got a flop ear and a tit frizzed off."

The structure of this folk narrative performance is classic: the dinner-table conversation leads up to reminiscences about William Wood; general background material is given about his deafness; then the specific situation is described, and finally the funny punchline arrives. Let me indicate briefly the sources I pointed my student to so that he would understand this anecdote as a traditional story beyond his family's folklore. The central motif belongs to the folk-narrative category "The Wise and the Foolish" *(Motif-Index* section J), with the theme of foolishness being operative here. This foolishness is a factor of old age and especially of poor hearing. There is a general category "Deaf Persons and Their Foolish Answers" in the *Type-Index,* with subtype number 1698G fitting best: "Misunderstood Words Lead to Comic Results." Once we have made this identification, it is an easy matter to gather and compare versions of Type 1698G from the published literature. My student found several version from Arkansas (via annotations in a Vance Randolph collection) as well as an Old World prototype in *The Handbook of Irish Folklore.* (Here it is a priest thought to be announcing the loss of the deaf man's sow.) Moreover, the BYU folklore archive had a variant about an anonymous old-timer living in Canada near the place where William Wood once actually lived; evidently this was a spin-off from the traditions about him, minus his name.

Once again, when a story fits, it becomes assimilated. This one is no less a part of the Wood family lore for having a genealogy outside of their immediate circle of relatives. The student's parents, however, still insist that the incident really happened to William Wood, although neither of them was present when it occurred.

Even the most up-to-date-sounding contemporary stories may turn out to have deep roots, for folk narrative tradition is far from dead. Let me conclude with a story discussed in *The Vanishing Hitchhiker,* the book that I began quoting. This text comes not from some ancient yarnspinner but from a California woman writing to Ann Landers; her letter was in the *Salt Lake Tribune* column for July 31, 1982:

> Dear Ann:
> I tell this story to everyone I meet, but I hope that by telling you others will get the message.
> A lady friend of mine got into her car to do some errands. She was in a hurry but had to stop for gas.
> The young attendant asked her to step inside his office because something was wrong with her credit.
> Reluctantly, she got out and followed him. Once inside he asked her if she was aware that a man was crouched down in the back seat of her car. My friend nearly fainted.
> Moral: Check your back seat before you get into your car. These days it is easy for an experienced rapist or mugger to open a locked car and hide in the back seat.[17]

Certainly a worthwhile lesson is drawn from that dramatic story. But it simply could not have happened recently to the writer's friend, having been told in numerous varying versions—always as a true experience—since the mid-1960s and probably earlier.[17] The story has also enjoyed semi-literary circulation in a book titled *Night Chase* written for fifth- to eighth-graders as a form of Christian, moral, and safety instruction.[18] Along the same line, I have a clipping from the Flagstaff, Arizona, *Sun* (July 17, 1980) describing how a Phoenix police officer tells the assailant-in-the-back-seat story as "a true incident of several years ago" in his crime-prevention lectures. So the telling of folk narratives goes on, and they continue to fill various needs in our current lives.

I want to sum up the few and basic lessons about folk narratives research that I have been trying to teach in this brief folklore essay.

Collect the verbatim texts in their multiple existence, and describe the contexts of folk narrative performance.

Note the degree and nature of variation among the texts.

Generalize the themes and motifs found in the variants; then look for parallels to the motifs and tales in the standard folklore indexes and in published collections of folk texts.

Develop—through comparative analysis—an awareness of how folk narratives evolve and what they mean.

Notice how elements of performance style and verbal style contribute to the stories' meanings.

Keep in mind that however true a tale may seem—even to the extent of preserving some verifiable historical facts—the process of folk transmission will inevitably introduce some non-authentic material.

Finally, remember that the *true* part, even in the tallest of tales, often consists of what the stories tell us about the people and the folk culture from which the narratives come.

Notes

1. Jan Harold Brunvand, *The Vanishing Hitchhiker: American Urban Legends and their Meanings* (New York: W. W. Norton & Co., 1981), p. 1.

2. Austin & Alta Fife, *Saints of Sage and Saddle* (Bloomington: Indiana University Press, 1956), p. 80. A paperbound edition was published by the University of Utah Press in 1980 with the same pagination.

3. The 1967 version is given in Jan Harold Brunvand, *A Guide for Collectors of Folklore in Utah* (Salt Lake City: University of Utah Press, 1971), p. 59.

4. Stith Thompson, *Motif-Index of Folk Literature* (1932-1936) (revised edition; Bloomington: Indiana University Press and Copenhagen: Rosenkilde and Bagger, 1955-1958).

5. Ernest W. Baughman, *Type and Motif Index of the Folktales of England and North America,* Indiana University Folklore Series No. 20 (The Hague: Mouton and Company, 1966).

6. See Antti Aarne and Stith Thompson, *The Types of the Folk Tale: A Classification and Bibliography,* Folklore Fellows Communications No. 184 (Helsinki, 1961), a translation and enlargement of Aarne's *Verzeichnis der Marchentypen,* Folklore Fellows Communications No. 3 (Helsinki, 1910).

7. See Butler H. Waugh, "The Child and the Snake in North America (Aa-Th 285)," *Norveg: Folkelivsgransking,* (1960), 7:153-182, drawn from Waugh's Indiana University dissertation.

8. See Jan Harold Brunvand, "Len Henry: North Idaho Munchausen," *Northwest Folklore* (1965): 1:11-19.

9. Vance Randolph, *We Always Lie to Strangers* (New York: Columbia University Press, 1951); Roger Welsch, *Shingling the Fog and Other Plains Lies* (Chicago: Swallow Press, 1972).

10. Mentioned as a traditional anecdote in my *The Study of American Folklore: An Introduction,* 2nd edition (New York: W. W. Norton & Co., 1978), p. 137.

11. My student Julie Newton reported this story, as her husband told it, in 1973; the published source is the Rawlins, Wyoming, *Daily Times,* "Perverley's Patter" column, undated clipping sent to me.

12. Jan Harold Brunvand, *Norwegian Settlers in Alberta,* Paper No. 8 (Ottawa: Canadian Centre for Folk Cultural Studies, 1974), pp. 36-37.

13. Vanna Hunter, "Three Southern Utah Storytellers," in Jan Harold Brunvand, *Folklore: A Study and Research Guide* (New York: St. Martin's Press, 1976), pp. 123-124; the story appears on pp. 9-10 of Vanna Hunter's 1975 term paper as reproduced in this book.

14. Vance Randolph, *Hot Springs and Hell and Other Folk Jests and Anecdotes from the Ozarks* (Hatboro, Pennsylvania: Folklore Associates, 1965), p. 41; and Mac E. Barrick, "Folktales from the Institute at Duke," *North Carolina Folklore Journal* (1975), 23:75-81.

15. Here I confess a horrendous scholarly lapse: I have lost the reference! The

student gave me these two versions of the story around 1978, but I can find only photoduplicated copies of them in my files lacking further documentation. Someday, I hope, I will find the original or the documentation.

16. See Gordon S. Wood, Jr.'s excellent essay "Did Great Grandpa Wood Really Talk about Tits in Church?" *Southwest Folklore* (1979), 3:29-35.

17. See "The Killer in the Backseat" in my *Vanishing Hitchhiker*, pp. 52-53, notes, p. 70.

18. Cheryl Herbert, *Night Chase* (Nashville: Southern Publishing Co., 1977), pp. 7-13; I am indebted to Barre Toelken for calling my attention to this book.

Testing for Reliability in Oral History

William L. Lang and Laurie Mercier

How reliable is oral history? This question is valid and important. Oral history is very reliable; in some ways it is the most reliable form of historical documentation. The strength of oral history, and the foundation of its reliability, is the source—the expression of honestly held opinions and remembered impressions of personal experiences. Whether the person's memories are filled with the wildest stories and tall tales or detailed descriptions of the smallest events, their expression is reliable. This perspective is the unique contribution of oral history: the unqualified individual viewpoint on the past.

But the question of reliability in oral history can mean something other than the accurate expression of a viewpoint; and it is this second kind of reliability that is to be examined here. The measure of reliability that draws the most scrutiny is that which is applied to the hard information recorded in interviews—the dates, statistics, explanations, events, and the like. Testing the reliability of these types of data in oral history is an important component in local history research. But how can we evaluate what we have on tape?[1]

One place to begin is to recognize that good, reliable oral history is undertaken with some purpose, whether it is biographical in scope or is part of a more complex research project. Oral historians must have their purpose well understood before they venture out with recorder in hand, and they should choose narrators with that purpose in mind. They should be aware of the kind of information that needs to be gathered, which individuals are most knowledgeable, which ones have been interviewed before, and biographical details of potential narrators.

In the choice of narrators, of course, the historian makes the first decision that directly affects the reliability of information that will be recorded. Oral historians working in local history must be sensitive to what roles individual narrators have played in their communities. Bankers, farmers, librarians, mechanics, and merchants all live in the same community, but their private and public lives have been much different, both in their own perceptions of themselves and in the perceptions that others in the community have of them. Each narrator, because of these differences in background and perceptions, requires an individually tailored approach if the highest quotient of reliability is desired. In short, the merchant who had wielded economic power in a small town for years cannot be interviewed in the same manner as the department-store clerk who felt powerless in town affairs. They have very different stories to tell, very different information to impart, and probably very different views of their community.

Reliability of information in interviews can depend greatly on the interview relationship itself—that relationship which develops between interviewer and narrator. Mutual trust, respect for individual opinion, honesty, and a high sense of propriety on the part of the interviewer usually produce the best interview and elicit the most reliable answers from the narrator. Beyond their demeanor, interviewers can have profound influence on reliability during the course of the interview itself. Interviewers must be aware of a number of potentially disruptive situations, misleading questioning techniques, and tip-offs in narrators' responses during interviews if they expect to gather the most reliable information. As the interview proceeds, interviewers must test for reliability.

There are obvious tests of credibility. Does the information agree with the written historical record? Does the narrator use dates accurately? Are the descriptions consistent and free of contradictions and inconsistencies? Foremost in the interviewer's mind and in the mind of the researcher using oral materials is the general reliability of the narrator. Basic questions to ask of the narrator are whether the narrator has information that is confidential and whether the narrator was in a particularly good postion to know unique information. Is the narrator describing a personal experience, or is the description a second-hand one? In short, the interviewer should try to ascertain from the narrator's background, occupation, and other factors how generally reliable he or she is.

There are no firm rules in this process. The rapport and sense of openness and honesty between interviewer and narrator may be the best general guide, but interviewers can easily be misled when a narrator reels off a series of statements that the interviewer knows to be either very accurate or wholly wrong. Narrators, no matter how knowledgeable, will not accurately recount each event they discuss. The schoolteacher, for example, who can vividly remember the personalities of students she taught over many years may not be a good source for the details of the construction of community buildings even though she offers information on the subject. The accuracy of a narrator's statements on subjects with which he or she is familiar is a test of general reliability, but it is not an absolute determinant.

In the pursuit of reliable narrators on local history, oral historians invariably are advised to interview certain individuals on specific topics. When asked about the fire of 1924, someone might say, "Oh, you better talk to George Peabody, he knows all about that fire; everyone else is gone who knew about it." The pitfall here is the expectation of the interviewer. If George's memory of the fire is incomplete or inaccurate, the tendency might be to discount most or all of the narrator's information. He was supposed to be an authority on one subject; failing in that, his memory becomes suspect. Conversely, the interviewer might miss an opportunity to ask another narrator about the fire because *only* George Peabody supposedly knew about it. It is important to avoid prejudicing interviews by carrying hard expectations into them.

If the interviewer has confidence in the overall accuracy of the narrator's responses, how confident should the interviewer be when the narrator offers seemingly unique information? The following excerpt from an interview with a Montana smelter worker who achieved a high position in his labor union is an example of a narrator who had given solid information on the tasks of his trade and then discussed highly important labor negotiations.

> *Int:* The Smelter workers had to do the negotiating?
> *Nar:* They did the negotiation . . . eventually, we did get joint negotiation so that we all negotiated together. In fact, we got a coalition bargaining where not only the workers in Montana but the workers in Utah and Arizona and back east and all . . . . Matter of fact, in 1959, I went back to Ansonia [Connecticut] to help those guys and when I sat down the personnel manager whispered to the manager and the manager looked down and he said, "Where're you from?" I said, "I'm from Montana" and he said, "Well, there are going to be no negotiations as long as you're here or I ain't got a job." He got the word.
> *Int:* What did he mean by that?
> *Nar:* Well, they knew I was going back there so they . . . seemed to feel that there was no communication between Montana and Connecticut I guess. So, we adjourned the meeting and I told them, I said, "I didn't come back to put you guys out on the street." I said, "Anytime you guys are negotiating and feel that there's something you'd like to discuss with me, why I'll be down at the union hall and you just adjourn and come down there." So they'd go up and negotiate and they'd say, "Oh, we've got to go talk it over with Dickson," and they'd come down and play cards for a couple of hours. And, the manager called up and said, "What's going on down there?" "Well, Dickson's thinking about it. Go ahead and deal."[2]

Is that how those labor-management negotiations truly developed in 1959? The narrator's information is unverifiable by any standard checks with other sources. Only interviews with other participants could determine the accuracy of this account, but the position the narrator held in the episode combined with the accuracy of his other statements gives credence to this information.

The reliability of a narrator's answers is often closely tied to the subject or principal purpose of the interview. If the point of an interview, for example, is to gather information on a particularly controversial event, the narrator might very well alter his or her answers to conform to popular opinion, to contradict popular opinion, or to protect himself. Even when controversy is not the subject of interviews, disturbing or sensitive subjects can suddenly arise during the course of an interview and take the interviewer by surprise. Thorough pre-interview preparation, of course, can prevent some of these "surprises," but evaluating the reliability of the information given under these circumstances remains a problem. It is more important when evaluating such material to ascertain the narrator's relationship to the subject under discussion. Was the narrator a victim of events? Was the activity discussed a very significant part of the narrator's life? Did the event have a personal effect on the narrator? These and similar questions should be asked.

Interviewing the principal actors in an historical event is the dream of most oral historians, but there is often irony in such a fortunate situation. Usually individuals who played central roles in key events are the ones who can provide the best and most accurate information, but the narrator's close relationship to important events might be cause in itself to question the reliability of answers. When a locally prominent western Montana citizen who had been instrumental in creating the new state constitution was asked about that historic process, his answers were assertive and informed, but they were also worthy of close scrutiny.

> *Int:* What is your remembrance of the politics leading up to the constitutional convention, the con-con?
> *Nar:* Well, if what happened in the constitution had been known, and I don't mean that document. You'd better put that another way. If the legislature had known what the court's decision would be, as to who could run for the constitutional convention—you can put this in but nobody's going to like it—You had a bunch of losers that wrote the constitution. You did not have any winners.
> *Int:* Because all of the winners were in the legislature and they could not run for the con-con delegate positions?
> *Nar:* The winners were in the legislature. They were all seconds. And all of them that re-ran [after con-con] got beat. If the legislators had known

that they could not run for that job [con-con] we would have never had a new constitution.
Int: And, of course, that decision came down practically at the eleventh hour.
Nar: It came down too late to change. See, the original constitutional study—I was on that. We worked on that constitution. It wouldn't have been near as sweeping and maybe this is good or bad. I don't know. But anyway, I think the average legislator had the dream of running for that and reforming it, in the manner they thought it should be, but it wouldn't have been near as sweeping as it is.
Int: Would it have been a more conservative document?
Nar: Probably. More clarification, qualifications and things of that kind but no great change of intent. I mean like some of the stuff they put in there . . . would never have gotten in there. And then legislators maneuvered themselves into a place where they ended up supporting it.
Int: How did that happen?
Nar: I suppose friendships and little things like that generate into a guy's life.
Int: Was there opposition to it that never surfaced?
Nar: A lot of opposition that never surfaced. Of course, a lot of people didn't think it had a chance [of passage by voters]. See, there's things in that constitution that I think are asinine.[3]

The narrator in this interview had an important role in the constitution-making process, yet his information suggested that the process had gone awry. The interviewer had to know that the narrator came from an area that was less than enthusiastic about the new document and that the narrator had represented that area in the state legislature for many years. When these factors are taken into account, evaluation of the accuracy of the information can be made with much more confidence.

When oral historians interview on topics that have great significance or notoriety, the narrator's reliability can be tested. This is especially the case when local opinion has already answered the main questions about the topic. Everyone knows what happened during the flood of 1948, for example, so the interviewer is prepared to hear the familiar story from the narrator, even if the narrator was an eyewitness to crucial events. The expectations of the interviewer can act as a block when the narrator offers information that seems to contradict current opinion. Interviewers must listen carefully to avoid this problem. An example of this comes from an interview with a native of Italy in Missoula, Montana, who had been an inmate of a detention camp in Missoula during World War II. Local citizens with some knowledge of the camp knew that Japanese and Italians had been incarcerated there and believed that the Japanese were inferiors of the Italians in that tense wartime climate. But the interview contradicted that viewpoint and posed a problem for the interviewer.

> *Int:* You mentioned that there was a barrier in the compound between your group and the Japanese. When did the Japanese come to Fort Missoula?
> *Nar:* The Japanese came right after Pearl Harbor, yeah, 1942 they came over here during the winter and it was very tough on the old people. To me I think they were all good people, they didn't have anything to do with the war, they were here in the United States from old time.
> *Int:* After a while did the Immigration Service take down the barrier?
> *Nar:* No, we were the ones who asked them to take it down because we were in the same camp. It was not long before we wanted to learn about Japanese culture. And they were nice people. . . . We had our own cooks and so did the Japanese, see, and sometimes we used to go over there and eat with Japanese and then they would come over here and eat Italian.
> *Int:* How did the Italian cooks get traditional foods for their meals in Fort Missoula?
> *Nar:* We used to get pasta and oil and all from Italian grocery in Missoula, but I don't remember how the Japanese got their food. But like I said, we were interested in sharing between the two groups. They used to come over and see our plays and we used to go over to their barracks to see their play. Like I say, we went over there a lot, because there was no news from home, the war was bad, the whole world seemed upside down and it was good to share.[4]

The narrator was determined in this sequence of questions to document the relatively friendly nature of the relations between the incarcerated Japanese and Italians at Fort Missoula, while the interviewer almost left the subject. The information contradicted a general view; yet given the informant's first-hand experience and his insistence on the point, there is every reason to accept his answers as reliable.

Reference to famous events of celebrated historical characters in local history can pose similar problems in evaluating oral history. People like to emphasize real or imagined associations with prominent individuals and events. The "I knew Elvis" syndrome can be found in most communities, and it is usually recognizable when encountered. But its appearance during an interview can affect the course and integrity of the oral history. Narrators may exaggerate their relationships with local celebrities or claim they witnessed specific well-known events, when their knowledge actually comes from secondhand sources. If the interviewer's questions produce such exaggerated responses, the reliability of the narrator's answers becomes even more suspect. In Montana, for example, many informants will claim that they knew the famous cowboy artist Charlie Russell, and they might well make such claim even if they were quite young when Russell died in 1926. One Utica rancher proudly discussed his acquaintance with Russell:

> *Nar:* I met him when he came to the ranch. The first time he came through he was going to stay with Jake Hoover, well I'm not sure he stayed with him . . . but he came from Helena here [Utica] and the first night he stayed with my dad. . . . Russell was just sixteen years old then. He had some colored crayons and watercolors . . . he painted to entertain us kids. My mother later burned them all up, it was just trash, she didn't want that "trash" and he was nothing but a bum of a cowboy anyway at that point . . . .
> *Int:* Then he was a frequent visitor at the ranch?
> *Nar:* Oh yes. He would come to visit Dad all the time.[5]

The narrator gave reliable information and he had met Russell, but there are perils in this line of questioning. The interviewer encourages the narrator to boast and exaggerate by asking him if Russell was a frequent visitor. Emphasizing relationships and contacts with well-known figures is natural enough for both interviewer and narrator, but interviewers must be aware how easily memories of these famous people can be altered by information about them from other sources.

The romantic, exotic, and anecdotal episodes in people's lives often generate the most exaggeration, even to the point of falsification. Stories or tales in this context are important because they can tell historians a great deal about the nature of the times or the range of popular opinion in a locality; but if the narrator introduces opinion that seems to be based on hard information, the oral historian must be careful. Asking narrators for "the most unusual event" in their lives or "the most frightening time" places the informant in an awkward position, and the results can detract from the reliability of the interview. In interviews with two ranchers who resided in eastern Montana just prior to World War I, the subject of outlaws—the Kid Curry or Hole-in-the-Wall gang—came up.

> *Nar:* In northern Garfield County you had an awful lot of people, when I was a kid, on the dodge out of Texas—this was in the [Missouri River] Breaks up there, and they were there. And to this day I never ask a man his name. I was trained as a kid to ask no questions. I've seen 'em come in and. . . . It was an unwritten rule there was never a lock on a door. . . . I'm telling you, and a woman was as safe as if she was in a guarded compound . . . . A lot of those old boys [outlaws] would not sit down in a house but what they looked at the door . . . .This was tough country.
> *Int:* Do you remember meeting any of these men?
> *Nar:* I met some and . . . . Well, I thought they were marvelous. They were just as square as I'm telling you . . . . A lot of these, you must remember, gets pushed and then they get, oh, they get mad.[6]

The image of the famous "Hole-in-the-Wall Gang" is, if this narrator is reliable, that the outlaws in the Missouri River Breaks country in 1916 were just like good neighbors. When the subject surfaced in an interview with a second rancher, this time a man who had homesteaded in the same country, the information was quite different.

> *Nar:* . . . of course, people were more self-reliant in those days [1916]. The Little Rockies is peculiar, in one respect, it was, I believe, probably the last holdout of all the worst outlaws in the whole damn United States.
> *Int:* It was still pretty wild when you were up there?
> *Nar:* Oh, yes. Now, I homesteaded five miles from Kid Curry's ranch. Thank God, he'd been gone ten or twelve years or he might have had my hide on the same press, too. But everybody in the country knew he was an outlaw. The Hole in the Wall gang used to come up there after robbing a bank or holding up a train.[7]

The first narrator was ten years old in 1916, the second was nearly twenty-two when he took out his homestead. The first claimed he "met" outlaws and thought they were gentlemen, while the second came a decade after the desperadoes had left and expressed fear at what might have happened to him had the gang been next door. The outlaws in question had already left the region about 1905, one year before the first narrator was born. It is very likely that his memories are remembered stories of their corner of Montana with some romantic overtones, but it is likely that the second is much more reliable.

That romantic backward look, which is prevalent in many local history interviews, is often the creator of other problems in evaluating oral history. Long-term memory, as several researchers have demonstrated, has terrific power. In older people it is often the long-term memory that is sharpest, and it is this truth that contradicts criticisms of oral history that human memory is not to be trusted for accuracy. But as sharp as long-term memory can be, the passage of time can alter perspective and distort a narrator's viewpoint. Of importance here is what the narrator has experienced since the described decades-old events took place, for what happened in the intervening years can affect how memories are presented.

An example of how an individual's role in events and subsequent history can change perspective occurred in an interview with a retired banker whose bank weathered one serious depression in the early 1920s and then went out of business in the following decade. The poor reputation suffered by bankers in the 1930s and his own career had a direct effect on how he remembered those tough years when asked about rural banking practices.

> *Int:* What causes banks to continue to loan out during trying times?
> *Nar:* There is an axiom in the banking business that people go in debt during good times and have to pay it off in bad times.
> *Int:* When individuals came into the bank how much encouragement did the bank give to these people to take out loans?
> *Nar:* To begin with the oldtime merchants trusted everybody . . . the only time they didn't collect their money was when the man was killed. . . . I remember an oldtime merchant in Sac [Montana] I used to visit with quite a lot and he was telling me about staking different cowboys when they went out on the job and he said, "You didn't need to worry; you'd fix 'em up with a saddle and bed roll and gear they had to have to go out to work," and he said, "if they lived they'd always get back to pay you. . . . These oldtime merchants were used to dealing with those people but when the flood of homesteaders came into the country they kind of felt that they were dealing with the same kind of people—and they all needed credit of one kind or another—but unfortunately about 9 in 10 of the homesteaders didn't make a go of it—maybe not that high a percentage but at least 50 per cent . . . . They simply owed too much money . . . [and] of course many early banks extended credit to these same homesteaders. The homesteaders weren't necessarily dishonest—they were just buckin' the proposition where the odds were completely against them.[8]

The narrator went on to explain how the other bank in town went bankrupt and his bank remained solvent. Looking back on his experience, he did not blame the homesteaders; but the historian who accepts this narrator's estimate of homestead farming failures or cowboy successes could be quite in error.

Changing political opinion over the years can do much the same thing. One narrator, when asked to describe the work of the infamous IWW labor organization in Northwest lumber camps before World War I, tried to dissociate himself from a radical organization that seemed similar to contemporary social troublemakers—without denying his membership in the union.

> Int: Were you working in the woods during the strike of 1917?
> *Nar:* Oh yes, I was working for W. B. Russell in Plains [Montana]. I was driving skid-team there, and I picketed there in Plains. We had a restaurant there of our own. . . .
> *Int:* What kind of restaurant?
> *Nar:* The union did—the IWW, International [sic] Workers of the World. Some of them was in the Dakotas, too, and they used to stick dynamite in grain and blow the threshing machine all to hell. But they didn't do that there. . . . People thought they ought to have better conditions, a place to take a bath, and of course the companies didn't want to, didn't want to furnish any bedding. . . . That's why they struck. . . . Then they started talking about the war [World War I], they didn't want the United

> States in that and all that crap. . . . There was rabble-rousers in that [IWW] but not in Plains. . . . You couldn't get drunk and go there and eat, at the IWW eatin' house. . . .
> *Int:* Why did you join the IWW?
> *Nar:* It was the custom of the country, I guess. You knew what they was fighting for, eight hours and beds and blankets, and that's what we should've had. . . . There was a radical bunch that got into it . . . putting dynamite in grain . . . but what did that have to do with the lumber business? It was just a crazy bunch of radicals . . . . The same thing is happening now with the dope in California and Florida . . . . They're killing and cutting throats. It's the same damn thing only in different form. . . . Look at that Jane Fonda, there's an example of your IWW. It's the same principle, she went over there [Hanoi]. Tokyo Rose, she was broadcasting to those Americans to lay down, well, that's no different than what the Wobblies were doing here against the [Germans] . . . it's the same form.[9]

The narrator's focus on the evils of radicalism overwhelms his responses. It distorts his answers and leaves the interviewer with little foundation for further questions.

One episode of such loss of perspective on the part of the narrator does not damage an entire interview, but an interviewer must be aware of these developments as an interview progresses. Often there is a shift in mood and emphasis in the narrator's answers when questions stimulate one of these tug-of-wars between long-term memory and subsequent feelings about a specific event. A political figure who was asked to recall sensitive developments over four decades old, for example, suddenly changed his descriptive tone. In response to questions about Federal Emergency Relief Administration field agents during the New Deal in Montana, the narrator took issue with the interviewer.

> *Int:* There's long files in there [Archives] of correspondence, most through field agents writing back to Washington from Montana.
> *Nar:* You know something, most of those field agents I wouldn't believe under oath.
> *Int:* Why do you say that?
> *Nar:* Well, damn them, they're hell; I could tell you stories about some of those buggers that would break your heart. . . . But I remember one fellow, I can't give you his name, and I took him at his word, but damn it, I was used to believing people, you know, living out there in the hills, but God, if you couldn't believe them you didn't want anything to do with them. He tells me this and so, we had to do this and do that one thing and another. He had me primed making these speeches and getting these bills through the Senate. By God, one day, he's sitting in the back of the back row [Montana Senate] and I'm in the second row ahead of

> him, the damn fool gets up and he absolutely lies about something I had said he said, so right then and there we fell. . . .[10]

Later in the interview the narrator goes into great detail about two phone conversations between field agents and New Deal administrators in Washington. How reliable is the information? How much should the interviewer accept, knowing that the narrator has strong feelings about the subject?

One other example from the same era, this time dealing with the New Deal's WPA work program in the 1930s, points up the need some narrators may have to explain their actions in a specific event or development. When asked about their experiences in the WPA, two narrators gave quite different accounts.

> *Nar:* I started out there [working for the WPA] one fall. I got $12 a day for me and four horses building these dams they built around the country. I worked there eight days and I was so disgusted with the way it was worked that I quit and left, no more of this. I took my outfit and went home. . . . I didn't go down there to stand around, I went down to work. . . . The people that ran it didn't care, they didn't have no push. The government was paying for it, it wasn't costing them anything, they didn't care and just let it go at that. Nobody worked. Nobody wanted to work.[11]

***

> *Nar:* A lot of people criticized us for working on WPA for us people that were poor, but yet the storekeeper and everybody else was dependent on that money too just as much as if they were on WPA. That's what always griped me—everyone else was just as glad to get that money as we was, we were just putting money in circulation. . . . The business people needed that money just as we did. . . . We worked for every doggone dollar we got out of that. I'd get up in the morning and take care of the horses and get the kids off to school and god, we'd be gone and at the job before daylight and get home after dark. . . . It wasn't no picnic working on that.[12]

Both narrators, of course, could be recounting accurate history. Undoubtedly there were "shovel-leaners" as well as industrious workers on WPA projects. What the interviewer must ask in these instances is whether the narrator's political views and experiences since the WPA days prejudiced their answers. The interviewer should be aware of these influences and pursue a line of questioning that avoids or blunts the narrator's prejudices while still probing for the details.

Another common problem in oral history that has an immediate effect on the question of reliability in interviews is familiar to everyone who has ever tape-recorded someone's memories: the recall of dates. Interviewers and narrators alike tend to assume accurate recall of dates, but most people do not have the ability to remember their lives in terms of calendar years or specific months. More often, people look upon their lives with little or no sense of chronology and associate time—even the passage of time—with memorable events. "When did you buy your first tractor?" an interviewer asks a farmer. The narrator struggles for a few minutes and replies, "I can't really remember when that was." "Would it have been before the depression of the '30's?" the interviewer asks. "Oh, I'm sure," the narrator replies, "that would have been in the '20's, because we had to go back to using horses during that depression." The interviewer, knowing the history of the region and the fact that 1926-1928 was when many farmers and ranchers purchased tractors, asked questions that aided the narrator in placing the time of his first tractor use, yet it is clear that the narrator was unable to specify a date.

When narrators are able to specify dates, even to the time of day, that are connected with memorable events, interviewers should be prepared to accept those dates as accurate. An interviewer who was asking for information about a rather notorious trial asked a narrator about when the trial took place. "Well, yeah, it was 1919. The reason I know, I had my girl and we were walking home and leading our horses [the crime took place after the dance they attended] and I proposed to her after the dance. I got married in 1919, April 29th."[13] Events associated with such singular moments in an individual's life are deeply etched in memory.

The inability to recall specific dates, however, is not a very solid measurement of reliability. People who held several jobs in the space of twenty-five years, for example, may have a devil of a time remembering the sequence of employment, to say nothing of dates. Focusing on the recall of dates can do more to damage an interview than the recording of a few dates could aid it. Interviewers and narrators will stumble, halt, and even threaten the process of interviews in the vain search for specific dates.

Sometimes chronology and dates can bewilder narrators. People can easily confuse one decade with another. Because most people remember the events in their lives in episodic fashion, the precise time the action took place—the actual year or month—does not loom as important as the event itself. A woman who had been discussing her son's involvement in World War II, for example, responded with the following answer when asked by the interviewer about the effect of rationing on her household:

Nar: We always had enough, plenty. I'll tell you what happened once. Lar [husband] went into town, they were giving away sugar—you could get so much, you know—so they brought the sugar home and I put it on

> [the stove] to make sugar syrup for the children, and what do you suppose? It was full of glass. The whole sack was full of glass. . . . I did use some of it. We melted it and strained it and used it, but imagine, it was full of glass. If you had put that on your breakfast food you'd have been eating glass. We never even turned it in. We just kept it and ate it.
> *Int:* Was that during the first World War or World War II?
> *Nar:* Yes, that was in the last war. It was terrible, wasn't it?[14]

It was not until the interviewer consulted with the narrator's son that it became clear she was referring to an incident during World War I. Her memory for the details was not faulty, and when asked later she clearly stated that it happened during the "first war." In fact, in subsequent questioning she went on to discuss the "flu epidemic" of 1918 with great clarity. Her information on the sugar incident was reliable; and even in her initial confusion, when she stated "that it was in the last war. It was terrible, wasn't it?" the narrator disclosed valid information about the impact on World War I on her.

Descriptions or labels used in association with specific dates can cause confusion in the minds of both interviewers and narrators and thus affect the interview's overall reliability. References to the "storm of 1958," for instance, might derail an interview if the narrator remembers only the large storm occurring in 1950 or earlier. The narrator can lose confidence in his or her answers or unnecessarily stumble trying to make date and event agree. In an interview with an eastern Montana homesteader who moved to California in 1919 and then back again to Montana in 1925, the interviewer asked how the family had fared in the years before the depression.

> *Int:* That year that you returned then, in 1925, and those years up until the depression, how did you manage?
> *Nar:* Well, you see, we were in California for five years. The depression was just about over when we came back here in '25. There wasn't much. Yes, of course, we didn't notice it out there in California at all. Jim had a good job and I had a little store and post office and we didn't know there was a recession at all. But, we soon found out when we got here and people had been leaving from about 1919, when we left. By 1920, most everybody was gone. Nobody left after we came here in 1925. All that was going to had gone.[15]

The "depression" referred to in the interviewer's question, of course, was the economic depression in the 1930s, while the narrator related the question to the severe agricultural depression of the early 1920s in Montana. The *real* depression for the narrator was the earlier one. If the interviewer had pressed the homesteader to discuss the depression in the 1930s, much valuable information might have been lost.

Forcing narrators to fit their responses into chronological patterns can limit the information they relate and distort what details they give. As narrators remember their lives, they may pursue a topic, leaping from decade to decade in no chronological sequence or discuss events in several different years to make a particular point or tell an important story. Interjecting questions about chronology might silence the narrator or prejudice his or her answers. It is often best to allow narrators a "stream-of-consciousness" freedom in interviews; rather than ask questions that attempt to establish chronology, the interviewer should pursue topics and events raised in the interview without any reference to time. After a story is told, the interviewer can ask questions to ascertain the sequence of events. But interviewers often lose patience before the narrator can tell a story or express opinions. The following exchange demonstrates the rewards of patience.

> *Nar:* I worked at the Glendive Steam Laundry for 25 cents an hour.
> *Int:* When did you do that?
> *Nar:* In 1935 when our house burned down. And I sewed. I upholstered 21 automobiles one winter. We had two very serious, very extensive gas explosions here in town. That was in the spring of 1937. They were sewer gas explosions . . . there was fire just like that. It seldom burns a building but there's nothing left in there that is any good. They had 21 or 22 automobiles stored down in Akins Garage, which is where the old Sawyer store used to be and Wagner's plumbing and that machine shop, on the corner across from the courthouse on the west. That was a big garage at the time, and they had them in there for winter storage. This happened along in January 1937. Our house had burned down in August 1936. Now, wait, we had gone to visit my folks in Missouri for Christmas in 1935. . . .[16]

The interviewer stayed with the narrator, let her ramble, and she was finally able to describe, in great detail, how she had aided her husband in upholstering autos in 1937. If the interviewer had pursued questioning the narrator about women's work, the information gathered might well have been lost. Patience in interviewing is a great virtue.

Remembering dates, speaking knowledgeably about subjects, being objective in remembering controversial events—when narrators can do these without difficulty, the question of reliability is easily answered. But usually the situation is quite different. Interviewers need to keep some of their attention on the areas that have been discussed, and they need to conduct their interviews at least partially with these problems in mind, but being overly self-conscious about them in an interview can be nearly paralyzing and self-defeating. In other words, interviewers must concentrate first on conducting good interviews and keep the pitfalls of unreliable narrators' answers as part of the numerous "do's and don'ts" of oral history—to be understood and applied but not to the point of distraction.

Researchers using oral history can ascertain the reliability of narrators, and interviews in general, by looking carefully at the factors discussed in this article. The biographical information on narrators, the place of the interviews, the context of questions and answers will all disclose how reliable the information is likely to be. There is no acid test of reliability in oral history, but we can say the same thing about information in letters and diaries. It is the historian as a skeptical believer in the process of collecting, sifting, and making sense out of historical materials who applies tests and sorts out the accurate from the inaccurate.

Notes

1. Although the question of reliability in recorded interviews has been dealt with in oral history manuals, none of them provide analysis of interview situations as are presented in this paper. For discussions of reliability in oral history and folklore see: Barbara Allen and William Lynwood Montell, *From Memory to History: Using Oral Sources in Local History Research* (Nashville, Tennessee: American Association for State and Local History, 1981), pp. 67-87; Richard M. Dorson, "The Oral Historian and the Folklorist," in *Selection from Fifth and Sixth National Colloquium in Oral History*, edited by Peter D. Olch and Forrest C. Pogue (New York: Oral History Association, 1972), pp. 40-49; Larry Danielson, "The Folklorist, the Oral Historian, and Local History," *Oral History Review* (1980), pp. 62-72.

2. Thomas Dickson, Anaconda, Montana, interviewed by Laurie Mercier, November 25, 1981. All interviews cited in this article are in Oral History Collections, Archives, Montana Historical Society, Helena.

3. Bill Groff, Victor, Montana, interviewed by William L. Lang, September 20, 1978.

4. Alfredo Cipolato, Victor, Montana, interviewed by Lang, January 9, 1981.

5. Bill Korell, Billings, Montana, interviewed by Mercier, July 20, 1982.

6. Charles Mahoney, Miles City, Montana, interviewed by Mercier, October 24, 1981.

7. E. E. MacGilvra, Butte, Montana, interviewed by Lang, August 4, 1978.

8. Charles Brocksmith, Glasgow, Montana, interviewed by Mercier, May 25, 1982.

9. Charles Kennedy, Dixon, Montana, interviewed by Mercier, April 23, 1982.

10. MacGilvra interview.

11. Ted Olsen, Lewistown, Montana, interviewed by Mercier, April 1, 1982.

12. Fred Blyth, Geraldine, Montana, interviewed by Mercier, March 16, 1982.

13. Roland Matthews, Lewistown, Montana, interviewed by Mercier, April 1, 1982.

14. Isabella Mogstad, Geraldine, Montana, interviewed by Mercier, March 13, 1982.

15. Mary Stephenson, Circle, Montana, interviewed by Mercier, October 29, 1981.

16. Edna Patterson interview, October 26, 1981.

Comment:
Truth and Deep Roots

Elaine J. Lawless

It seems a coincidence that the papers by Jan Brunvand and by Laurie Mercier and Bill Lang have nearly identical focuses: ascertaining the difference between "truth" and "folklore." Given that one of the speakers is an oral historian and the other a folklorist, I expected their speeches to be more polarized. But, I found them to be quite parallel in their thinking, and therein lies my concern: both seem inordinately concerned with Truth with a capital "T," and by pursuing that concern they may, I fear, run amuck. Permit me to play devil's advocate.

My concern about our attitudes in collecting oral history will not be the same as those who assume tape-recorded interviews may be "half-truths, outright falsehoods and tall tales." I worry when reliability is couched in these terms: "Does the information agree with the written historical record? Are the descriptions consistent and free of contradictions and inconsistencies?" Wherein lies our awe of the written record? Can we not gain enough perspective to admit that the record was written down by men and women, human beings just as susceptible to the very same prejudices, strong feelings, and influences as we oral narrators? And by already having a "true" model in mind, do we not set ourselves up to ignore what our narrator is telling us—about the era, about his or her attitudes and emotional make-up, about human nature in general?

It is my understanding that when history books are written, they are written with the goal in mind of recording the "facts"—and that the emergence of a new technique in gathering "history," that is, oral history, has been developed in large part to provide information left out by the historians: the "folk history," if you will, of the ordinary people who actually experienced events or lived in a particular town at a particular time. Yet here, throughout this presentation, I hear only the pursuit of facts and truth: a preoccupation with "reliability and accuracy." Only once do the oral historians admit to what I would consider the most valuable information the oral histories can provide: "gathering those opinions and retelling of what life was like years ago is what oral histories can offer historians that few other sources can; in part, *it is what oral history is all about*. But that is only one type of reliability . . ." and the authors proceed to discuss *only* the other kinds of reliability (the most important ones?) in their pursuit of Truth.

Both the oral historian and the folklorist seem to equate "truth" with carbon-copy "sameness" and folklore with inconsistency and variation. I am not at all comfortable with these equations. For example, it seems to me quite plausible that the two WPA workers could have had two completely different experiences. Yet, because of the well-known attitudes and stereotypes about the WPA, the oral historian automatically questions the memories, believing they have been prejudiced. If reliable information is the goal, then perhaps these two stories should be pursued futher, rather than categorized based on the collector's perceptions. Where were the two camps in question located? Who were the bosses at each? What was each town's attitude toward the WPA? It seems quite plausible that both accounts are accurate; if they both turned out to be so, then oral history would have, indeed, taken steps to dispel a prevalent stereotype.

More than anything, I am dismayed to find oral historians avoiding the human emotions that are bound to erupt when people talk about times and events that were significant for them. We are asked to "pursue a line of questioning that avoids or blunts the narrator's prejudices." Strong feelings are felt to taint the materials; we are warned that emotions may "get in the way" of accuracy. Are we expecting our oral narrators to be mechanical historians? Do we want them to be? Or could we instead listen carefully to what *becomes* emotional in our interviews and write a local history that focuses on the most poignant and important events in the lives of its people? Frankly, I would rather know which elections had emotional content than when they happened; I believe it may be very important to isolate which issues are likely to elicit strong feelings—education, religion, morals, moonshine? I find myself satisfied about how to collect oral history, but I find I have many unanswered questions about what oral historians can tell me or how I can best interpret the materials I might collect.

As trained folklorists, Brunvand and I both know how to collect stories, place them in their performance context, and search out analogues in folklore indices. Yet, for the local historian or amateur folklorist who may intentionally or inadvertently collect "folklore," I wonder if we can be more helpful in providing ways for them to interpret what they collect.

First of all, I know that the primary popular concept about folklore that folklorists must battle all the time is the equation of folklore with falsehood. If someone suggests rubbing a cut potato on a wart, someone else is likely to chuckle and comment, "Oh, that's just folklore." In my own classes, I must first try to erase this popular concept of folklore before I can successfully tackle such sensitive issues as, for instance, folk religion, where such a connotation automatically suggests that folk religion is false. I fear the layperson will come away from these presentations with the popular misconceptions about folklore firmly intact. Brunvand seems to be assuring us that if a story can be labeled as "folklore," then we automatically remove it from the realm of possibility. For example, the story of the child and the snake is included in the category of a "true tale;" how then can it also be folklore? Does "true tale" refer only to tales that are plausible or really happened? Did this story—and perhaps the "man in the back seat"—really happen once, with all subsequent retellings folklore? Or is the story "just a folktale?" Does placing it in its historical, folkloric context really help us understand why Mormons keep telling the story?

I do not believe it is quite clear, either, whether family anecdotes are to be labeled as "real" or as "folklore." They have been placed in the "tall tale" section of the paper and are described as "different in style and content" from the "true" tales that circulate in oral narrative tradition. Yet the grandmother teacher story is referred to as a "factual family anecdote" and appears to be believed (by the folklorist) as a "true" story having really happened to the teacher, who even wrote down her own version of the story. To me, a family story told and retold, passed down from family member to family member, cherished and remembered, is folklore—whether or not it contains folkloric motifs and "even" if it is true. Isn't it equally possible to assume that grandmother of the splinter was a delightful storyteller, both in oral performance and on paper?

On the other hand, the Grandfather William story is treated as a "tall tale"—why? Because there are folkloric analogues? Because it is a more "fantastic" story than the one about the grandmother? Why are we concerned that "the student's parents still insist that the incident really happened to William Wood, although neither of them was present when it occurred?" I am further concerned about the interpretation of the Grandfather William story. Why was it important for the student to understand the anecdote about William as "a traditional story beyond his family's folklore?" In a presentation such as this one do we rush too quickly to our folklore indices (which, quite frankly, intimidate most people) and point out national and international analogues? Might we more usefully tackle the issue of family folklore—that lore about family members that is told and perpetuated in family circles? Would it have been more beneficial for that lad to query why his family told that story about Williams? Why was it funny for them? In their religion was it a release to imagine those words spoken in the church? Could it be more usefully compared to the Mormon stories about J. Golden Kimball? How many members of Williams' family told this and other anecdotes about William? How do the other anecdotes compare with this one? Was this incident completely plausible given William's character? It seems to me the student might have gotten a lot closer to the importance of the telling of this story by staying home and asking questions than by tracing motifs and discovering that the story was only a "traditional story beyond his family's folklore." Such an approach, it seems to me, may negate the significance of the narrative in the lives of those who tell it and for the amateur collector who collects. Such comparative work, performed by trained folklorists, is, of course, important.

Perhaps Brunvand's most important statement, a bit hidden, is "folk narrative tradition is far from dead." But even this remark is firmly attached to the subsequent "even the most up-to-date-sounding contemporary stories may turn out to have deep roots." Is this what makes them folklore or points to what is important for us to notice, record, and analyze? Has Brunvand successfully distinguished for us the difference between "tall tales" and "true tales"?

Can, or should, the local historian and amateur folklorist who collect what we would classify as folklore do the kind of comparative work that has been described? I doubt if they could; I doubt if they would want to; and I personally hope they do not. Rather, I would want them to recognize the storytelling as traditional in style and content and important in its performed context, but concentrate their analysis on the folks who told it and the importance of the story (or personal experience) in their lives. They are better equipped than we to do that, and I think the results are more important.

In conclusion, I would suggest that, in our interpretation of the materials that we collect from real human beings, we listen more carefully to what people are actually saying and avoid trying so hard to pin down facts and truth and authenticity. We should try instead to determine what the collected materials say about the people from whom we collected them. After all, are we not all really in the pursuit of understanding ourselves?

Response:
On Truth

Jan Harold Brunvand

It is not really such a coincidence that both papers for this panel focused on the word "truth," since among the themes suggested to us by the conference planners some months in advance were "historical vs. cultural truth" and "the trustworthiness of oral tradition." Also enjoined to include "techniques of identifying traveling tales and motifs" in my talk, I naturally strove to please. I hope I did not "run amuck," though I may have gone astray somewhat.

Probably my excessively alliterative title—chosen more for sound than for strict sense—has slightly misled Lawless. It is not "Truth with a capital 'T' " I refer to, but "truth" in quotation marks to signify the kinds of stories that people *regard as true* but which comparative analysis often reveals to be traveling tales. One of my major points is that the "truth" in such folk stories may be more a cultural or a psychological kind than a historical or scientific kind. In any case, I certainly regard stories that are orally repeated and that become stylized in structure and performance as being genuine "folklore," whether or not they contain traditional motifs. And I don't just "seem to," but *do* associate oral folklore with variation.

Besides the assumption that by "truth" I meant only literal, historical Fact (with a capital "F"), there is another fundamental misunderstanding in the commentary. There are no "true tale" and "tall tale" *sections* of the paper; rather, there are several different legend genres illustrated, including anecdote, dialect story, family tradition, and urban legend. A lengthier and more subtle discussion of the kinds of analysis appropriate for each of these varied but related narrative forms would have taken far more pages and minutes to present, but the essentials of verbatim collecting, performance analysis, and comparative study would have been the same.

I stand by my suggestion that even amateur folklorists can and should make use of the standard bibligraphic tools of our field. My students (like Vanna Hunter and Gordon Wood, quoted in the paper) have done it successfully for years, which is not to say that they have not also stayed home sometimes and asked questions. Among Gordon Wood's conclusions in his published article, besides the Type and Motif numbers, are astute comments about how the story probably became connected to his ancestor, why his Mormon family still treasures the tale, and what the family tradition (branching off from an international story cycle) finds meaningful about this apocryphal tale.

Elaine Lawless raises some excellent points about oral narrative research and interpretation in her commentary, though she seems to score me at times for stands I have not taken or for lacking insights that I sometimes have. I urge readers' attention to the last two points in my summary, especially the ultimate sentence of the paper that concludes: "the true part, even the tallest of tales, often consists of what the stories tell us about the people and the folk culture from which the narratives come." Here, I am sure, Lawless and I are in perfect agreement.

Response: *Historians and Truth*

William L. Lang

Reconstructing and interpreting the past are the prime responsibilities of the historian. In pursuit of that business, the historian will err in interpretation and stumble over her or his own prejudices in the process. The result can hardly be called the "truth," but historians vainly hope that their version will be accepted as the best and most truthful account. What historians must be, above all, is honest about the data they uncover and honest in their use of those data. It is because of this responsibility that concern over reliability is so important to historians.

Reliability in historical sources is difficult to evaluate. Diaries, letters, and other documents all have built-in biases and contain errors of fact. Historians are wary of accepting anything found in these sources without careful scrutiny. Oral history must fall under the same critical glare. What is so different about oral history, however, is the unique opportunity for historians to be *involved* in the creation of an historical document. Now the historian has the advantage he or she did not have in deciphering the accuracy of a decades-old diary—the source can be questioned. But this great opportunity is not without potential hazard.

Because the interviewer is intimately involved in creating a historical resource, oral historians must proceed with care. It would be illegitimate, for example, to encourage a narrator to make up a false version of events in the pursuit of novelty, excitement, or other understandable reasons. Lawless, in her comments, misunderstands the caveats about "prejudices" and "emotions." The danger is distortion. How different are questions that ask "How has predator control affected your sheep operation?" from "What about the use of 1080 to kill helpless coyotes in sheep country?" Which question is likely to "create" the more reliable historical resource? If the narrator believes that all coyotes ought to be vaporized, let the narrator offer that fact freely without inducements.

Lawless asks whether narrators are expected to be "mechanical historians." The answer, of course, is no, because that is an impossibility. What Lawless desires—the emotional dimension—will be there regardless, for the genius of oral history is the involvement of two people in creating the resource; the beauty and joy of oral history are in that interaction between the interviewer and narrator. But again the question is before us: should the interviewer try to elicit the emotional? Is history served by that approach?

Folklorists and oral historians record what narrators believe to be the truth, whether it is a tale told them by their fathers or their memories of what their mothers did twenty years earlier. Folklorists collect what is current and repeated in the community at large. Oral historians collect reminiscences about yesterday. Accuracy in recording this information is important for both folklorists and oral historians. In the case of oral history, however, the recording creates something new—a new resource that other historians will use.

Oral History and the Images of Seneacquoteen:

A Crossing of the Disciplines

Sharon Boswell

The large wooden historical marker situated along Highway 2 near Laclede, Idaho, reads:

> SENEACQUOTEEN
>
> Long before white men discovered this river, Indians used to camp here at this important early crossing.
>
> White fur traders, surveyors, and miners followed the old Indian trail that forded the river here at Seneacquoteen – a Kalispell word meaning crossing. During the Kootenay gold rush of 1864, a wagon road came from Walla Walla to a ferry here. The Wild Horse Trail – a pack route – ran on north to the Kootenay mines in British Columbia.

As an inveterate reader of roadside signs, I can remember stopping to study this description of Seneacquoteen's history the first time I traveled in northern Idaho. I also have a distinct recollection of craning my neck as our car pulled out of the graveled turnout where the marker is located, trying to catch a glimpse of this important river crossing. Instead, I could only see a string of rather rusted railroad cars, sitting on the track behind the sign, and a development of nondescript tract homes – all of which blocked any possible view of the river or the ford.

Despite many subsequent trips past the marker after my husband and I actually moved to northern Idaho, I could never quite erase from my mind this initial image of Seneacquoteen. Although over the next few years I learned much more about the background of the site, and heard local residents discuss the significance of "the deep water crossing" or "delightful crossing of the water," as they called it, I continued to associate Seneacquoteen with what I had seen of the land immediately surrounding the sign. In fact, for a very long time, my recurring mental image was of all those Indians, miners, and surveyors winding their way past ranch homes and railroad cars to arrive at the crossing.

Only recently, when I was asked to help with a project examining the historical development of Seneacquoteen, did I gladly begin to alter these initial impressions of the site. The project I participated in was designed to provide a multidisciplinary look at Seneacquoteen, combining the techniques of oral history, archaeology, and standard archival research.[1] The basic premise of the study was that the land on the southern bank of the crossing had developed as a camping place, ferry station, trading post, and then possibly a town, and that this site could be used to illustrate the impact of geographic location on historical development. Archival researchers could discover some of the individuals who had utilized the site; oral historians could document its more recent history and help to pinpoint the location of previous buildings or unique features of the area; and archaeologists, utilizing all of this information, could make test excavations and interpret artifacts and other data to produce a fairly complete record of activity at Seneaquoteen and how it had changed through time.

The major focus of this research would be the one structure still standing on the site. Since it was the only tangible remains we had at the time, that particular building became Seneaquoteen to me and to other project participants. My visions of the Seneacquoteen of the railroad cars and the tract homes faded and was replaced by an image of a fairly dilapidated log-and-frame house that several farming families had occupied and that, according to local tradition, had originally been a trading post, possibly of Hudson's Bay Company origins.

As is sometimes the case, our preconceived notions of what we would uncover at Seneacquoteen did not always agree with the information our research produced. Among the findings were that a town of Seneacquoteen as we had envisioned it may never have existed, that the archaeological remains seemed to show that the existing structure was not as old as we had suspected, and that oral sources generally indicated that our site may not have been as important in the history of the crossing as another site approximately one-half mile farther downstream. Although our site did prove to be significant, it was not entirely for the reasons we had initially assumed.

Perhaps equally as important as these new directions were some of our methodological conclusions. Although our studies supported the value and effectiveness of a multidisciplinary approach, oral history seemed to emerge as the one technique that served as an essential link. Oral history, in essence, accomplished a "crossing of disciplines," not only by providing detailed site-specific information for archaeologists and informant corroboration of the written records for historians, but also by placing the building and the entire site in the broader context of the community and of the people who had used it. Just as I had adopted several different images of Seneacquoteen based on my own particular experiences, so oral interviewing revealed that the people of Seneacquoteen had their own ideas about the importance of the site. In particular, we found that a detailed examination of the architectural and historical significance of the building could not be separated from an understanding of its image in the minds of the community.

Using a few examples from our experiences at Seneacquoteen, I will examine further the role that oral history can play in interpreting sites and specific buildings, especially when used in conjunction with other disciplines. In particular, I will concentrate on oral history's effectiveness in relation to folk or vernacular architecture—structures such as log cabins, barns, or other similar buildings erected by ordinary people to suit their daily needs. In addition, I will address the question of how this technique might be used by local historical groups and individuals who are seeking a broader understanding of their own community and its past.

In our Seneacquoteen project, oral history served two important functions. One was to provide detailed information on buildings, their architecture and specific location, in order to guide archaeologists in their test excavations and to help them interpret what they found. The second function was to fill in the gaps in the historical record, particularly in the modern period where few, if any, written accounts existed, and to clarify, if not corroborate, documentary evidence with personal remembrances.

The oral history portion of the project began with a compilation of the names of potential informants, supplemented by some informal interviewing of these individuals to discover how much they knew about Seneacquoteen. One of the first to be interviewed was Grace Roffey Pratt, who had published two articles on Seneacquoteen.[2] Much of her writing was based on interviews conducted with Hilda Christianson Crockett, whose family had run a store and post office in our Seneacquoteen building in the late 1890s. Conversations with Mrs. Pratt and other local residents produced the names of a few Christianson descendents and relatives who proved to be good informants.

A title search of the property and additional community suggestions also yielded the names of several individuals whose parents had owned or leased the Seneacquoteen site and who could give more recent perspectives on the nature of life there. In addition, since the community encompassing Seneacquoteen was very close-knit and its population relatively stable, there was an unusually large number of neighboring families whose members had spent time working, playing, or visiting at the Seneacquoteen site through several successive generations and were available for interviews.

Approximately half of the interviews were conducted after the basic archival research had commenced but before any archaeological work was undertaken. Questions covered the whole gamut of personal experience and memories of the site, with informants providing information on its role as a store and post office in the late 1890s, its use as a farm by new owners or tenants who often had difficulty making it pay, and its eventual purchase by a family who first tried to make it a dairy and later kept it mainly as a summer retreat. An effort was also made to gather very specific details about the construction of the remaining building, any remodeling that had taken place, or changes made in its layout. In addition, the location of barns, sheds, and other outbuildings, the types of equipment, utensils, and other items used in everyday life, and any pertinent information on other physical aspects of the site were sought.

Interviewees were encouraged to describe specific aspects of the building in as much detail as possible and to draw diagrams or sketches when they might be useful. Photographs taken at various periods of time were also important aids in identifying and describing the site. An added benefit of the oral interviewing process was that it helped to turn up the majority of photographs we were able to locate. Informants would quite often pull out old albums or boxes of family pictures relating to Seneacquoteen that they had, prior to the interviews, considered to be inconsequential or of purely personal interest.

This type of interviewing produced some very vivid, detailed descriptions of the Seneacquoteen building and helped to identify specific areas that might be productive sites for excavation. Archaeologists on the project, for example, wanted to find the location of outhouses and dump sites, which often contain important items of material culture. An interview with Gordon Mead, who lived at Seneacquoteen when his parents purchased the property in the 1920s, provided not only a sketch of the area but also the following description of outhouse locations:

> You wanted to know where the old outhouses were. Well, if you'll walk around this shed part, you might see first a little old dip here—a little recession. Maybe you'll see another recession, and then you'll see another recession. As far as I know, the outhouses were in these three positions. And then the last time, outhouse was way on over . . . across that gully and a walk went across . . . that was where dad put it—it was about 50 feet from the house.
>
> There was only one when we first came (next to the lean-to) and then when dad put up one, he hauled that first one off and burned it up. . . . They moved it three times. I remember that dad covered the ground here and then he put boards down and said there was old outhouses set there. And he told us kids to keep off the ground and not to dig. . . . I'd say it was close to the edge of the lean-to—within five feet—I guess five feet or six feet.[3]

When this information was corroborated by other informants, archaeologists used the descriptions to place several auger holes that pinpointed the outhouse locations on the ground. Test pits were then dug in these spots and yielded, among other artifacts, an almost complete earthenware crock as well as a variety of other household items, silverware, bricks, metal pieces, and even an old toy gun, all of which could be used to interpret everyday domestic life at the site.

No other actual dump sites were located, and oral history also seemed to explain the lack of archaeological evidence.

> We used to throw a lot of stuff down there in the river. We used to take old hay wire—not baling wire, but barbed wire, and we used to row out in the river and drop it in the water to get rid of it. Then if you had a gunny sack, dad always made us put tin cans, whatever tin cans we did have, we put in gunny sacks, and then he'd take them and weight them, and row out into the river and sink them. We wouldn't throw over the bank like a lot of people did.[4]

The river, as corroborated by several informants, was the major dumping spot for most people who lived above its banks, and thus very few refuse pits could be found on the ground.

In interviews conducted during or immediately after archaeological fieldwork, informants were asked about particular artifacts and other findings that puzzled the archaeologists. For example, among the numerous artifacts found at the site were oddly shaped pieces of broken metal that archaeologists could not immediately identify. An interview with an informant who lived at the site produced the following possible explanation:

> I'm surprised they haven't found any of those old logging brands. Some way, way early logging brand, we had a lot of those. We kids used to play with those—like a hammer and put a line on them and play slinging that hammer like for sports. You made your own toys.[5]

Oral history could also provide a key to understanding why and when structural changes had been made. Archaeologists wondered why so many fairly modern nails were contained in the original log part of the Seneacquoteen structure and why the interior log walls were in such a deteriorated condition. Harry Kenny, whose family had leased the house in the early 1930s, first described this portion of the building as follows:

> The lower part of the log building there, that was cellar. I guess they used that for storage in the days when it was a trading post. . . . Nothing in it really but a few shelves. . . . Logs didn't show in the house, they

showed in the cellar part. . . . It was pretty thick. I imagine the walls were about that thick [a couple of feet]. It was chinked.[6]

Clues as to why the structure was changed after the Kenny occupancy were then found in an interview with Gordon Mead:

> The log part was the original old, old building. It also had walls 30" thick log-to-log, and the center was filled with clay. . . . (It was) framed in two layers. My older brother and I took the inside frame out. It started dryrotting—the clay in between it started to dryrot. It was the only thing we had to live in—times were tough. . . . It seemed pretty large to me because we had bins in there—potato bins and vegetable bins, and everything for our food. It would never freeze.
>
> We took out a layer of logs on the side facing the road and the side facing the lean-to. . . . The building was settling real fast. And so we took the inside ones out, and as we took it out we had a big screw jack and put posts in to hold it. . . . By the way, we found very few nails—pegged mainly, I think, with wood pegs.
>
> Interviewer: Did you ever put any nails in it yourself in order to keep it together?
>
> Oh yeah, lots. But nothing after late 1939 or 1940. Nothing was done after that.[7]

As might be expected, informants who had actually lived in the structure had particular vivid memories of the exact details of building construction and interior appearance. Neighbors and friends were generally more vague in their descriptions, except for individual rooms such as the kitchen or parlor that they might have frequented. For all informants, particular features of a building were most often remembered because of their association with a memorable incident. Gordon Mead, for example, recalled that the floors of their house had been covered with linoleum and a prized Persian rug when he related the story of an insensitive logger who walked across the floor in his caulked boots and had then been banned from the house by Mead's mother.[8]

Mrs. Charles Sebring, whose mother had been one of the earliest teachers at the Seneacquoteen school and had boarded for a term with the Christianson family, had difficulty describing certain elements of the interior of the Christianson house. Her memory was pricked, however, when she began to relate a story her mother had told about one of the Christianson children, who had fallen down an open staircase from the upstairs bedrooms into the store below. This incident helped to pinpoint the actual location of the store and the stairway in the house and to corroborate the information that the upstairs rooms in the log portion of the building were used for bedrooms.[9]

The effectiveness of oral history in illuminating the personal side of the life of a structure seems even more apparent when attempting to understand that structure in its broader context in the community. Too frequently, it seems, people (including site-survey personnel, representatives of federal or state agencies, archaeologists, and even members of local historical groups) become so immersed in the specific architectural details of a building that they lose any sense of the role that the site played for the community at large. This particular issue led us into using oral history in a second way at Seneacquoteen—to supplement the written record and, more importantly, to add a personal perspective to the documentary evidence we uncovered.

Archival research produced a surprisingly long and varied array of travelers who had utilized the site at different periods in its history prior to established settlement. Beginning with the Kalispel and other Native American peoples who undoubtedly frequented the area as a fording and camping place, the list of Seneacquoteen visitors includes explorer and trader David Thompson, other Northwest and Hudson's Bay Company personnel, missionaries, Governor Isaac L. Stevens' 1853 railroad exploration party, members of the United States and British boundary survey teams, and freighters, tradesmen, and prospectors rushing to take advantage of the Wild Horse and Montana mining booms in the 1860s.

Although oral interviewees could offer no first-hand accounts of these early days, and few had any knowledge of the extent of nineteenth-century activity at the site, questioning produced a very strong oral tradition about its use as a trading post. Every informant who was interviewed had heard stories that described the site as the location of a Hudson's Bay Company post, and most interviewees were thoroughly convinced of the authenticity of these accounts despite their consistently vague recollections of the sources of their information.

Because of the persistence of this tradition, project historians decided to seek documentary support for the story, even though several regional scholars totally rejected the idea that the site had ever served as a Hudson's Bay Company operation. This new research turned up a 1903 volume, *The History of North Idaho*, which contained a biography of Francis Markham, an early area pioneer and owner of land adjacent to our Seneacquoteen project site, who was listed as having recently torn down a building on his property erected by the Hudson's Bay Company.[10] An Arrowsmith map from 1959, which marked the site with the words "old post," was also located.

More evidence would certainly be needed to support the claim, since archaeology seemed to show that neither the dilapidated Seneacquoteen building nor the artifacts found around it were old enough to be of the Hudson's Bay era. In fact, it is possible that informants confused the store run by the Christianson family in the 1890s with one of earlier Hudson's Bay Company origins. Yet, whether this Hudson's Bay post tradition is deemed plausible enough to pursue by historians probing further into the archival records or by archaeologists digging, perhaps, at another nearby location, or whether it is classified as part of the folklore of the area, it still remains a very important indicator of community perspectives on the significance of the site.

Oral history also revealed that, aside from the Hudson's Bay post legend, community perceptions of Seneacquoteen and what that term represented were extremely varied. My own images of the Seneacquoteen of the historical marker or the Seneacquoteen of the decaying log building in no way reflected all possible images of the site. To the families who had lived in the old structure, it was indeed the Seneacquoteen that we on the project had envisioned. But to their neighbors and other members of the greater community, Seneacquoteen was much more. To some, including the man who still tended the graves, Seneacquoteen was the cemetery—the final resting place for pioneer families on both sides of the river. To several others who had grown up in the area, Seneacquoteen was the school, first housed in a log structure and then moved to a newly built frame building a mile further down the road. To the Markham family, who had operated boats on the river, Seneacquoteen was the ferry crossing and the site of their family home. And to another neighbor whose house sat on a hill overlooking the area, Seneacquoteen was the entire valley—the land running along the river that encompassed the school, the cemetery, the ferry crossing, and a number of homes and farms.

Seneacquoteen, in a sense, *was* the community. The building and the crossing, although important to all residents, were only part of a larger entity that was Seneacquoteen. Without oral history we would never have been aware of this larger significance. In fact, if we had failed to document these multiple community perceptions through oral interviewing, then our treatment of the site would have been as shallow and inaccurate as my initial impressions of Seneacquoteen and the railroad cars and tract homes.

As we came to learn, Seneacquoteen was important not only for its use by travelers of the past, as the historical marker suggested, but also for its everyday uses in modern times. Seneacquoteen in this latter sense was really a very ordinary place that represented a way of life common to many other small communities in the area. As a result, local historical groups or interested individuals may be able to use some of the techniques that proved effective at Seneacquoteen to gain a better understanding of their own past.

Initially, it is essential that these local groups try to set aside their preconceived notions and broaden their perspectives in order to examine the history of the whole community, rather than to concentrate solely on its outstanding features. Too often historical societies, museums, and other similar organizations focus only on the first settlers or the famous people who have had an impact on the community, rather than documenting the role that common people played in its growth and development.

This narrow perspective also quite often extends to the built environment of the community. If the architecture of a town is examined, it is the notable buildings—the fashionable homes of the wealthy or the famous, the theaters, courthouses, and other public structures that are admired, preserved, and displayed proudly to visitors, not the structures that were the homes and workplaces of the everyday people who built the community. Although the notable structures obviously should not be ignored, very often the less imposing buildings can offer more important insights to the attitudes and influences that helped to shape local development. Even if it means they must concentrate on sawmill buildings, mining operations, log cabins, barns, retail shops, and saloons, local groups must remove their historical blinders and make sure that their interpretation of the past reflects what is truly significant or representative in the community.

No matter what aspects of its history a community chooses to emphasize, a multidisciplinary approach to interpretation may prove to be extremely effective in achieving a more complex picture of the past. Researchers should not only make use of letters, diaries, published accounts, and newspapers available in local archives, they should also not ignore the personal reminiscences of their residents as well as the physical remains of life in the past. I am not advocating that local history buffs immediately pick up a shovel and start digging around the nearest homestead cabin or dump site, nor am I saying that, untrained, they should march out with tape recorder in hand to interview every resident over 65 in their area. What I do suggest is that local groups can expand their interpretation of their own past by understanding and, when possible, utilizing the insights of other disciplines. These disciplines may include history, archaeology, and oral history, which we used at Seneacquoteen, and folklore and architectural history as well.

People already living in the community may have an educational background in some of these fields, but if not, professionals can be brought in to present new perspectives or even to provide training in methodology. When local funds are limited, grant organizations and speakers' programs may possibly be able to provide financial assistance to bring these experts to the area. Nearby colleges and universities may have faculty members who would be willing to help in an advisory capacity. In the case of archaeology, a number of federal and state agencies such as the Forest Service, Bureau of Land Management, National Park Service, state historic preservation offices, and historical societies usually have trained archaeologists on their staffs who can offer information, if not direct support, for historically significant projects.

Oral history, as we saw at Seneacquoteen, is also an extremely effective technique that is not beyond the scope of local historical groups. With appropriate training in interviewing techniques and strategies, residents can become competent interviewers, gathering and preserving important information on the lifestyles and attitudes of people in their community as well as on the use of particular structures. Some states, including Idaho and Washington, have oral history offices, while in others the state historical society, libraries, and some colleges have staff members who are knowledgeable about oral history methodology. A wide variety of published materials is also available that deals specifically with interviewing techniques and methods of informant selection that are appropriate for local historical groups.

Finally, when these new perspectives have been explored and adequate techniques developed, it is important that the interpretations derived from them be available to the general public. Museum displays, public lectures, newspaper articles, guided excursions, and the examination and preservation of significant sites are only a few of the possible ways to provide this interpretation. Many of these activities can be financed on a limited budget with the use of volunteer labor and with small donations from local businesses, chambers of commerce, tourism boards, and other similar organizations. Occasionally, state or federal agencies may also have grant funds available for such projects.

Above all else, remember that local residents need and want to be exposed to their roots. Just as I, while studying the site, learned that Seneacquoteen was more than a historical marker or a dilapidated building, so a community must be able to discover all the various possible perspectives on its own past.[11]

Notes

1. The project was funded in part by a grant from the Association for the Humanities in Idaho (now the Idaho Humanities Council), a state-based program of the National Endowment for the Humanities. The North Idaho Cultural Resource Information Center was the project's sponsor, with Nancy Renk serving as primary researcher and Lorelea Hudson, chief archaeologist. Helpful research assistance was also provided by Dave Osterberg.

2. Grace Roffey Pratt, "Ghost Ferry in Hoodoo Valley," *Old West* (Winter, 1967), pp. 46-47; Pratt, "Seneacquoteen," *Incredible Idaho* (Summer, 1976), 8/2:18-21. *The Sandpoint News-Bulletin,* December 30, 1965, also carried an article on Seneacquoteen whose contents were essentially the same as the *Old West* article with some additional material included.

3. Hereafter, any quotations from taped interviews will be cited by the last name of the informant, the tape number, the tape side, and the minutes into the tape. An example of this citation method is as follows: Mead I, ii, 25-28. All taped

material referred to in this article was recorded by the author as part of the Seneacquoteen project. Copies of the tapes are available at the Idaho Oral History Center in Boise and the Bonner County Historical Society in Sandpoint, idaho.

4. Mead I, ii, 28:00-32:15. See also interview with Edith Calvert and Mel Markham in Markham III, ii, 24:45-27:15.

5. Mead I, ii, 28:00-32:15.

6. Kenny I, i, 3:30-10:45.

7. Mead I, ii, 10:00-14:30.

8. Mead I, ii, 17:00-18:15.

9. Sebring I, i, 22:30-26:00.

10. *An Illustrated History of North Idaho* ([Spokane?]: Western Historical Publishing Company, 1903), p. 911.

11. A few of the many works which might be useful to local groups interested in oral history projects are: Willa Baum, *Oral History for the Local Historical Society* (Nashville, Tennessee: American Association for State and Local History, 1973); Cullom Davis, Kathryn Back, and Kay MacLean, *Oral History From Tape to Type* (Chicago: American Library Association, 1977); William G. Tyrrell, "Tape-Recording Local History" Technical Leaflet 35, *History News* (May, 1966), 21/5; and Stacy Ericson, *A Field Notebook for Oral History* (Boise: Idaho Oral History Center, 1980). One of the few articles that specifically examines the use of oral history in site-related work is Madeline Buckendorf and Margot K. Knight, "Oral History and Historic Preservation: A Case Study in Washington and Idaho," *The Oral History Review* (1981), 9:97-114.

Comment:
Evaluating Oral Material

Barre Toelken

These two fascinating papers by Laurie Mercier and Sherry Boswell bring up a number of issues dear to the heart of a folklorist. Both papers express a proper and admirable regard for fact and factuality, and both speakers have made it clear how the element of reliability relates to our constant attempt to learn more about our past and present cultural contexts. Without denigrating anything said in either of these papers, I should like to go a step further and suggest that there are details in both presentations which are clearly valuable to us even though it may be impossible to determine in any objective way how specifically factual they are. Moreover, I would like to suggest that even if an informant is lying outright, there may be historically important reasons for it which are interesting to examine. If an informant is "performing" and entertaining the interviewer with personal anecdotes the details of which may not be subject to verification, one still has a rich document of personal attitude and perspective that cannot be derived in any other way. Since perspective is what we often lack in historical and cultural studies, my insistence here will be that in addition to ascertainable facts, which we all agree have an importance for our understanding, other kinds of materials—even if they are totally nonfactual—may be equally exciting.

For example, many towns in the American West were split by competition and conflict between families who raised cattle and families who raised sheep. In many cases the cattle families became wealthy sooner than the sheep families, and a status system arose in which the sons and daughters of cattle barons often went to the university and came home as leading citizens, doctors, lawyers, and other people engaged in the hierarchy of the town, while the sheep people occupied—for a time—a "lower" social level. In many towns, it is said, these conflicts gave rise to open warfare between families, to mistreatment by doctors, mishandling by lawyers and judges, and a number of discriminatory procedures and attitudes that either are probably impossible to document or may never have happened except in the imaginations of those who felt these local tensions very deeply as aspects of their everyday lives. Since these are the kinds of details that seldom get into the newspapers, the written record of the time is likely to tell us very little about what actually went on. But even if we could find substantial written accounts of the factual details, we would still be left with the knowledge that people *felt* a deep and abiding discrepancy in the ways of life that had become central to their communities and that governed the dynamics of community deportment, politics, and cultural development. To overlook these tensions, even though we may hear of them today only by rumor and unverifiable reminiscence, would be to overlook an important aspect of the West: the emotional system that brought about key historical development.

This means that whether we are dealing with lies, exaggerations, errors in memory, or intentional manipulations of the facts by people who wish to create a rosy (or overly dramatic) picture of the past, we are nonetheless dealing with real people and their opinions. Opinions, perspectives, fears, tensions, anxieties, and joys form just as important a part of American history as do the various dates, Important Personages, and verifiable political and economic processes. We overlook them only if we want to see history as a fossil lacking the animation of a real culture.

But there are other exciting possibilities as well: much that exists in oral history and reminiscence *is* more accurate than many of the written accounts. We know, for example, that a number of American Indian tribes have very strong oral traditions concerning peoples who inhabited their area before they themselves moved in. In many cases, working from these oral traditions of Indian tribes, archaeologists have been able to find remnants of cultures that were previously unrecorded, unknown, or ignored. As well, we know that a number of American Indian orators, having memorized the fine details of treaties they recall having signed, have become some of our best sources for recapturing what a given treaty actually meant and how the people who signed it actually understood its provisions. Even though we may have a written document in hand, especially given the misspelling and other minor incompetencies of army clerks in another era, the oral tradition often provides us with a much more satisfactory account of what indeed took place.

Historians in recent times have found numerous examples of political actions across the early United States in which a newspaper editor, say, in concert with political colleagues, published false information in a newspaper in order to dishearten or confuse the other party. Historians working only from newspaper accounts, or from other formally published materials, are often unknowingly subject to fact-manipulation that took place at a time and place from which the details have become vague or untraceable. The oral traditions of families in those same towns often detail down to date and name the people who were involved in the economic or political interplay and are often at odds with news items in the paper. In one celebrated case, the white editor of a Texas newspaper reported the death of a well-known and beloved black politician and successfully broke the cohesion of a black voters' coalition. It has been determined through other sources that the black politician indeed did not die on that occasion, nor in the manner reported. The facts are more easily reached through the reminiscences of families in nearby Texas towns than they are through a study of the printed documents. Thus, on the one hand, oral information is interesting even if it cannot be verified as accurate; on the other hand, in many cases oral history may give us the only clearly accurate perspectives available, even when it will be impossible to verify the details through print. In both cases, I think it is clear, what we are dealing with finally is perspective, human attitude, shared values, and those other abstract expressions of a communality of interest without which specific items and dates in history have very little meaning of their own.

The essay that examines oral traditions about the Seneacquoteen building provides us with many fine examples of the importance of collecting oral history. Only through oral history were Boswell and her colleagues able to deal with the possibility that this building had been located at different places (or that other similar buildings had been identified with it). The oral traditions allow us to see not only where the bins, rooms, and other physical items were inside this building, but where the people were and what they did. It is interesting to note that the excavations of the outhouse sites, which produced many fascinating items, led to solid objects whose history or use could only be surmised because oral traditions at this late date cannot supply enough of the factual details of life at that site. One could not find a better example of the need for oral history in archaeological work: the object (the building and its contents, along with its layout and setting) is there for all to see, photograph, sketch, and dissect. But the life of the building, as experienced through its various inhabitants and owners, is reachable for us now only through the means of oral tradition. What we find when we look at that oral record is not so much a list of verifiable dates or "reliable" and separately attested scientific facts, but rich and moving testimony about the dynamics of the lives of people who inhabited the building and who made local history. Often in our museums we pay more attention to these objects, and in our archaeological finds we often spend a great deal of energy interpreting them, without fully appreciating the live dimensions of the cultures and peoples who produced them. A chief advantage of recent archaeological sites, of course, is that we can still find people who can give us these important perspectives.

Beyond all of these things, a folklorist would want to point out that there are still other kinds of oral traditions that are extremely accurate on one level but are, on another, intentional lies. Here I refer to a genre of oral tradition called the tall tale. The tall tale is—from one point of view—an attractively performed and humorous lie. People in desert areas will tell strangers that it gets so dry during the summertime that trees follow the dogs around town. The land is so fertile that one has to shoot corn seeds with a shotgun and jump back out of the way. The tale is told of a farmer who doesn't step back fast enough and who gets carried off the ground by a corn plant that grows through his suspenders. People in desert towns feed cracked ice to the chickens to keeps them from laying hard-boiled eggs. One town in Missouri is so healthy that the people had to shoot someone just to start a cemetery. A man on the Olympic Penisula can show you where his rain barrel turned over in a heavy rainstorm and the rain forced its way into the bunghole faster than the water could flow out the open end, and he was able to water his stock all summer with the compacted rain from that one barrel. In eastern Oregon and some parts of Idaho the wind blows so powerfully that the cows have had to learn to stand on their hay to keep it from blowing away from them. A Montana rancher sees his cows all lying down and thinks that they have died, but taking a closer look he notices that each one is hunkering down behind a fence post to get out of the wind. People who live in parts of the country where their survival is not threatened by wind, rain, dry weather, or blazing sun do not need to make up such stories.

Rather than a collection of lies, the American tall tales are a wonderful array of hyperbole, dramatic cameos if you will, of attitudes about real locale and real weather. Some people could not make it in the West and went back home. Others went broke and killed themselves. Those who remained, and this probably represents the majority, had not only the land and the weather to cope with but their own thoughts, fears, and apprehensions about survival with their families. The tall tale is not only testimony to specific geographical and meteorological conditions which are indeed true in and of themselves, but is also proof of an ongoing element of human spirit that goes farther to explain pioneer successes than any number of dates and names. The ability to make up humorous and hyperbolic statements about weather is not a sign of senility or lack of reverence for historical facts; rather, it is testimony to the way humans deal with psychologically traumatic conditions and triumph over them.

For all of these reasons, it is clear that when we talk about evaluating oral materials we need to expand our notion of what we mean by "evaluation." We need to include not only verification of facts but expansion of our awareness of how people act in the tremendously trying situations of new settlement such as those which set the keynote for history here in the Northwest. I think we want not only to check orally transmitted information against the written historical record, but to *induce* reminiscence, induce tall tales, induce performances. In these human expressions of attitude and value, we find the real kernels—perhaps better said, the real mother lode—of the history of ordinary people. Up until recently, history books have focused on the adventures of the wealthy and powerful: the Presidents, Founding Fathers, Generals, Empire Builders. Historians now are more anxious to clarify the record for all those people who actually did the work and settled the land. This does not necessarily stand in contradistinction to the history of Worthy Personages, but it adds to that record the valuable and rich dimension of human frustration and triumph which took place on all levels in the development of this country. Without the oral tradition of our neighbors, friends, and relatives, it would be very difficult indeed to develop this perspective very far. In this sense, we are all colleagues in an ongoing effort not only to understand the historical past but to understand ourselves.

Response:

Oral History and the Written Record

Laurie Mercier

In his comments and responses to the papers on "Evaluating Oral Materials," Barre Toelken offers additional insights regarding the evaluation and verification of such materials. Certainly, the attitudes and perspectives expressed by narrators make the oral history interview an invaluable tool for teaching us about our past. In the first paragraph of "Testing for Reliability in Oral History," we noted that the strength of oral history is "the expression of honestly held opinions and remembered impressions of personal experiences." Most oral historians agree that this is the oral interview's essential contribution.

Considering the wide acceptance of oral history, apparent in the burgeoning number of oral history projects, programs, and collections across the country, there is no need to defend its virtues. What *is* needed is more guidance concerning the evalution of these oral materials. Bill Lang and I attempted to deal with the question of reliability of certain kinds of remembered information, since this type of information undergoes the most scrutiny by historians. Concern for facts and factuality did not supersede the perspectives revealed in the reminiscences. The interview excerpts used through the paper were intended to illustrate how the interviewer/researcher should prepare to accept new and unexpected information as reliable, avoid having expectations of the narrator, and refrain from forcing narrators to fit responses in chronological sequence or dismissing information because of inaccurate dates.

The oral history interview is not sacrosanct. True, as Toelken says: many oral accounts *are* more accurate than many written accounts, but the historian must apply the same tests to the oral reminiscence as to any other source. A good historian is not "unknowingly subject to fact manipulation" from newspaper accounts. The conscientious researcher recognizes the pitfalls of relying solely on newspaper accounts or any other single source of information.

Toelken holds that even lies and intentional manipulations of facts offer as important a view of American history as do verifiable political and economic processes. But how do we interpret this material? And how does this give us a greater understanding of our past? Meteorological tall tales are certainly reflective of local attitudes toward weather and reveal how people have dealt with traumatic conditions, but how are they "proof of an ongoing element of human spirit which goes farther to explain pioneer successes than any number of dates and names"? As researchers of local history and culture, we need more instruction in interpreting the tall tales found in reminiscences.

Toelken emphasizes the value of oral history in understanding the trials of new settlement in the West, the cattle and sheep battles of the nineteenth century, and the pioneer spirit. It may be too late to accurately reconstruct what life was like for people at the turn of the century through the use of oral history. Oral historians have the opportunity to make a much greater contribution to the available body of historical knowledge of twentieth-century life by recording the memories of people about their own, first-hand experiences. There is so much to be done in the way of documenting men's and women's work, ethnic heritage, community life—the lives of ordinary people. The reminiscences from the Montana Historical Society oral history collection used in our paper reflect the diversity of the people living in our state, none of whom would have considered writing down their recollections. The excerpts demonstrate how the oral history interview can expand, enhance, and enliven the written record.

III. *Rethinking Cultural Stereotypes*

The Frontier through Women's Eyes

Susan H. Armitage

When we think of "the West" and "the frontier," what images come to mind? Most of us, influenced by movies and other media, imagine a vast region populated by cowboys, Indians, outlaws, miners, and perhaps a few Marlboro men. More seriously, the experience of the frontier has deeply influenced our literature at all levels, from dime novels to enduring classics. In fact, the frontier myth is *the* American myth, the story of how we made this land "our land." The stages of the frontier process are familiar to us all: the encounter with wilderness; the risk, challenge, and commitment; the final slow surrender of freedom to advancing civilization.[1]

Frederick Jackson Turner's famous "frontier thesis" is the most compelling theory in all of American history.[2] Turner argued that the frontier was a liberating influence both personally and socially. The individual who moved west was freed from the economic and psychological constraints of the civilization left behind. In the broader sense, Turner said that the frontier was both a "safety valve" that vented dangerous social tensions and a democratizing example that kept American society fluid and open.

Physically, as well, the frontier is always with us. As we live and work in the American West, our frontier heritage is always present—as near as the stark, beautiful, and challenging landscape which surrounds us.

The idea of frontier *is* evocative and appealing, but it contains some deeply disturbing elements. The frontier image is a male myth, preoccupied with stereotypically male issues like courage, physical bravery, violence, honor, and male friendship. While these are important themes, they by no means encompass the reality and complexity of the frontier experience.

This paper treats three frontier themes—adventure, individualism, and violence—through women's eyes. I will draw on the vast accumulation of women's materials, including diaries, letters, journals, memoirs, novels, poems, children's books, and oral histories, that historians of women have recently rediscovered and are now using to fill out the historical record.[3]

What do the Overland Trail diaries of women tell us about the adventure of pioneering? Lillian Schlissel's recent *Women's Diaries of the Westward Journey*[4] clearly shows that women's experience was different from the well-known male accounts of the Overland Trail. The women's story of the westward journey is one of worry, privation, and loss. In one of her most striking observations, Schlissel points to the way in which women never lost their personal awareness of death: they counted graves. Men tended to aggregate and abstract the figures; women kept precise daily counts and lived with their impact.

In *Women and Men on the Oregon Trail*, Johnny Faragher concludes:

> For men, the trip west was an active test of competition, strength, and manliness. It meant measuring themselves against the already romanticized images of their heroic pioneer fathers and grandfathers traversing the Wilderness Road and the Cumberland Gap. For women the trip west was a test of their inner strength. They did their part and more; they were comforting wives and attentive mothers, to the many single men of the trail as well as their husbands. They did all this, because of, not in spite of, their not wanting to leave home in the first place.[5]

The evidence that men and women experienced the Overland Trail differently is fully in accord with recent research in eastern nineteenth-century women's and family history. The two sexes inhabited separate spheres: men's was the public sphere; women's was the home. What women did was dramatically different from what men did, and their perceptions were shaped accordingly. This contrast illustrates that there were two pioneer experiences: one male, one female.

Simply put, many women were reluctant pioneers. At first, many feminist historians found this fact upsetting and disconcerting. We are so accustomed to the West as a land of freedom and opportunity that this new evidence is unwelcome. We may also fear that the women themselves must have been at fault and too weak or genteel to adapt to pioneer life.

It is instructive to look at an individual case in more detail. Amelia Buss moved to Fort Collins, Colorado, in 1866. She came west unwillingly, leaving friends and family behind, because she believed it was a wife's duty to follow her husband. She filled her diary with details of daily housekeeping in a primitive cabin and with complaints about hard work, isolation, and loneliness.

> George went to the mountains yesterday morning to be gon all week . . . after he had gon gave vent to my feelings in a flood of tears. it may seem foolish to those that have neighbors and friends around them. I get a long very well through the day but the long evenings and nights are *horrible.*

Amelia developed rituals to sustain herself in her new surroundings. On Sunday she held Bible readings with her young daughter, evoking warm memories of companionable Sabbaths in the East. She lived for letters from home. And she used her diary, which was given to her by her sisters as a parting gift, as a place to acknowledge her private fears:

> I have not had a letter in over two weeks till today I got one from A. and one from L. there was good news from home but some how I have felt very low spirited ever since and that old homesick feeling comes back to me an other week is gon and O how cold the wind sounds tonight. G. and V. are a sleep and I am alone.

Amelia's diary ends with a retrospective entry, dated exactly one year after her arrival in Colorado. She has become resigned: "Now I have settled down with the belief that here I shall end my days and the sooner I make it home the better."[6]

Amelia Buss appears to be a perfect example of the western stereotype of the lonely, pathetic woman longing for female companionship. She is pitiful and frail, too gentle for the harshness of the West.

But consider how congruent her experience was with the nineteenth-century notion of separate spheres. Women, confined to domestic life, built strong female support networks within their sphere. Recent work by Carroll Smith-Rosenberg and Nancy Cott[7] has demonstrated that while men were experiencing the risks and rewards of the new competitive individualism, many women derived primary emotional sustenance from a traditional sharing, female subculture composed of mothers, sisters, and female friends. This female subculture did not easily develop in the pioneer West. On the plains women were too far apart, and in the mining camps diversity and mobility of the population seem to have created something like modern suburban privatization. Women were no longer embedded in a tight community with all the customary attendant female supports. Frontier individualism was forced upon these women: they had to be more self-reliant and less communal than they had been before.

Most women keenly felt their isolation from other women and from a shared female value system. As soon as they could, once the hard early years of settlement were past, they joined together with other women to help build community institutions such as churches and schools. This role is celebrated in frontier literature in the image of woman as "gentle tamer," as the culture-bearer who brings civilization to the West. Not so noticed is the criticism of male values which this female "civilizing" activity represents. The first stage of pioneering required that both men and women adopt the individualism and the self-reliance which we have been taught to view as the result of the frontier process. However, what becomes clear from a close look at female sources is how much most women disliked that very process. They did not accept individualism willingly; they missed the shared support of the female subculture; and they re-created that network when they could. In the meantime, they worked side by side with their men.[8]

At its deepest level, the frontier myth celebrates violence and conquest over the land, over the native inhabitants of that land, over fear of the unknown, and finally, over the temptation to succumb to wilderness and revert to savagery. To justify this violence, the historical reality of the encounter between Indians and whites has been distorted.

Presentations of another reality provide, however, a different perspective. In this scene, the woman and her children are alone and "unprotected"—because the white man is elsewhere—when the Indians arrive. The result is not a massacre. The Indians want food, not scalps. The woman, while afraid of the Indians, is even more afraid to refuse their demands. She cooks the requested item, or regretfully offers up scarce store-bought food. The Indians leave peacefully. When the white man returns home, he praises the woman for her courage and common sense.

This same scene appears again and again in women's writings. One of the best known examples occurs in Laura Ingalls Wilder's *Little House on the Prairie*.[9] Wilder recalled that when her family lived on the Kansas-Oklahoma border, visiting Indians took all of the family's cornmeal and tobacco, which could not be replenished without a four-day round-trip journey to the nearest store. Nevertheless, when informed of the Indian visit, Mr. Ingalls reassured his wife, "You did the right thing. . . . We don't want to make enemies of any Indians."

Frequently the encounter between new settlers and Native Americans was not a violent event but a mundane aspect of daily life. To recapture the experience of culture contact as ordinary white settlers of my own region remembered it, I researched three fine local oral history collections compiled by the Latah County Historical Society, the Whitman County Historical Society, and the Idaho Rural Women's Oral History Project. I will focus on the experiences of women and children.

When whites began to settle the Palouse country in the early 1870s they were, of course, not moving into uninhabited territory. The region was the home of numerous Indian tribes who had long-established trails and settlement sites. The whites, generally ignorant of Indian practice, often settled on or near a well-traveled trail. This conjunction provides the largest single source of oral history stories.

Whites came into contact with Indians as the latter passed through on a seasonal basis, or as they camped where they always had, except that now it was close to a new barn or house. The white women usually were frightened of the Indians, either because of fear of violence or because Indians, like gypsies, were reputed to steal children. Nevertheless, the white women had to cope. Minnie Brandon in Whitman County remembered that her mother, although frightened, offered passing Indians some of her homemade bread.[10] The Indians liked the taste so much that they subsequently brought huckleberries to trade for more bread, and so a friendly bartering relationship developed. Another version of the same basic encounter was offered by Edward Swenson of Latah County. One day Indians camped in what had become an oats field:

> Father and the older boys were away that day, so it was mother and my sister and I. And so mother told me, she said, "You better go and tell them to move their horses off of the oats." Well, I had heard the Indians were wild, you know, and I was pretty well scared of it, but I managed to get over there and showed 'em where they should stake their horses. And they did, they started to move, put their horses over. I ran back to the house. Then mother told me, she said, "They were nice to you," so she said, "ask them to come in and have their meal." Well of course I couldn't talk to them, but somehow or other I got the message across. So they came to the house. There was five or six of 'em. And mother set the table, but they put the table back where it was, and they sat down on the floor in a circle and had their dinner. And mother had coffee for them, and sugar and cream and things like that, you know, a little fruit. So they really enjoyed it. . . .[11]

When the Indians came back in the fall, a trade for deer skins developed. The Indians originally offered fifty cents for deer hides, but Mrs. Swenson successfully held out for a price of seventy-five cents per skin.

Initial contact was often made through food, as in these two stories. But although white women served the food, they did not always control its disposal. For example, one reminiscence captures a women's grudging hospitality:

> [The Indians] used to come right by my folks place . . . They knew my dad well . . . and they always stopped. They'd come sometimes around dinnertime . . . and mother had soup, and dad would always invite 'em in. And they'd eat . . . and then . . . what they had left, the bucks would take it outside and give it to the squaws . . . . After they'd left mother

> used to put the boiler on the stove and put the dishes in and boil [them].[12]

Furthermore, although initial contact might be made over food, and therefore require the participation of the white woman, permanent trading relationships were usually managed by the white men, not by the white woman.

Although women may have been afraid of Indians, many tried to encourage their children to be less fearful. One narrator recalled, "[Mother was] scared to death of Indians but she used always tell us not to be afraid of them," and went on to describe the interest and excitement of watching the Indians on the move.[13]

A particularly nice written reminiscence comes from the Tekoa region, which was the chief trading center (and for a time the site of the agency) for the Coeur d'Alene Indians. Because of frequent contact, many local white people stopped being fearful. Bertha Williams wrote:

> I recall . . . when I was an adult meeting a group [of Indians], riding on a trail in the mountains in Idaho going huckleberrying and one Indian woman reaching down with her horse-urgin stick and tickling me with it. We both laughed, but my companion, reared on horrible Indian tales, was sure, for a moment, [that] there were evil intentions.[14]

In literature, and I suppose in reality as well, violence is often the expression of hidden fear, and a means of resolution. Presumably many whites would have liked to express their fears of Indians violently. But often that was impossible, and we see instead the anxious, placating response of these everyday, mundane encounters. But this reality has been hidden in neglected women's stories and in oral histories. We need to use the information they contain to counterbalance the violent accounts which we once thought were the whole story.[15]

Our pioneer heritage holds a powerful and evocative fascination for us today. Films, novels, and histories tell and retell the stories we want to hear. Again and again the stereotyped figures act out adventurous, individualistic, and violent dramas. Clearly, these stereotyped images express a psychological truth. But is it historical truth? If we want to see the pioneer experience as it really was, we must do our best to discard the stereotypes. Women's accounts, because they are largely new and unexplored, and because their perspective is just a little different from what we are used to, can help us see familiar events and circumstances in a new light. Thus women's sources are valuable not only for what they tell us about women's lives on the frontier but also for what they tell us about the pioneer experience as a whole.

When I think of what western history can be, I often think of the stereopticon, that fixture of so many Victorian parlors. The card with two nearly identical photos is uninteresting until placed in the viewer and focussed: then a sharp three-dimensional picture emerges. Women's history, like the picture in the stereopticon, can contribute a missing dimension to our frontier history. We will all benefit from a wider and fuller sense of our western heritage.

Notes

1. Richard Slotkin, *Regeneration Through Violence* (Middletown, Connecticut: Wesleyan University Press, 1973), provides a thorough discussion of the frontier in literature.

2. Frederick Jackson Turner first read his paper "The Significance of the Frontier in American History" at the American Historical Association meeting in Chicago, July 12, 1893, and thereupon launched a new and important field in American history.

3. For bibliography, consult Joan M. Jensen and Darlis A. Miller, "The Gentle Tamers Revisited: New Approaches to the History of Women in the American West," *Pacific Historical Review* (May, 1980), 49:2, and Sheryll and Gene Patterson-Black, *Western Women in History and Literature* (Crawford, Nebraska: Cottonwood Press, 1978); recent journal issues devoted to women's sources include *Journal of the West* (April, 1982), 21/2, and *Montana the Magazine of Western History* (Summer, 1982), 32/3.

4. Lillian Schlissel, *Women's Diaries of the Westward Journey* (New York: Schocken, 1982).

5. John Mack Faragher, *Women and Men on the Oregon Trail* (New Haven, Connecticut: Yale University Press, 1978).

6. Diary of Amelia Buss, 1866-67, Special Collections, Colorado State University Libraries, Fort Collins; a published version, *The Diary of Amelia Buss: The Record of a Reluctant Pioneer,* is forthcoming from Cottonwood Press.

7. Carroll Smith-Rosenberg, "The Female World of Love and Ritual," *Signs* (Autumn, 1975), 1:1, and Nancy Cott, *The Bonds of Womanhood* (New Haven, Connecticut: Yale University Press, 1977).

8. For further exploration of these themes, see my "Reluctant Pioneers," in Helen Winter Stauffer and Susan J. Rosowski, editors, *Women and Western American Literature* (Troy, New York: Whitston Press, 1982), 40-51.

9. Laura Ingalls Wilder, *Little House on the Prairie* (New York: Harper and Brothers, 1935).

10. Minnie Brandon Interview, Whitman County Oral History Collection, Holland Library, Washington State University, Pullman.

11. Edward Swenson Interview, Latah County Oral History Collection, Latah County Historical Society, Moscow, Idaho.

12. Seth Harris Interview, Whitman County Collection.

13. Agnes Jones Interview, Latah County Collection.

14. Bertha Engelland Williams, letter in *Standard Register* (Tekoa, Washington), May 8, 1980.

15. For further exploration of these themes, see my "Women's Literature and the American Frontier: A New Perspective on the Frontier Myth," in L. L. Lee and Merrill Lewis, editors, *Women, Women Writers and the West* (Troy, New York: Whitston Press, 1979), 5-13.

Mexican Heritage and Experience in Idaho

Patricia K. Ourada

My initial experience with Mexican and Mexican-American people consisted of watching them in the cherry orchards each summer at Sturgeon Bay, Wisconsin. Closer experiences, when teaching a class on the history of minorities in the United States in the bilingual program at Boise State University during the spring of 1977, enlarged my awareness. During that semester, two students received their United States citizenship and two dozen others discussed their experiences in border crossings, on the migrant trail, and in the heavy field work in which they and their families engaged. That class made me interested in the people of Mexican descent in Idaho. I was not too surprised that these people were omitted from the state histories, and everything else written about Idaho. Yet the state's billion-dollar agricultural enterprise came to fruition on the backs of the Mexican and Mexican-American laborers. In 1978, with the help of a Faculty Research Grant, I undertook to write a history of migrant workers in Idaho.

The search for information took me to the State Historical Society library, where the major suggestion made was that I use the state newspapers. The state departments of Labor and Agriculture furnished bulletins and statistics; the Department of Education offered school information; the United State Bureau of Immigration and Naturalization provided information on illegal aliens; the Idaho Migrant Council told me of their work, as did the president of the Utah-Idaho Sugar Company at Burley. The National Archives housed some information on farming in Idaho through the years in their Region XI files of the United States Department of Agriculture. A large number of books have been written on migrant labor, especially in California and Texas. These were utilized for generalizations in the paper. A trip to the labor camps in the eastern part of the state and to the Marsing camp in Owyhee County clearly showed the present plight of the migrant workers.

I have drawn from this migrant study for the present paper, but I have broadened my base to include the 30,000 people of Mexican heritage who reside permanently in Idaho. The first question to be asked is: "Who are these people?" The answer is somewhat complex, since there are four distinct groups of people with a Hispanic heritage living in Idaho.

1. Mexicans—persons who are Mexican nationals and reside here in accordance with their visa provisions, or illegal Mexican nationals who cross the border to work.

2. Mexican-Americans—persons of Mexican heritage who are citizens of the United States through either naturalization or birth.

3. Spanish-Americans—persons of Spanish ancestry from the Southwest who are citizens of the United States and who maintain strong ties with relatives in the Southwest.

4. Chicanos—either Mexican-American or Spanish-American youth, who are militant and opposed to the adoption of American culture.

The fact that members of these four groups reside permanently within the state runs counter to the stereotyped belief that all Hispanics are migratory workers. It further indicates that each group has a different self-image and thinks differently about its culture.

Most Spanish-Americans live in Boise, Burley, and Pocatello. They are engaged in railroading, trucking, and construction. These people speak English and, if they speak Spanish at all, it is the language of the eighteenth century that they use. Their traditions go back to the old Southwest Spanish culture, and they cherish what they know to be their aristocratic ancestry. Mexican people are found in southern Idaho, along with most Mexican-Americans. They engage in agricultural work and food processing in the Magic Valley, Treasure Valley, and Upper Snake River Valley. These people may be bilingual. Adults over thirty have an average of four or five years of formal schooling. Among the Mexican-Americans there is a growing middle class that live in the urban communities and have assimilated into the mainstream. Most Mexican-Americans, however, prefer to live in a *colonia:* a small settlement apart from or in a distinct location in a town, where they live among themselves and rely upon one another for companionship and support. Such settlements exist at Sunny Slope, North Nampa, Caldwell, Wilder, Burley, Pocatello, and Twin Falls, and in the towns of eastern Idaho. Together, the people comprise 30,000 permanent residents, 10,000 Mexican-American migrant workers, and 5,000 illegal Mexican aliens.[1]

Collectively these people possess a rich Mexican-American folklore, evidenced by song in the form of lyrical ballads, romances, and tragedies. The ballads comprise the popular music of the people; the romances are the serenades, lullabies, and love songs; and the tragic ballads include the church music and the music for funerals and wakes. This common folklore also includes drama, dance, medicinal practices, and religious and festival observances. The rich traditions of the Hispanic people are synthesized within a common Indio-Spanish background.

How the people of Hispanic background view themselves and their culture differs sharply from the way in which they have been perceived and received within our national experience. In the nineteenth century, Mexicans in the Southwest were caricatured as "ignorant and degraded" and worthy of conquest. This early pattern of anti-Mexican prejudice continued into the twentieth century. The general attitude was that Mexican people were the kind of people who could be exploited for their labor. They were considered too "dirty" and too "lazy" to keep up their homes or to contribute to the welfare of the community. Thus, people of Mexican ancestry quickly came to be viewed as a national problem.

The years from 1900 to 1930 can be called a dark age of racism in the United States. Americans preached Anglo-Saxon superiority, and all minority groups received bad press and were negatively portrayed in novels, textbooks, and motion pictures. In this climate, hundreds of thousands of Mexicans crossed the borders into the Southwest and California. Such action made nativist Americans seek restrictive immigration legislation with renewed vigor. The *Idaho Daily Statesman* in a June, 1916, editorial expressed Idaho's sentiment: "We all know what a thieving, scoundrelly, marauding lot the Mexicans are." In that same editorial the Mexicans were referred to as "poor little greasers."[2] Spokesmen on the national level uttered the same prejudicial slurs. David Starr Jordan, president of Stanford University from 1891 to 1913, described the Mexicans as "ignorant, superstitious, ill-nurtured, with little self-control and no conception of industry or thrift."[3] Still others shouted for national exclusion.

The number of Mexicans or Mexican-Americans in Idaho for this period remains unchronicled, but the papers bear evidence of the Mexican's presence through reports of deaths, murders, and injuries to Mexican workingmen. In 1924, Mexican gang laborers were hired by the Union Pacific Railroad in Idaho, and the Utah-Idaho Sugar Company announced that it would provide Mexican field hands to sugar-beet growers where twenty-five acres or more were planted. The influx of foreigners into the country spurred the Ku Klux Klan into action, and at a Klan rally in Boise on June 9, 1924, the Reverend H. H. Mow of the Payette Christian Church deplored the "flood of undesirables" coming into the country.[4]

During the Depression years, Idaho "loomed like the biblical garden of Eden in a dust-stormed and drought-stricken nation."[5] Waves of workmen and their families arrived from the scorched earth of mid-America, and Filipino and Mexican laborers competed in the fields with the newcomers. The 1930s produced the first crackdown on Mexican laborers. Thousands of Mexican-American families were repatriated. A common method of encouraging families to leave was to threaten to end relief and emergency assistance. Families that reached California found that their train fare would be paid by the state as far as the Mexican border.[6]

World War II produced a rapid drain of farm workers to the war production factories of the Pacific coast. The loss of farm labor to the war effort threatened Idaho's agricultural productivity at a time when the demand for crops was critical to the nation's war aims. In 1942, a *bracero* program to bring Mexican workers into the United States was instigated. This was a program for contracted Mexican nationals that lasted from 1942 until 1964 with a brief interruption from 1947 to 1951. Idaho enthusiastically participated in the program, and the Mexican workers pursued Idaho's agricultural interests side by side with Japanese-American internees from Minidoka, conscientious objectors from Camp Downey, Indians from the Navajo reservation, Jamaican workers, and German prisoners of war. The Mexican nationals were moved about the state to fill specific or unexpected needs. They not only worked the orchards and potato fields but were used to plant white pine seedlings and to fight blister rust and insect infestations in the national forests of the state. Mexican nationals joined the war prisoners and conscientious objectors in fire-fighting in northern Idaho and the Idaho Primitive Area. The use of *braceros* in this hazardous work brought a formal protest from the Mexican government and a threat to withhold workers.

The Mexican nationals, many of them from Mexico City, who worked in Idaho met discrimination and general hostility throughout the state. After the war, they became the major source of field laborers in the state. Frequently, there were strikes in the hope of raising the hourly wage for those not on a piecework scale. Strikers were usually quickly dispersed by closing down the camp kitchen until the men went back to work. The Mexican nationals complained of poor housing, bad food, poor working conditions, and hostile community attitudes. There were signs in seven beer parlors in Caldwell and eleven in Nampa that forbade Mexicans from entering; stores often asked family members to wait outside, permitting only one Mexican shopper into the store at a time.

The distortion that accompanied the Mexican or Mexican-American in the United States was widespread. Their resistance to injustice was ignored by the history books. Mexicans were bandidos in the event of violence. Anglos were pioneers by comparison. The Mexicans' fight to protect their property, preserve their religion, or assert their rights was ignored. Few studies contributed to a fair understanding of the Mexican people either in the United States or Mexico.

Two exceptions to this generalization are the works of Hubert Howe Bancroft in the nineteenth century and Herbert Eugene Bolton in the early twentieth century. Carey McWilliams gave new meaning to acceptance and understanding in his book entitled *North from Mexico,* written in 1942. That book and the American veterans coming home from World War II helped awaken a new respect for persons of Mexican heritage who were citizens of the United States and had served in the war. Through them the term Mexican-American came into common use.

In 1947 a new labor agreement was worked out between Mexico and the United States. In that agreement 55,000 illegal Mexican wetbacks in the United States were given legal status and offered permanent residency. The following year Mexico banned the use of Mexican national laborers in the state of Idaho because of poor housing, contract violations, and general discrimination. In 1955, Governor Robert E. Smylie created the Governor's Migratory Labor Committee to investigate and bring compliance in migratory housing. This committee functioned until 1968, and during its existence housing improved considerably.[7] The committee reports were made public, and this not only created awareness but forced violators to improve living conditions for their employees.

The 1960s witnessed power movements among minority groups, including Mexican-Americans in California and the Southwest. Tired of prejudicial reporting in the newspapers, tired of prejudice in the courts, tired of derogatory remarks from teachers and civic leaders, Mexican-Americans began to stand up for their rights. Perhaps surprisingly, it was the youth that initiated the movement that came to be called Chicano Power. In 1968 school children in the deprived *barrio* schools of East Los Angeles went on strike, demanding that they be recognized and given a meaningful school experience. These "blow-outs" or strikes produced the Mexican-American movement of 1968 in which parents, children, teachers, and civic leaders joined together in the first acts of militancy among Chicanos in Southern California.[8] Because of their effort, bilingual education became a national byword, and programs such as the one at Boise State University sprang up around the country.

The California "blow-outs" triggered a conscious movement enlisting a variety of groups including MECHA; the *Catolicos por la Raza* (CPLR); the Priests for Religious, Educational, and Social Rights (PADRES); the Mexican American Legal and Education Defense Fund (MALDEF); the United Farm Workers; a new political party, La Raza Unida; and a militant group called the Black Berets. Activists precipitated a full-blown international grape boycott by 1969; a confrontation with and resignation of Cardinal James Frances McIntyre of Los Angeles; a lettuce boycott in 1972; a new political awareness in state and national elections;

and a major educational push in higher education and throughout the elementary and secondary systems where Hispanics are involved.

It was in this era also that the Hispanic community rose up against national advertisers who made fun of Mexican people in their radio, television, and national-magazine advertisements. The depiction of Mexicans as dirty, fat, lazy, dumb, comical, or thieving made an impression on young and old alike. People formed a mental image of the Mexican-American without ever having met one. This commercial usage of Mexican inferiority was practiced by Taco Time, Frito-Lay, R. J. Reynolds, Philco, Arrid Products, and General Motors, to name a few such companies. La Raza Unida won a series of civil rights cases against such firms, and the advertising has disappeared.[9] This same kind of change has taken place in children's books. No longer is the Mexican child shown as someone quaint, although the majority of children's books about Mexican children still place them in a rural setting. (Stereotyping is not confined to Hispanics: one finds that Chinese children all wear pigtails; African children wear no clothing and watch lions and elephants.)

When Public Law 78 terminated the *bracero* program on December 31, 1964, Basque sheepherders remained as the only legal foreign nationals in Idaho who were part of the work force. When the Spanish government refused permits in 1970, Idaho first recruited Peruvian sheepherders. In 1974, Idaho began legally contracting with Mexican sheepherders for one-year periods of time with the possibility of receiving three-year extensions. This practice continues to the present.[10] From 1967 to 1969, the Idaho Department of Employment also recruited up to 5,000 sugar-beet workers and 1,000 sprinkler-pipe movers into the state from Mexico annually. Most of these workers were assigned to farms under contract to the Amalgamated Sugar Company in eastern Idaho.[11] Because of poor housing, the state stopped the program, and recruiting was left to individual farmers.

Almost at once, the advertised demand for workers dropped to a trickle. The illegal alien had come to work! Since 1970, the major source of interstate labor in Idaho has been the undocumented workers from Mexico. By 1977, it was estimated that 10,000 illegal aliens worked the fields and ranches in Idaho.[12] According to Harrison V. Rhodes, supervisory investigator for the United States Immigration and Naturalization Service in Boise, "the illegals are here in such large numbers that it's beyond our control. We apprehend large numbers of them – send large numbers back. We are working on this, but it is out of hand."[13] Two or three thousand illegal aliens are apprehended yearly at the Idaho borders, in labor camps, and in the fields by agents of the Immigration and Naturalization Service. In 1971, the United States returned 400,000 illegal aliens to Mexico. In Idaho such workers were being apprehended at the rate of 150 a month.

Such figures do not begin to give a true count of undocumented workers in the state of Idaho or in the United States. H. Fred Garrett, state employment director, commented on the situation in 1973:

> There's no way in the world you can get a count on them. It's like grabbing a handful of quick-silver. But they've been able to keep their labor supply in balance. We simply have an inadequate supply of labor to do all the jobs on the farm. If the supply dried up, we'd be short of labor.

In discussing the problem further, Garrett continued: "Of course the farmer will deny having them . . . The illegals themselves, don't dare complain about treatment, about substandard housing . . . they might expose themselves."[14] Besides substandard housing, very low pay, social isolation, and insecurity, the illegal alien kindled the fires of racial prejudice, and the Mexican-American is paying the price. No effort has been made to distinguish the Mexican-American citizen who has remained in agriculture from the illegal. No effort is made to distinguish citizens from illegals in reporting stabbings or barroom brawls in the newspapers. Mexican-Americans in Idaho have empathy for their Mexican brothers but resent the system that brings the undocumented workers into the state and the system that is permitted to exploit them. While the bill for immigration reform and control is pending in Congress, the Hispanic community deplores the use of penalties against those who hire illegals for fear of reprisals against all who are "brown." They oppose a renewal of the *bracero* program and resent the initiation of a quota system for Mexican immigration.[15]

For the legal or illegal migrant worker without skills, the problems remain unsolved. For them, the back-breaking jobs in the annual harvest, in the sugar-beet fields, and in the sprinkler-pipe moving industry have not changed. Mechanization in the sprinkler business has been slowed by the high cost of automation. The cold, wet, and strenuous seven-day-a-week job of moving sprinkler pipe goes on, dependent upon the unskilled manual-labor force that travels through Idaho each year. Such workers remain invisible to mainstream Americans. They belong to the "other" America, the America of illiteracy and poverty, where aspirations are destroyed and hope does not exist. In the midst of Idaho's billion-dollar agri-business, it is unfortunate that workers toil in jobs where their labor is exploited and where they and their families do not begin to enjoy the opportunities available to the average American citizen.

In Idaho the Idaho Migrant Council is a major spokesman for the Mexican-American community and its concerns. The Migrant Council, established in 1971, provides protective, legal, educational, and health services to low-income and migrant-worker families in Idaho. The Roman Catholic Diocese of Idaho sponsors an Office of Hispanic Ministries that has an educational and spiritual program for persons of Mexican heritage in Idaho. The Migrant Education Resource Center in Nampa promotes educational literature, books, films, and classroom materials for use in the area schools.

The problem of prejudice has not been resolved, but the 1980s can go a long way in establishing labor controls and a fair program of treatment for the agricultural force in the nation. A widespread movement emanating from libraries, schools, and local historical societies throughout the state could produce a beneficial acceptance of the Mexican-Americans and their culture in Idaho. Such organizations would gladly give assistance in planning a program or exhibit. They will assist in securing speakers and films. The Office of Hispanic Ministries has prepared a booklet concerning the story of Guadalupe and honoring the Mexican-Americans in Idaho.

Each person or organization will need to construct his own conclusions from the information presented. However, exhibits can be prepared to help the Hispanic community celebrate festival days; articles pertinent to Mexican-American accomplishments or interests can be published in local papers; a speakers' program can be initiated; a fiesta can be held by a church group or community in conjunction with a festival. A simple activity recognizing the Mexican-American people in a community can help foster mutual respect among all Idahoans for our varying cultures and our similar American heritage.

Notes

1. Padre Mauricio Medina, Our Lady of Guadalupe Parish, Nampa, Idaho, interviewed by Patricia Ourada, June, 1977. Interview in the Migrant Collection at the Boise State Library Archives.
2. "Gringoes Won't Fight," *Idaho Daily Statesman,* June 19, 1916, p. 4.
3. Edward McNall Burns, *The American Idea of Mission* (New Brunswick, New Jersey: Rutgers University Press, 1957), p. 196.
4. "Speaker Outlines Principles of the Klan," *Idaho Daily Statesman,* June 10, 1924, p. 3.
5. "They Came to Idaho" (editorial), *ibid.,* May 14, 1935, p. 15, c. 1.
6. Rolando Bonachea, "Mexican American Relations," manuscript in the Migrant Collection in the Boise State University Library Archives, p. 8. The reference cited is an article by Frank del Olmo in the *Los Angeles Times,* February 23, 1976.
7. *Reports on Idaho Migrant Labor Camps,* Annual Report, 1955-1965 (Boise: Employment Security Agency, 1966).

8. David F. Gomez, *Somos Chicano: Strangers in Our Own Land* (Boston: Beacon Press, 1973), pp. 112-113.
9. Julian Nava, *The Mexican American in American History* (New York: American Book Company, 1973), pp. 150-151.
10. *Annual Farm Labor Report, Idaho, 1974* (Boise: Department of Employment, 1975), p. 49.
11. *Ibid.*, 1969.
12. William Chapman, *Washington Post*, "El Dorado in North Still Draws Wetbacks, But New Breed," in the *Idaho Daily Statesman*, December 23, 1973, Sec. B, p. 15.
13. Harrison W. Rhodes, interviewed by Patricia Ourada, July, 1977. Tape in the Migrant Collection, Boise State University Library Archives.
14. "Wetbacks 'Earn' Place," *Idaho Daily Statesman*, September 17, 1973, p. 17.
15. *Idaho Daily Statesman*, October 20, 1975. From the clipping file of the *Statesman* office.

Comments:
Historians and Minorities

Robert C. Sims

The two subjects treated in the panelists' presentations have much in common. In our interpretations of the past, they have both been victims of what Mark Twain once characterized as "the great lie of silence." What is explicit in Armitage's paper and implicit in Ourada's is that this condition is due to our methods of assessing the past. In its most general form, we have relied on an approach that tells the American story as one of an east-to-west "conquest." In specific form, we have the "frontier myth," seen in Armitage's paper, which celebrates, as it focuses on, those characteristics and activities we identify as "male." Thus, in viewing the American past as one of conquest, those essentially male characteristics have been the critical ones. Armitage's paper is an effort to confirm the recent observation by Carl Degler that "our generally accepted conception of the past has been derived from the interests of man."

Is there a conception of the past derivable from the interests of Woman? If there is, what will that history be? Degler, Armitage, and a growing number of people believe that the answer to the first question is yes, and that it is quite different from men's history.

The implications of this notion are important. It is one thing to call for a different perspective on the same history and quite another to propose a different type of history. The latter change will require a reconsideration of women in American history: one that views them not as powerless men, but as participants in the American past with very specific sets of experiences. The justification for such an approach is well established by Armitage's presentation, and the implications are clear: In order even to adequately assess the meaning of those experiences, some more enlightened conceptual frameworks are needed, informed by women's values just as the frontier myth and the larger concept of conquest are derived from men's values.

Like the subject of women, Mexican-Americans as historical actors have been victimized by a view of American history as an east-to-west story of conquest by Europeans. Specialists in this area have noted that two principal factors impede effective understanding of that experience. One is the general lack of knowledge about Mexican-Americans and the other is the rigidity of traditional frames of reference for examining that experience. In the case of the latter, failures of historical understanding are attributable to the same reason as those involving women.

To understand why women and minorities have not been adequately dealt with in historical scholarship is only the beginning, of course. The important thing is to do something about it, and our two papers today represent significant steps in that direction. Both move toward providing more significant information about their subjects and both demand a new conceptual framework. There is some hope for improvement.

In both women's studies and historical studies of specific minorities, expanding opportunities have resulted in women and minorities entering academic departments or positions of influence as self-conscious women or Mexican-Americans. And, as in Ourada's case, scholars of ability and sensitivity have begun to work in these areas even though there is no personal identity with the group studied. One result of the former circumstance has been and will likely continue to be that the work they produce will be related to their values as women or minorities, in exactly the same way historical studies reflected the male consciousness of earlier scholars. There are those to whom such work appears not only faddish but perhaps irrelevant as well. In order to meet this criticism it may be necessary to first determine to what extent American history has been dominated by men who wrote history to meet their needs and concerns as men. Is it possible that when men looked to the past for guidance, understanding, and identity, they produced a certain type of history? Now that more women and minorities are writing history they are producing a different account because, as human beings, they need history, too. The result will likely be a fuller, and thus more accurate, accounting of what the American past was like for all Americans. The papers presented today are part of that much-needed effort.

Euro-American Attitudes and the Native American Experience

Alan G. Marshall

Euro-American attitudes have strongly influenced the Native American experience.

Although few would dispute such a statement, definitions and descriptions of both Euro-American attitudes and the Native American experience remain elusive. The Native American past and present are difficult for non-Indian observers to interpret because we are just now beginning to circumscribe the lens of Euro-American attitudes and values. The only way we can grasp the one is to understand the other.

I will describe Euro-American attitudes by showing how they incorrectly describe "the Native American experience" as exemplified by the Nez Perces. This example will show that interpretation of local history requires that we understand our own values. Further, we must verify our interpretations, not only by reading other historians, but through oral testimony by local people. Finally, history is made of the lives of individuals; therefore, our efforts at gathering their testimony is essential.

The testimony of many different people is essential. Everyone talks about "good" things or wrongs done to them: few people talk about their mistakes or wrongs they have done. Either way, people reveal their attitudes and experiences. No story can be told accurately without many perspectives. Our knowledges of Euro-American values and the Native American experience is growing because many local historians and others have begun to listen more carefully.

Images of American Indians are in a state of flux. During the past twenty years, Indian people have become more effective in impressing themselves on the consciousness of other United States citizens: some through the means of demonstrations, others through control of vital resources, still others in the political arena. Partly in response to these developments, a philosophic re-evaluation of Native Americans has also taken place.

The most significant re-evaluations appear in historical, sociological, and anthropological thought. American Indians now seem much more complicated – indeed, much more "human" than they did before. I want to discuss this issue of complexity: look at analyses of Euro-American views of the American Indian, then turn to the expression of these views in scientific thought. Finally, I shall describe the Nez Perces as an example of some new views of American Indians.

One of the fundamental premises of anthropology is that people judge others with a set of ideal standards. When applied across cultural boundaries, such judgments are ethnocentric and lose their validity because the same event may have very different meanings. Many events calling for such judgments occurred between Nez Perces and Euro-Americans; two, with far-reaching impacts, were the treaties of 1855 and 1863. At both treaty sessions, Euro-Americans assumed that there were Nez Perce leaders who could commit their followers to giving up immense areas of land. The Nez Perces, on the other hand, believed that no one could speak for anyone else, that no leader could make such a commitment. These different beliefs epitomize two radically different ways of judging a person's humanity. For Euro-Americans, civility and public order required leaders who could make a commitment and make it stick; otherwise only savagism, a war of all against all, would follow. For Nez Perces, a person incapable of making his or her own decisions was barely human; anyone who forced his desires on others reduced their humanity and committed a terribly violent act.

The concepts of savagism and civility have been examined by Bernard Sheehan in the context of colonial Virginia.[1] He shows that the ethnocentric views of American Indians held by Europeans resulted in a two-faced policy toward them and, indeed, toward the land itself. This policy was not to be denied; nor did information contrary to Euro-American stereotypes change those images significantly. Early views were of an earthly Paradise untrammeled by the adulterating influence of ignoble, sinful humanity. When the land did not yield its fruits easily, as it should in Paradise, it became a wilderness excluded by fences, governed by man, and eventually placed on "reservations" such as the Selway-Bitterroot Wilderness. When the noble savage did not bend to the sweet voice of reason, did not enter into the harmony of the social contract, and acted sinfully by European standards, he, too, suffered the same fate.

American Indians continued to suffer from these stereotypes for the next 350 years. Robert F. Berkhofer has described Euro-American stereotypes of the first Americans in his book *The White Man's Indian.*[2] He finds the same kind of process at work in the arts, humanities, and science. On the one hand, there is the noble redskin, at one with the land, innocent of the corrupting influence of civilization; on the other, a degenerate, polygamous murderer: Uncas and Geronimo.

The curious thing about these stereotypes is that the noble redskin lies over the hill while Geronimo lives next door. The noble savage lived in the past, his degenerate child lives now. Sometimes these images are embodied in the same person. In 1877, Chief Joseph and his band were murderous savages; with defeat, the passage of time, and the distance of removal, he is the Red Napoleon. This distinction suggests that the white man's stereotypical Indian never existed, that the noble redskin and the ignoble savage were both figments of the European imagination and remain so.

The denigration of American Indians has occurred in scientific views of Indian people as well. The image of social and cultural simplicity of Indian people in the United States (but *not* in Mexico – by the marvel of distance) has fascinated anthropologists. In the nineteenth century, American Indians were used to exemplify the most primitive levels of human society; they were a kind of cultural fossil. In the twentieth century, American Indians are important in an antiquarian way; but nothing very interesting about modern people could be discovered from studying them. American Indians were essentially assimilated, the argument ran, and their experience was of little scientific value. A few "long hairs" remained out in the hills, and capturing their memories of the "good old days" was all the research that remained.

By the 1950s and '60s, however, a sea change in this image occurred. Indian people began to enter the field of anthropology as co-workers rather than objects of study. This change was in part forced on anthropologists. American Indians perceived accurately that virtually all rights to environmental use would be extinguished – there were demonstrations over fishing rights, the Indian land claims commission and individual tribes hired anthropologists to determine the extent of land claims against the federal government, and other intellectual and physical confrontations occurred.

Further, new demographic and archaeological data added to the mounting evidence that American Indians were more than simple hunters and gatherers or gardeners. Estimates of overall Indian populations north of Mexico in 1492 have increased more than tenfold, from roughly 1,000,000 to more than 10,000,000. Archaeological studies of Cahokia, an Indian city near St. Louis,[3] Missouri, show that it was occupied by at least 50,000 people in its core area. It was larger than any European city except Paris at the time.[4] Still other finds have jolted the anthropological community.

Taken together, these elements are causing widespread re-evaluation of American Indians, and they make it clear that social scientists and others interested in American Indians have been subject to the cultural myth of the "golden age" and its degradation to the present. In consequence, a perverted picture of American Indians has been produced. Besides this bias, Alice Kehoe, an anthropologist, has identified "the cant of conquest" as an important element in past views.[5] That is, denigrating American Indians made some justification of the subjugation of alien peoples possible. Kehoe points out that both myths are cultural in nature and, therefore, especially difficult to overcome, even for scientists.

The nature of Euro-American stereotypes of the American Indian can be briefly summarized. In a significant way, Euro-Americans define themselves by using the Indian people as a foil. I can remember parents telling their children, "Don't act like a wild Indian." If Euro-Americans act civilized, Indians act savagely. If Euro-Americans live together, Indians live in distant places. If Euro-Americans are the people of the present and future, Indians belong to the past. If Euro-Americans progress, Indians degenerate – or at best have reached the end of the trail. We can extend these images: if Euro-Americans are reasonable, Indians are unreasonable; if Euro-Americans are increasing in population, the redman is vanishing.

When these stereotypes are transgressed or shown to be wrong, Euro-Americans, like members of any other culture, react strongly. They respond with disbelief or intervene to show that they are correct. Hence, the cant of conquest, war, and so on. These elements have all appeared in the way American Indians of the Northwest are studied. Much ethnographic work has focused on memory culture descriptions – studies of the way things were. The region, especially the interior plateau, has been distinguished primarily by negative traits: that is, by the absence of formal political organization and so on, especially when contrasted with coastal people. This essentially negative image of this region's native population remains important in most anthropologists' views of this region, known as the Plateau culture area. In fact, the area has sometimes been characterized as having little anthropological significance. Most studies have been of the so-called "acculturation" of Plateau people, or how native lifeways are replaced by Euro-American ones. Clearly, a degeneration hypothesis is at work here.

The Nez Perces, as one of the ethnographically best known of the Plateau groups, reflect these views. They first appear as the noble savage, yearning for enlightenment by missionaries; then as an obstacle to progress. With the defeat of off-reservation Nez Perce in 1877, a noble-savage image reappears on a national level, but locally they are seen as degenerates. Anthropologic views of them first stressed a pastiche of coastal and high plains traits,[6] then virtually nothing for fifty years but memory culture studies, then acculturational studies.[7] But the Nez Perces are much more complicated as a cultural group. Three issues reflecting those complexities are especially significant: the image of Nez Perces as simple hunter/gatherers; images of Nez Perces as nomadic, or partially sedentary; and the image of the Nez Perces as living in bands. The basic images refer to pre-reservation life.

The Nez Perces are often viewed as simple hunters and gatherers. To anthropologists, this characterization implies people with little material culture. In the most extreme view, hunter/gatherers have little impact upon their environment and certainly do not improve the productivity of the environment. The Nez Perces never fit this image. Nez Perce people significantly altered regional environments through the use of fire. The use of fire by the Nez Perces to improve game habitats as early as 1892 was noted in 1900 by John Leiberg, a forest ecologist. His studies of the Bitterroot Forest Reserve showed that two-thirds of it had been burned at least twice in the previous 150 years. Nez Perces both then and in the present have maintained that such burning increases game populations, especially elk and deer. Thus, the very character of this region's forests was affected by the Nez Perce management practice. Fire was similarly used on the region's prairies; reportedly, camas meadows were also burned.

In other words, the view of the Nez Perces as simple hunter/gatherers cannot be sustained. And there were other efforts to increase productivity. For example, Nez Perce women collected a variety of roots and regularly returned to the same harvesting places each year.[8] To increase plant productivity, women waited to gather roots until after the seeds had matured. Then they "chunked up" the earth with digging sticks, took the largest roots, replaced the unwanted ones, and scattered the seed. This appears to be cultivation rather than simply gathering the land's bounty.[9]

The fact that agriculture was quickly introduced to the Nez Perces is significant because hunters and gatherers rarely make the transition to settled agriculture quickly. The difficulties of introduction encountered by missionaries were not in getting the ideas of planting, cultivation, and harvest across but of getting *men* to do it. Even so, by 1862 the Nez Perces were growing enough agricultural products to supply the Orofino and Florence mines.[10] Further, the efficiency of Nez Perces as cattlemen was widely known. The point is that adoption of agriculture followed immediately upon the substitution of foreign plants and animals in the economy—*not* of new ideas.

The Nez Perces have also been pictured as "semi-sedentary": as being only partially tied to a particular place. In the view's most sophisticated form, they are seen as spending the winter in the same village from year to year, and traveling in the other seasons to where resources are most abundant. This view is also incorrect.[11] In fact, given the use of root crops, a nomadic picture could be rejected out of hand.

Nez Perces lived at several places throughout the year; in a sense, the pattern can be likened to a family with a summer home. These several places were referred to as a /wi-ses/.[12] A person was tied to this pattern by social and spiritual bonds. The social bonds included those of family and use: a person growing up in a family had a right to use the same resources as did other family members. As new families formed through marriage, this right to the product of other resource patches extended outward as well. Without those social bonds, nothing outside the /wi-ses/ could properly be used.

Spiritual bonds reinforced the social bonds. Every individual was thought to have a spiritual guardian. This guardian spirit revealed itself to a person, giving him or her special abilities. Many of these were from particular places of the /wi-ses/. Another significant way of obtaining such a spirit was to inherit it. That is, before a person died, she or he might transfer the power to a chosen successor. In both instances, a person became spiritually tied to a particular /wi-ses/. There were many variations on this theme. In many cases, however, a person remained on his own /wi-ses/ and did not disrupt the relationship between other people and their places.

These concepts could be developed further, but suffice it to say that an image of Nez Perces wandering willy-nilly across the land in response to variations in productivity is incorrect. Instead, there was a complex system of resource tenure, reinforced by social and cultural bonds.

The last anthropological image to be discussed is the idea that the Nez Perces lived in bands. This concept implies that there are no separate formal economic, political, or religious organizations; that leadership is familistic and egocentric; and that group sizes rarely exceed 200 to 300 people. These implications are closely tied to the ideas of a hunting/gathering mode of subsistence and a nomadic lifestyle.

Bands, as the term is used by anthropologists, are characterized by familistic and egocentric leadership. Leaders obtain their position on the basis of kinship relations with other people and by virtue of greater ability than others. For example, simply being a grandparent means that you are closer to the spirit world, and therefore the religious leader for your descendants. Of course, there are at least four grandparents; the one who shows the greatest facility in religious thought is the leader. This means that all economic, religious, and other functions are firmly embedded in kinship relations.

This pattern clearly does not apply to the Nez Perces. Political leadership positions extended far beyond the family and included governance of up to 400 to 500 people. Some economic leaders represented groups of 1,000 or more. Religious leaders often had adherents from many families and several villages. Indeed, hints of voluntary religious organizations of several kinds exist.[13] In anthropological parlance, this means the Nez Perces were a tribal society.

This probably occasions no surprise to most people. One might ask why it has taken an anthropologist so long to discover the obvious. But the answer is that it is not obvious. When Euro-Americans think of a tribe, a hierarchy of chiefs, sub-chiefs, and so on is pictured. Each chief is thought of as an arbiter, able to make legal agreements binding upon his followers. This concept has little to do with the social reality of Nez Perces 150 years ago. Two points about tribal society are important. One concerns leadership, the other group size.

Leadership, as we have seen, is context specific in tribal societies. A person becomes a leader through having the appropriate social connections and superior performance. But these evaluations, and the extension of power, rarely exceed about 1,200 people. Thus, the people whom we now call the Nez Perce Tribe were probably members of one of about five tribes. This fact is especially pertinent to understanding Nez Perce history and the 1877 war. We can also see that leadership had a powerful moral basis as well: it was evaluated on moral terms, not in terms of behavioral competence. Consequently, the composition of social groups was extremely fluid.

This new way of thinking about Nez Perce society allows for the development of an image more accurate than previous ones. It is more accurate in the sense that the destruction of the Nez Perce Tribe becomes moot. Euro-American were tilting with a windmill: the defeat of the tribe could not occur simply because the tribe did not exist. The Nez Perces remained members of significant social entities following the war and have transformed these into new, but nevertheless Nez Perce, social entities active in today's social life. This is important because it removes the stigma of "acculturation": that is, a dismal account of cultural loss and degeneration. It frees us somewhat from the strain of justifying two contradictory images, images that cannot be rationalized because of their very nature. And the re-evaluation of Indian people is the starting point for Euro-American recognition of the place of Native Americans in American history.

The kind of re-evaluation discussed here results from "getting the story straight": it requires local history work with people of many backgrounds. This work is basic and, therefore, essential. Like all historical research, it tells us about our values: values built in conversation with our friends and relatives. Oral history and local history are the only way to get the story. Through these means, we will gain insight into Euro-American attitudes and the Native American experience.

Notes

1. Kenneth M. Ames and Alan G. Marshall, "Villages, Demography and Subsistence on the Southern Columbia Plateau," *North American Archaeology* (1980-81), 2:25-52.

2. Robert F. Berkhofer, Jr., *The White Man's Indian: Images of the American Indian, from Columbus to the Present* (New York: Alfred A. Knopf, 1978).

3. William M. Denevan, editor, *The Native Population of the Americas in 1492* (Madison: University of Wisconsin Press, 1976).

4. Henry F. Dobyns, "Estimating Aboriginal American Population: An Appraisal of Techniques with a New Hemispheric Estimate," *Current Anthropology* (1966), 7:395-412.

5. Morton H. Fried, *The Notion of Tribe* (Menlo Park, California: Cummings Publishing Co., 1975).

6. Alice B. Kehoe, "Revisionist Anthropology: Aboriginal North America," *Current Anthropology* (1981), 22:503-509.

7. John B. Leiberg, "The Bitterroot Forest Reserve," in *Twentieth Annual Report of the U.S. Geological Survey*, Part 5 (Washington, D.C.: Government Printing Office, 1900), pp. 317-410.

8. Alan G. Marshall, "Nez Perce Social Groups: An Ecological Interpretation" (Ph.D. dissertation, Washington State University, 1977).

9. Field notes, 1972, in the possession of the author.

10. Bernard W. Sheehan, *Savagism and Civility: Indians and Englishmen in Colonial Virginia* (Cambridge: Cambridge University Press, 1980).

11. Herbert J. Spinden, "The Nez Perce Indians," *Memoirs of the American Anthropological Association* (1908), 2:167-224.

12. Deward E. Walker, Jr., *Conflict and Schism in Nez Perce Acculturation: A Study of Religion and Politics* (Pullman: Washington State University Press, 1968).

13. Donald N. Wells, "Farmers Forgotten," *Idaho Yesterdays* (Summer, 1958), 2/2:28-32.

Comment:
Western Stereotypes

Glenn Mason

Stereotyping is a trend becoming more and more common today in America. We all know that cowboys chew Copenhagen, wear Wrangler jeans, are muscled and tanned, and, when the hard work is done, drink Millers!

The influence of the media is so powerful that we begin to develop thinking in stereotypes without really knowing it. LeRoy Ashby gives us many examples in his essay. Few, if any, of us have ever been Hell's Angels. Yet, if asked to describe a Hell's Angel, I would wager that at least eighty percent of us would give essentially the same description. Why? Because of media exposure and the exploitation of the attention it creates in the form of movies and books that reinforce the sensational.

In a way this pattern is no different from the nineteenth-century pulp writers who took real people like Buffalo Bill and Davy Crockett and turned them into national heroes who became the stereotype of the American frontiersman and Indian scout. The West and its development were ripe for the creation of myths, legends, and stereotypes. Those who wrote about the nineteenth-century West during its settlement were writing largely for an eastern audience who, although they had never been there, were avidly interested in that vast and mysterious region. Many writers exploited that desire to learn about the West by mixing fact and fiction, a distinction not discernible by the uninformed reader. Some authors, selling themselves and their works as authentic, had never even been to the West. Or, if they had made a brief journey, they only recorded the superficial or the campfire tales of the old trapper or miner trying to impress the tenderfoot reporter. With these kinds of circumstances, coupled with a young nation preoccupied with its own destiny and influenced by a wave of romanticism, it is no wonder that the myths and legends of the West were perpetrated and perpetuated.

Bret Harte's characters (the prostitute with the heart of gold and the gambler whose last act was one of compassion) still survive in grade-B movies.

Remember the "good old days" when we, as kids, could play cowboys and Indians without feeling guilty? We all knew the difference between right and wrong. It was as obvious as white and black hats. It was Roy Rogers, Gene Autry, and Hopalong Cassidy with both guns blazing, defending the hardworking pioneers. Today, historians delight in shooting down our childhood fantasties. And because of recent scholarship, we often find that the old black and white begin to turn gray.

Because of the social consciousness movement that is so popular today, the first stereotypes to be examined were the obvious: those associated with visible minorities. Blacks, Native Americans, women, and Chinese were topics ripe to be researched because they were easily identifiable. Ironically, that visibility is one of the reasons those groups became prime candidates for stereotyping during the nineteenth century in the first place. Many cultural stereotypes are easy to develop because of their immediate recognition. The images and the comment reinforce each other. Alan Marshall mentions as an example the phrase "acting like a wild Indian."

It is popular now for some historians and writers to reassess the past in such a manner as to make us all feel guilty. I do not understand that. We need not be apologetic for the past. It serves no purpose. What a proper and closer-to-the-truth reassessment of a topic can do is provide us with more information on how to proceed in the future. Is that not one of the time-honored virtues of history?

So what can we do to better serve the future when we find evidence that what was formerly perceived as truth is in error? What can those of us in the museum and historical society business do? The first thing we can do is interact with the scholarly researcher and be receptive and openminded to their findings based on new evidence. Scholars need to be aware of that necessary interface as well. More people visit museums in a year than ever read the latest Bureau of American Ethnology report or the *Journal of American History.* Exhibits in museums are critical to the issue of perpetuating stereotypes. All that we can ask of our museum exhibits is that they accurately portray events and help to explain those events based upon the mindset of the period.

I do not feel that any of us, museums included, has the right to judge behavior or past events. Museums do, however, have the responsibility to record an event as accurately as possible and help visitors to understand the causes or ideas that led to that particular behavior or action. I advocate the use of first-person narrative to help portray an event or theme in an exhibit. The proper use of primary source materials enables us to get as close as we possibly can to a person actually involved in an event. The contemporary letter or diary entry not only gives that observer's account of the action but also often allows us to begin to understand the perspective of the observer-author.

History itself is viewed differently by different people. Philip Brooks, writing about the use of primary source materials in his book *Research in Archives,* says:

> The study of the past is the study of events that took place, what people said or wrote then, and the trends that developed. Such matters cannot be changed, but the evidence of them varies widely, and their description and interpretation are often revised. The closer the student can get to direct observance of them, the closer he can come to being a witness himself, the more accurately he can narrate or understand them. With intelligent imagination he may visualize events, or sense their reality.[1]

All of us in the museum profession have had experience with the visitor who comes up to the front desk to challenge the label content in an exhibit. How do we treat him? With a superior attitude that we know better because we are the museum experts? Listen and be aware that any verified new information could enable us to more correctly and effectively interpret history to others.

History is a continuing process. It never ends. New data are constantly being added to our knowledge bank. Likewise, the interpretation of history, in both fact and method, is constantly changing. Historians and scholars must interact with museum folk. And museum people must be receptive to new evidence and the constant need to re-evaluate and change our exhibits if the evidence so dictates.

Interpretation through proper exhibition is only one area of responsibility that history museums have in helping to accurately portray the past. Another has already been alluded to: the need to collect primary source materials that can bring us closer to the actual event.

The collection of artifacts presents another problem. What should be collected? Often what museums collect becomes the basis for creating stereotypes. The pioneer shrine approach of the sacredness of relics that came across the plains, the overabundance of wedding dresses in our history museums, and our fervor for saving elegant Victorian houses can unconsciously lead museums visitors astray with false impressions of the past. What museums collect can influence what the future will think about the past. Historians sometimes decide what was important by what survives. Therefore, as collecting agencies, history museums have a tremendous responsibility.

I believe history museums should be collecting the present for the future. But, how do we determine what is representative of today's culture? Museums have a responsibility not only to watch out for perpetuating stereotypes of the past but to also guard against the creation of new stereotypes by thoughtfully collecting the present. It is not an easy task.

As long as Madison Avenue makes millions of dollars in creating them and we keep buying into them, stereotypes will continue to be generated. As consumers, perhaps we can alter that fact. I don't know. But I do know that as responsible historians and museum and historical society personnel, working together, we can help to eliminate the cultural stereotypes of the past.

Note

1. *Philip C. Brooks, Research in Archives: The Use of Unpublished Primary Sources* (Chicago: University of Chicago Press, 1969), p. 2.

Contributors

Susan H. Armitage is professor of history and director of the women's studies program at Washington State University. She is the author of *So Much to be Done: Women Settlers on the Mining and Ranching Frontier.*

LeRoy Ashby, professor of history at Washington State University, has written *The Spearless Leader: Senator Borah and Progressivism in the 1920s* and a biographical volume on William Jennings Bryant.

Judith Austin is editor of *Idaho Yesterdays*, the journal of the Idaho State Historical Society.

Sharon Boswell is a doctoral candidate in history at the University of Washington.

Jan Harold Brunvand, professor of English at the University of Utah, has written extensively on American and particularly western folklore. He is the author of *The Study of American Folklore: An Introduction.*

T. Allan Comp, formerly of the National Park Service, Seattle, Washington, has published numerous historical site surveys, including one of the Ebey's Landing National Historic Reserve.

Lawrence de Graaf is associate professor of history at California State University, Fullerton.

G. Thomas Edwards, professor of history at Whitman College, Walla Walla, Washington, has published widely on the history of the Pacific Northwest, most recently *Sowing Good Seeds: The Northwest Suffrage Campaigns of Susan B. Anthony.*

John R. Jameson is associate professor of history at Kent State University and the author of *Big Bend National Park: The Formative Years.*

William L. Lang directs the Center for Columbia River History of the Washington State Historical Society.

Elaine J. Lawless, associate professor of English at the University of Missouri, has written *Handmaidens of the Lord: Pentecostal Women Preachers and Traditional Religion*, and *God's Peculiar People: Women's Voices and Folk Tradition in a Pentecostal Church.*

Alan G. Marshall is associate professor of anthropology at Lewis-Clark State College, Lewiston, Idaho.

Glenn Mason directs the Eastern Washington State Historical Society.

Laurie Mercier, an independent historian, was formerly oral historian at the Montana State Historical Society.

Patricia K. Ourada, professor of history at Boise State University, is well known for *The Menominee Indians: A History.*

J. Sanford Rikoon, research assistant professor of rural sociology at the University of Missouri, is the author of *Threshing in the Midwest, 1820-1940: A Study of Traditional Culture and Technological Change.*

A.J. Simmonds is curator of special collections at Utah State University. His work includes *The Gentile Comes to Cache Valley: A Study of the Logan Apostasies of 1874 and the Establishment of Non-Mormon Churches in Cache Valley.*

Robert C. Sims is professor of history and dean of the School of Social Science and Public Affairs at Boise State University.

Barre Toelken is professor of English at Utah State University. He is the author of *The Dynamics of Folklore.*